# MANAGING THE CURRICULUM

**Educational Management: Research and Practice**

Series Editor: Tony Bush

---

*Managing People in Education*
Edited by Tony Bush and David Middlewood

*Strategic Management in Schools and Colleges*
Edited by David Middlewood and Jacky Lumby

*Managing External Relations in Schools and Colleges*
Edited by Jacky Lumby and Nick Foskett

*Practitioner Research in Education: Making a Difference*
David Middlewood, Marianne Coleman and Jacky Lumby

*Managing Finance and Resources in Education*
Edited by Marianne Coleman and Lesley Anderson

*Managing Further Education: Learning Enterprise*
Jacky Lumby

---

This book, *Managing the Curriculum*, is the reader for the module
Managing the Curriculum, one of the core modules of the MBA in
Educational Management offered by the EMDU, University of Leicester.

The modules in this course are:
*Leadership and Strategic Management in Education*
*Managing Finance and External Relations*
*Human Resource Management in Schools and Colleges*
*Managing the Curriculum*
*Research Methods in Educational Management*

For further information about the MBA in Educational Management,
please contact the EMDU at emdu@le.ac.uk. For further information about
the books associated with the course, contact Paul Chapman Publishing at
www.paulchapmanpublishing.co.uk.

EDUCATIONAL
MANAGEMENT
DEVELOPMENT
UNIT

# MANAGING THE CURRICULUM

### Edited by
### David Middlewood and Neil Burton

Paul Chapman
Publishing

First published 2001

Reprinted 2003

Paul Chapman Publishing
A SAGE Publications Company
6 Bonhill Street
London EC2A 4PU

SAGE Publications Inc
2455 Teller Road
Thousand Oaks, California 91320

SAGE Publications India Pvt Ltd
32, M-Block Market
Greater Kailash - I
New Delhi 110 048

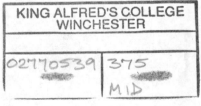
**British Library Cataloguing in Publication data**

A catalogue record for this book is available from the
British Library

ISBN 0 7619 7031 2
ISBN 0 7619 7032 0 (pbk)

**Library of Congress Control Number available**

Typeset by Dorwyn Ltd, Hampshire
Printed and bound in Great Britain by Biddles Ltd,
Guildford and King's Lynn

# CONTENTS

*Series Editor's foreword*                                                    vii
Tony Bush
*Preface*                                                                      ix
David Middlewood and Neil Burton
*Notes on contributors*                                                       xiii

**Section A: Strategic management of the curriculum**                           1
  1  Framing teaching and learning in the twenty-first century                  2
     *Jacky Lumby*
  2  Models of curriculum organisation                                         18
     *Neil Burton and David Middlewood, with Roy Blatchford*
  3  The management consequences of different models of
     teaching and learning                                                     35
     *Peter Silcock and Mark Brundrett*

**Section B: Operational management of the curriculum**                        53
  4  Managing the planning of learning and teaching                            55
     *Neil Burton*
  5  Managing monitoring of the curriculum                                     70
     *Brian Hardie*
  6  Curriculum evaluation: measuring what we value                            89
     *Margaret Preedy*

**Section C: Roles and responsibilities in curriculum management**            105
  7  Leadership of the curriculum: setting the vision                         107
     *David Middlewood*
  8  The subject leader                                                       122
     *Christine Wise and Hugh Busher*

9   Cross-curriculum co-ordination                                      135
    *Les Bell*
10  Managing individual needs within an inclusive curriculum           155
    *Daniela Sommefeldt*

**Section D:  Resourcing the curriculum**                              173
11  Managing the learning environment                                  175
    *Ann Briggs*
12  Managing curriculum support staff for effective learning           190
    *David Middlewood and Richard Parker*
13  The management of resources for learning                           204
    *Ann Briggs and Neil Burton*

*Glossary of terms*                                                    217
*Index*                                                                219

# SERIES EDITOR'S FOREWORD

In many parts of the world, education is increasingly regarded as a vital element in the drive for economic growth. In developing countries, the focus is often on extending and improving basic education so that all young people acquire a minimum level of literacy and numeracy to contribute effectively to an emerging economy. In more highly developed nations, the emphasis is on increasing knowledge and skills to enhance their ability to compete in a global economy. This may be partly a matter of creating or improving the educational infrastructure, particularly in developing countries, for example in post-apartheid South Africa. In many advanced economies, however, there is increasing stress on the need to improve the quality of provision, often within the context of limited budgets for education.

'Quality' is one of the 'buzzwords' of the new millennium. It is frequently advocated, widely used and rarely challenged; few would admit to being anti-quality. However, the concept lacks clear definition and also suffers from a plethora of alternative terms, equally compelling but inevitably leading to overlapping meanings and lack of clarity. In education, as in other sectors, the term is value laden but there can be little doubt that it should relate primarily to classroom processes and to the management of these activities. The prime task of the education service is to promote learning, whether this be of young children, adolescents or adults.

The definition of quality in schools and classrooms in England and Wales is increasingly dictated by the Office for Standards in Education (Ofsted), whose remit has recently been extended to include further education. The periodic inspection visits and reports set the agenda for many institutions whose leaders are understandably nervous about being labelled 'failing'. The inspection relates primarily to the National Curriculum and to successive governments' concern to ensure that it is delivered effectively and that national achievement targets are reached.

Managing the curriculum, and the linked management of teaching and learning, are at the heart of the educational process. Heads and principals, senior and middle managers, and classroom teachers, all have a responsibility to promote learning and to ensure the implementation of both the prescribed and informal curriculum. It is this aspect of management which clearly delineates the role of educational leaders from that of leaders and managers in other organisations. What the Americans call 'instructional leadership' is the core task of managers in education which makes the British government's obsession with 'best practice' in industry and commerce all the more surprising.

The development of effective managers in education requires the support of literature which presents the major issues in clear, intelligible language while drawing on the best of theory and research. The purpose of this series is to examine the management of schools and colleges, drawing on empirical evidence. The approach is analytical rather than descriptive and generates conclusions about the most appropriate ways of managing schools and colleges on the basis of research evidence.

The aim of this series, and of this volume, is to develop a body of literature with the following characteristics:

- Directly relevant to school and college management.
- Prepared by authors with national and international reputations.
- An analytical approach based on empirical evidence but couched in intelligible language.
- Integrating the best of theory, research and practice.

*Managing the Curriculum* is the seventh volume in the series and it is underpinned by the view that the prime purpose of educational organisations is to facilitate effective learning. The editors challenge the notion that the 'curriculum' is simply that defined by government and encourage readers to develop their own concepts of the term. The book examines different aspects of curriculum management, including planning, evaluation and monitoring, and focuses on the roles of managers at different levels of the organisation as well as stressing the importance of resourcing the curriculum. The purpose of the book is to present and debate the most effective ways of managing teaching and learning, the central task of leaders in any educational organisation.

*Tony Bush*
*University of Leicester*
*November 2000*

# PREFACE

The *raison d'être* of educational institutions such as schools and colleges is to facilitate effective learning. With hindsight, it may be found surprising that the focus in the management of schools and colleges was until recently much less on this and more on organisational systems, resources and staff management and such. These continue to remain critically important but the study of these areas now has at its heart the concern as to how they facilitate learning.

For virtually the whole of the twentieth century (and many would claim it is still so), the primary means of facilitating learning has been teaching, which is why so much of this book concerns itself with learning and teaching. Indeed, the phrase 'learning and teaching' is gradually taking over from 'teaching and learning', as if to emphasise a shift in the relative importance of the two. An examination of a typical school or college in most developed countries, up to the mid-1980s at least, would have had the features of Carl Rogers's (1980) 'teaching organisation'. The context in which schools and colleges exist at the beginning of the twenty-first century is beginning to be different at least in developed countries, and changing rapidly the whole time. We may describe it as a new context for learning.

This context for learning resembles what Ferguson (1982) argued for as a 'new paradigm' of learning. He stressed the learning rather than methods of instruction or teaching. 'Learning is kindled in the mind of the individual. Everything else is more schooling' (ibid., p. 316). This new paradigm, as adapted by Law and Glover (2000), focuses on features such as:

- learning how to learn
- learning as a process, a journey
- learning as a lifelong process
- the teacher as a learner.

There are a number of developments in the 1980s and 1990s which have significantly influenced the current emphasis on learning, including:

- increasing discovery of how the brain works (it is claimed that 80 per cent of all we know about the human brain has been found out since 1990)
- ideas of multiple intelligences (Gardner, 1993; Handy, 1994)
- the recognition of the importance of emotional intelligence (Goleman, 1996)
- understanding of the different learning styles of individual (e.g. Visual, Auditory, Kinaesthetic (VAK) or the reflector, theorist, pragmatist, activist model of Honey and Mumford (1986))
- the influence of information and communications technology (ICT) upon education
- the interest in schools and colleges, as with businesses, in being learning organisations.

As this new emphasis is likely to increase as new discoveries occur, so the role of the teacher in learning will continue to evolve. Thus the management of the learning in a school or college and of the role of the teacher in facilitating it will continue to be central to the organisation's success or otherwise. At present, it is still possible – and convenient – to call this management of the curriculum.

Curriculum, according to Richmond (1971, p. 87), is a 'slippery' word, meaning in the broadest sense the 'educative process as a whole' and, in the narrowest sense, 'synonymous with the syllabus, a scheme of work, or simple subjects'. Curriculum management therefore is a concept that is not easily grasped and its development may be 'more piecemeal and incremental and less rational and coherent than is generally supposed' (Law and Glover, 2000, p. 178). The ability to 'manage' teaching and learning in this context is further complicated by the very indirectness of the impact of teaching upon learning outcomes.

A book on 'Managing the Curriculum' therefore cannot possibly embrace all the definitions in terms of their application in all contexts. What it can do, as this one attempts to, is to focus on the needs of the educational managers at school or college level with a view to helping them to become more effective through understanding, reflection, awareness of effective practice, and application of the fruits of these to their individual contexts.

Since the needs of the learner lie at the heart of educational management, especially at school or college level, our belief is that effective leadership and management begin with clarification and understanding of the values and philosophy that underpin concepts of the curriculum. One of the depressing situations for the editors and colleagues is to hear some teachers occasionally refer to 'the curriculum' as if its exclusive meaning was that national curriculum prescribed from the centre by governments such as those in the UK, South Africa or Hong Kong. The first section of the book therefore enables readers to explore concepts of the curriculum in order to clarify their own thinking. As the chapters in Section A illustrate, particular concepts of the curriculum inevitably have implications for which model of organisation the school or college will have and what choices may be made concerning approaches to managing learning and teaching.

The task of the manager of the curriculum at school or college level is to ensure effectiveness. In that respect, planning the curriculum and then monitoring and evaluating its effectiveness are essential. Section B has chapters which deal with these three aspects respectively.

As mentioned above, the role of the teacher continues to evolve but it remains pivotal in learning. However prescribed the curriculum, whatever the level of resources available, teachers still have what Kelly (1999) calls a 'make or break' role in curriculum development. Constant decisions and judgements by the teacher at classroom level remain crucial and these are made with an appreciation of the rationale of any activity. If the curriculum is seen as essentially about 'education', not merely learning via instruction, then this appreciation and understanding of educational experience at school or college level is the business of all those operating there, from headteachers and principals to classroom teachers and support staff. No matter how widespread and stringent are the measures to influence or 'control' curriculum activities at school or college level (assessment processes, inspections, performance appraisal, etc.), the influence of those working in schools and colleges is paramount. Section C therefore examines some of these key roles and some of the tensions referred to here.

Talk of a new context for learning may sound remote for circumstances in some countries where one teacher may have a class of 50 children in a building of minimal sanitation, and access to ICT is a fantasy. Yet even in Zambia where one in ten families is headed by a child and one out of three children has a parent who has died of AIDS, relationships between children and teachers are seen as on a par with the importance for schools of running water and cool classrooms (Riley, 2000). This is a perhaps surprising parallel to the research carried out in the UK on an effective classroom climate. In Section D therefore, which deals with resources, the word 'resources' embraces human and physical as well as financial support.

Debate about the meaning of 'curriculum' is destined to continue, but deciding upon a precise meaning is unimportant compared with ensuring that the learning experiences of children, young people and adults in individual schools and colleges are of the highest order for the appropriate purpose. Achieving this is ultimately the business and responsibility of those who lead and manage in these places. If this book helps some individuals and organisations in some part of this, it will have achieved its purpose of clarifying and understanding aspects of curriculum management and relating them to practice.

We are above all extremely grateful to all the contributors to this book for their time and commitment, as well as their scholarship. The book would not have been possible without the support of colleagues at the Educational Management Development Unit (EMDU), and we particularly thank

Felicity Murray for all her work on the manuscript, as well as Christopher Bowring-Carr for the index and our families for their support during the period of working on this volume.

*David Middlewood and Neil Burton*
*November 2000*

## REFERENCES

Ferguson, M. (1982) *The Aquarian Conspiracy*, London, Granada.

Gardner, H. (1993) *The Unschooled Mind*, London, Fontana.

Goleman, M. (1996) *Emotional Intelligence*, London, Bloomsbury.

Handy, C. (1994) *The Empty Raincoat*, London, Hutchinson.

Honey, P. and Mumford, A. (1986) *The Manual of Learning Styles*, Maidenhead, Honey Publications.

Kelly, A. (1999) *The Curriculum: Theory and Practice*, London, Paul Chapman.

Law, S. and Glover, D. (2000) *Educational Leadership and Learning*, Buckingham, Open University Press.

Richmond, K. (1971) *The School Curriculum*, London, Methuen.

Riley, K. (2000) Speech to National Union of Teachers Conference, Stoke Rochford, April.

Rogers, C. (1980) *A Way of Being*, Boston, Houghton Mifflin.

# NOTES ON CONTRIBUTORS

**Les Bell** joined EMDU of the University of Leicester as its second Professor of Educational Management in October 1999. His research interests include school organisation and management. He has written extensively on educational management and has worked throughout the world as an educational consultant and is a member of the editorial board of the *British Journal of Educational Research* and the *Journal of Educational Administration*.

**Ann Briggs** is a lecturer in educational management in the EMDU of the University of Leicester. She has considerable experience of secondary and further education, including a range of middle management posts. She has researched and written on issues of resource management and accessibility to learning. She contributed to the *Managing Finance and Resources in Education* text in the Research and Practice series, and is co-editor and contributor to the forthcoming volume *Research Methods in Educational Leadership and Management*.

**Mark Brundrett** is programme leader for the MBA in Educational Management by Distance Learning at the EMDU of the University of Leicester and is highly experienced in National Professional Qualification for Headship (NPQH) training. Prior to moving into higher education, Mark gained experience of teaching and managing in both primary and secondary schools, becoming a primary school headteacher for a number of years. He has most recently edited *Principles of School Leadership* for Peter Francis Publishers and is currently editing a second volume of case studies focusing on Beacon Schools, with Neil Burton.

**Neil Burton** is a lecturer in educational management with the EMDU of the University of Leicester on Ed.D and MBA courses and course leader of the BA (Hons) in Primary Education. Neil has taught and managed in both the primary and secondary sectors as well as having posts in initial teacher training and a school curriculum advisory service. He has published journal articles and chapters on educational management (most recently in Brundrett (ed.) *Principles of School Leadership*) and is currently editing a second volume of case studies focusing on the experience of Beacon Schools, with Mark Brundrett.

**Hugh Busher** is a senior lecturer in the school of education, University of Leicester. Having taught in comprehensive schools for many years, he is particularly interested in the interactions of individuals and organisations and the policies and processes of change. His publications include work on teacher professional development, managing school exclusions and subject leaders as middle managers in schools.

**Brian Hardie** has taught children and adults in a variety of schools and universities for 35 years and is currently an associate tutor with the EMDU of the University of Leicester. Ten years were spent in three secondary schools including being a head of department. Fifteen years were spent teaching in primary schools, first as a teaching deputy and subsequently as head of a middle school. In three universities he has taught master's students Education Management for over ten years in the UK, USA and Israel. He has published books on educational management, including *Evaluating in the Primary School* (1995, Northcote House) and contributed a chapter to *Strategic Management* in the Research and Practice series.

**Jacky Lumby** has taught in a range of educational phases including secondary schools, adult and further education. She is currently a Deputy Director of the EMDU of the University of Leicester. She has written extensively in the field of educational management and edited the titles *Strategic Management* and *Managing External Relations* in the Research and Practice series. She has also authored *Practitioner Research in Education: Making a Difference* (with Middlewood and Coleman) and *Managing Further Education: Learning Enterprise* within the series.

**David Middlewood** is Director of School-Based Programmes at the EMDU of the University of Leicester. Prior to joining the university in 1990, David spent many years teaching in schools, inclu ling ten as a headteacher. David's publications include *Managing People in Education* (with Tony Bush) and *Practitioner Research in Education*, and he has edited and contributed to other volumes in the Research and Practice series. His main research interest lies in staff development and teacher performance and appraisal. His next book on this topic reflects international research undertaken in countries such as New Zealand and South Africa.

**Richard Parker** is headteacher of Lodge Park Technology College in Corby, an 11–18 comprehensive technology college in the East Midlands of England. Prior to his appointment there in 1993, Richard had teaching and management experience in a number of secondary schools. Since gaining his MBA in 1997, Richard has written articles on staff development with David Middlewood and his school is the most successful in the country for school-based management training. Richard is co-editor of *Headship Matters* and is on the management committee of the Technology College Trust Council.

**Margaret Preedy** is a lecturer in the Centre for Educational Policy and Management at the Open University. She has written extensively in the field of educational management including, most recently: *Educational Management: Strategy, Quality and Resources* (1997) and *Organisational Effectiveness and Improvement in Education* (1997) and contributed a chapter to the Research and Practice series' *Managing External Relations in Schools and Colleges.*

**Peter Silcock** is visiting Professor of Education at the University of Hertfordshire and national chair of the Association for the Study of Primary Education. He has published widely on theories of teaching and learning and their implications for school curricula. His most recently published book is *New Progressivism* for Falmer Press.

**Daniela Sommefeldt** is a senior tutor at the EMDU of the University of Leicester where she co-ordinates the Headlamp programme and is also involved in the East Midlands NPQH Centre, as well as teaching on the school-based MBA programme. Before joining the EMDU, she worked for many years as a headteacher of a special school for children with severe and profound learning difficulties.

**Christine Wise** completed her doctorate with the University of Leicester and is a lecturer in the Centre for Educational Policy and Management with the Open University. She has published and made conference presentations on the role of middle managers in schools, the training of subject leaders, the role of Advanced Skills Teachers and the change for former grant-maintained (GM) schools to foundation status.

# Section A: Strategic management of the curriculum

These three chapters focus on the theoretical perspectives underpinning the construction of a curriculum and the management structures that support it. In Chapter 1 Jacky Lumby discusses the factors which influence the development of a curriculum and the interaction this has with the nature of learning and teaching. Neil Burton and David Middlewood in Chapter 2 then take these concepts of learning and teaching and explore the paradigms of curriculum organisation that develop as a result of adopting a particular view of the nature and purpose of the curriculum. They offer three specific case studies of different phases. Finally, Peter Silcock and Mark Brundrett examine the management implications, in terms of institutional structure and culture, of following generic models. Together, they offer a coherent view of how an institution is shaped by the way that it corporately defines a vision of the nature of the curriculum.

# FRAMING TEACHING AND LEARNING IN THE TWENTY-FIRST CENTURY

## *Jacky Lumby*

## INTRODUCTION

Accurate crystal-ball gazing is a very rare talent. In attempting to look forward to discern what managing teaching and learning will mean in the first half of the twenty-first century a mental kaleidoscope of possibilities form and re-form, but arriving at a satisfactory conclusion is undermined by two difficulties: first, the images are based upon what we know of the past. The images, language and concepts are retrospective and may be an inadequate basis for responding to the fast changing world. For example, there is a general belief in many industrialised countries that the growth of computer-assisted information exchange and communication must profoundly transform education but the imagination of most, whose own education was very much people and book based, struggles to grasp what this might mean and over what timescale. The second difficulty is that, though much will change, the polarities in the resources available between countries and within countries will persist (Devoogd, 1998). Thus imagining a future high-tech virtual classroom will have little meaning for those who currently teach a class of 60 with no resources beyond a bare building, a blackboard and chalk. Other influences, such as cultural, social and political perceptions, are discussed later in the chapter.

Differing concepts of learning, of educators, of the proper relationship between learner and educator and the variation in the available resources may suggest that there are no universal truths in managing teaching and learning. In contradiction to this conviction, despite acknowledging the incorrigible plurality of education, it may be that the international community of educational managers can share some understanding of just what the heart of their endeavour, supporting learning, means.

Defining the core task of education managers is problematic, often based upon unspoken values and visions of education. For some, helping each learner to fulfil his or her individual potential is key. In other societies, helping learners to become productive members of society with less stress on individuality (Satow and Wang, 1994) or obtaining high examination marks to gain a job with the highest possible salary (Chan and Watkins, 1994) is the aim. Whatever the differing goals, this volume focuses on the requirement of all educational managers, to provide an environment, within the parameters of the available resource, in which learners can grow individually and be equipped to take a place in society.

## DEFINING THE KEY TERMS

Further to the points made in the Preface, managing the curriculum and managing teaching and learning are sometimes used as if synonymous and sometimes as if different. 'Curriculum' is used at national level to indicate a syllabus and sometimes its means of implementation, assessment and the required learning outcomes. The National Curriculum in England, the Outcomes-Based Education of South Africa (OBE) and the Target-Oriented Curriculum of Hong Kong (TOC) define content, teaching method, assessment and outcomes. All are national curricula which attempt to influence the process of teaching itself and, thereby, learning. Consequently, 'managing the curriculum' takes on one meaning, that of implementing national directives on what should be taught and how, the means of assessment and the expected outcomes.

Managing the curriculum is also used in another sense, to indicate the internal arrangements within a school or college to facilitate learning, what Clark (1996, p. 93) calls 'the organized learning process'. The implication is that managing the curriculum involves not only the formally recognised process of teaching, but all other processes. Interpreted in this way, managing the curriculum could be seen as equivalent to managing the whole institution.

Managing teaching and learning has become the preferred term because it directs attention to the core purpose of schools and colleges. It has also gained ground in response to criticism throughout the 1990s that educational managers had been diverted from their primary task of supporting learning (Cordingley, 1999; Randle and Brady, 1997). The disadvantage of this term is that it makes no distinction between those who manage at team, department, faculty or whole organisational level and individual teachers who manage their classroom or workshop.

An additional term is posited by Watkins and Mortimore who define pedagogy as 'any conscious activity by one person designed to enhance learning in another' (Watkins and Mortimore, 1999, p. 3). This definition may be helpful as a means of differentiating between the individual teacher's classroom management and management by those with a wider responsibility. A whole range of individual teachers, lecturers, classroom assistants, instructors, assessors, technicians may be involved in pedagogy, that is the craft of managing the learning of the individuals for whom each has responsibility. Managing teaching and learning may be defined for the purpose of this chapter as not only implementing the curriculum 'the form in which knowledge, skills, and attitudes are configured for delivery' (Dimmock and Walker, 1998, p. 585) but also other organisation- or department-wide processes directly related to the process of learning.

## CONCEPTS OF THE LEARNER

The literature is rich in exploration of concepts of learning. The predominance of a discourse on learn*ing* rather than the learn*er* reflects the relative powerlessness of learners in discussions about teaching and learning. School students are rarely involved in any meaningful way in making choices about the teaching and learning they will receive. Once they move into post-compulsory education much more attention is given to their views. This may reflect a belief that having become adults they are more able to participate in educational choice-making. Equally it may reflect the financial need to take more account of those who can walk away from what they do not like thereby removing possible resources. Different cultures may vary in what they believe to be the proper relationship between learner and educator, from an overt expectation that learners will be passive, respectful and dutiful, for example in China (Dimmock and Walker, 1998) or South Africa (Pell, 1998), to an apparently greater expectation of encouraging independent thinking and challenge, as in the UK. However, as Bowring-Carr and West-Burnham (1997) point out, even in this environment in which there is a rhetorical commitment to supporting children's growth to autonomy, we tend to teach children to make decisions by not giving them opportunities to make any.

The experience which many learners bring to schools and colleges is bleak. Even in developed countries such as the UK, Ireland, USA, Canada and Australia, (Regan, 1998; Stoll and Fink, 1996) a large percentage of children live in poverty. In some developing economies, such is the level of physical deprivation that the first essential step in managing teaching and learning may be providing a minimum level of nutrition. The combination of change in family arrangements with many more single parents and other carers and high levels of poverty means that many children 'cannot be given the attention they deserve' in their home (Regan, 1998, p. 160). Learners therefore bring to schools and colleges a range of possible positives in their experience and culture, and negatives in what may be a background of physical and emotional deprivation. A holistic view of the whole of a learner's experience, social as well as educational, is the keystone of beginning to think about learning.

## PARADIGMS OF LEARNING

Interestingly Stoll and Fink (1996, p. 1) argue that schools follow a path which would be appropriate 'if this were 1965'. The path reflects a paradigm of learning, focusing on a particular range of educational outcomes, which Bowring-Carr and West-Burnham (1997) characterise as assuming a fixed intelligence which can be measured, where knowledge is imparted in a sequential process and the ultimate aim is to pass tests through replicating the knowledge which has been taught. Learners experience teaching as a wave which passes over them, lifting them briefly on to a high of knowledge but then planting them firmly back on the ground, the knowledge forgotten and often no longer relevant. The ultimate aim is to sort children and adults into groups with different life paths. Parents and children are well aware of this. In Japan competition to get into the right stream is fierce:

> Schools have become fact-grinding and knowledge-based institutions even at elementary level. In 1976, 26.6 per cent of primary school children attended after schools classes ('Juku') and by 1993 the figure was 41.7 per cent (Sugimine, 1992). Such attendance is felt by parents to offer a better chance of passing examinations for entry into famous high schools.
>
> (Sugimine, 1998, p. 121)

In this system, learning is not so much teacher or teaching centred as assessment centred. What is to be assessed dominates the decision on what is taught and how. The individual needs of the learner risk being made peripheral. For a fuller discussion of the assessment-led curriculum and its implications, please refer to Chapter 2.

The changing global context is undermining this paradigm. Those with World Wide Web access have a vast amount of raw knowledge literally at their fingertips. The previous role of teachers in transmitting knowledge is fast becoming redundant in many parts of the world where the Internet has taken hold. Changing career patterns demand a capacity to learn and adapt throughout life. Additionally, the need not just to reproduce but to manipulate knowledge as a basic economic commodity demands higher-level skills. The emerging paradigm suggests that learning is continuous and pervasive, that it results from an interaction between the learner and the environment in which formal education is an important but not unique part, that what is intended to be taught will always be metamorphosed by the individuality of the learner and that there are different sorts of intelligence involving the use of emotion as well as rationality (Gardner, 1983; Goleman, 1996; Handy, 1994). The teacher can promote or inhibit learning through the teaching of learning and information handling skills and can influence but not control its course. The objective of education is to achieve 'profound' (Bowring-Carr and West-Burnham, 1997) or 'deep' learning (OECD, 1996) where what is learnt is related to the holistic pattern of what has already been experienced and learned and what may happen in the future. The aim is to make it possible to continue learning and to do so independently, that is, not alone, but making choices about what, how and with whom to learn.

Such an interpretation could be accused of a bias based on narrowly defined cultural assumptions. Thinking for oneself rather than accepting authority is not universally accepted as preferable (Wang and Mao, 1996). Yet even within countries whose culture may have a profound commitment to continuity, to the collective, to the acceptance and reverence of established knowledge, there is an incipient acknowledgement that national culture must be balanced with global culture in order to thrive in the twenty-first century and, therefore, some accommodation must be found which respects traditional didactic approaches but which opens the door to more fluid forms of education. Additionally, as in Hong Kong, learners themselves in receipt of a traditional, expository style of teaching are 'unhappy with . . . a rigid controlled environment' (Chan and Watkins, 1994, p. 236) and may be exerting a pressure towards the new paradigm of learning.

## THE LEARNER'S VIEW

The traditional powerlessness of learners is being reversed to some degree by the global trend to expose educational institutions to market forces, resulting in more emphasis being given to the views of customers, that is, among others, learners. United Kingdom based learners appear to agree generally about what in their view makes for effective teaching and learning (Harrison, 1997). They see the conditions for effective learning in two ways, as dependent on their relationship with the teacher and on the process which the latter leads. Learners like teachers who maintain a balance between discipline and friendliness. They do not relish relationships where the power differential is stressed by an overemphasis on control but nor do they desire too little authority where the focus slips from working effectively. They wish the teacher to work with them, leading but not controlling. Their preference in the process of learning is to work collaboratively, communicating with their peers, at a timescale that allows them to truly absorb and understand. They admire teachers who find alternative ways of helping them comprehend, so that if one approach does not result in understanding another is tried. Evidence from elsewhere in the world shows the same preference for a partnership relationship between learners and teachers and a range of teaching and learning activities which foster deep learning. A study of student preferences in Hong Kong secondary schools showed that:

> Clearly many of the students would prefer their science classroom to be a friendlier place where both students and teachers enjoyed working together planning a variety of interesting but challenging

activities. Such an environment would encourage both the deeper
level and more achievement-oriented learning strategies that students
would prefer.

                                        (Chan and Watkins, 1994, p. 245)

Learner's views are therefore very much in key with the new paradigm of
learning, which assumes a partnership between learner and educator and
where the aim is not to proceed through a sequence of teaching but to
achieve learning.

## THE ROLE OF THE TEACHER

Throughout history, teachers have generally been given the freedom to
decide what to teach and how (Galton, 1996). This autonomy was based
on the assumption that teachers are professionals and therefore best
placed to make such decisions. In the last two decades of the twentieth
century, an international trend strengthened central control of the curriculum, leaving teachers less room for manoeuvre. Additionally, the advent
of a wider range of technologies to support learning has resulted in a
perceived threat to their control and centrality within teaching. Replacing
the Platonic model of the teacher imparting knowledge and wisdom,
some see a new concept of teaching which is reductive and conceives of
the teacher's role as 'technician' (Devoogd, 1998, p. 152), 'paid servants'
(Beattie, 1990, p. 31), 'quasi-professional or skilled tradespeople' (Stoll
and Fink, 1996, p. 119). Teachers relish large power differentials as little
as learners. Many are affronted by the assumption that they will implement a national curriculum with no power to adjust it in relation to the
needs of the individual, the group or their own strengths. For some there
is also unease that many more quasi-professionals are being employed,
often at lower salary levels, to support learning in a range of ways. The
role of the classroom assistant is growing. The use of computer-aided
learning is often supported by a technician. Practical lessons may be
taken by an instructor. Part of the concern of staff is personal anxiety at
the potential erosion of status and pay when tasks previously undertaken
by qualified staff are fulfilled by those who are not qualified teachers and
who are paid less. Part of the concern is a professional belief that teaching
is a skilled role which requires considerable training and should be undertaken by qualified staff who are adequately recompensed. (Refer to
Chapter 12 for a full discussion of these issues.)

The concept of educator will vary between phases of education and
between different cultures, for, as Dimmock and Walker (1998) remind us,
national boundaries do not equate to cultural boundaries. The international
imperative to educate larger numbers of people to higher levels with resources which are unlikely to be increased substantially demands a variety
of solutions. One possible strategy is to ensure that highly skilled and

adequately rewarded teachers are used only to achieve those educational objectives which the less qualified and paid cannot.

The role of the manager of teaching and learning is to ensure that the right balance of staff is in place, taking into account the current conceptualisation of teachers in their culture. For some the traditional concept of the teacher will remain predominant and their expected role and relationship with learners will be on the Platonic model. For others, teachers will become the leaders of a varied team of different types of staff, where they can confound the limitations of being 'tradespeople' or 'paid servants' by moving to the new paradigm of learning, where all their skill, professionalism and commitment will be tested by working in partnership with learners to move beyond current didactics to education which is neither teacher nor assessment centred but learner centred. However, many teachers will say that they sympathise with the wish to help learners acquire the range of skills they will need for the future but are trapped by a system which imposes a full curriculum which must be 'covered', and expectations from state and parents which are very much assessment focused (Pell, 1998). The manager's task is to find the fulcrum for change and to engineer room for progress, which may be incremental rather than dramatic, but which provides a vision of moving towards the education which is demanded by the twenty first century.

## MANAGERS OF TEACHING AND LEARNING

All teachers manage the learning process and are engaged in what in this chapter will be referred to as pedagogy as defined by Watkins and Mortimore (1998). Dimmock and Wildy (1995) discuss the range of terms applied to managers of teaching and learning with a wider responsibility. They suggest that in North America instructional leadership is used, while in the UK curriculum management and educational leadership are alternatives. Australia uses all three terms. The advent of the expression 'managing teaching and learning', with it being used as synonymous with both pedagogy and managing the curriculum, as discussed earlier in the chapter, can be added to the list. In this chapter, managers of teaching and learning will be taken to be those who have a responsibility for promoting learning beyond those individuals whom they personally teach. This responsibility can be assumed at different levels. First, the principal and senior management team have the task of establishing a whole-organisation culture or ethos, and whole-organisation policies and strategies. Middle managers such as heads of faculty or department will contribute to this process but will also be responsible for implementation at subunit level. Finally, there may be a range of team leaders or cross-organisation co-ordinators who focus on supporting learning in one particular curriculum area or a particular set of curriculum goals such as key skills. Some may have direct responsibility for the management of staff. Others may not.

In theory a manager could decide to revolutionise his or her organisation/department by introducing radical innovations in teaching and learning. In practice it is not usually possible. Managing teaching and learning is a political as well as a technical process and any innovation will be accepted in proportion to the degree of support that exists or has been constructed. In creating alliances to achieve change, the leader will need to have an empathy with the views of teachers, for after all, they do the teaching and can support or subvert progress. However, the manager's view will not necessarily be the same as the teachers' views, even supposing there is agreement among them. The beliefs, wants and expectations of learners, parents, the community and the state may all be equally legitimate, with those of the learner holding particular weight. The foundation of improving teaching and learning is to build agreement on which staff can overlay the macro structures needed to support learning.

## WHO MANAGES TEACHING AND LEARNING?

It is a point of debate whether the different levels of management usually conform to a common differentiated pattern of responsibilities, for example the principal responsible for vision and strategy, middle managers for the day-to-day and mid-term implementation of teaching. I have argued elsewhere that the evidence suggests that dispersed leadership means that no such straightforward pattern exists and that middle managers contribute to vision creation and maintenance and to boundary management, for example, tasks associated with senior management (Lumby, 2001). The research suggested that senior managers were unlikely to be directly involved in curriculum management but had an important effect on teaching and learning through putting in place macro systems, for example, culture and structure. Dimmock and Wildy reach a similar conclusion in their case study of an Australian school where high levels of academic performance appeared to be related to the work at departmental level, not to the management of senior staff. They concluded that: 'The absence of direct instructional leadership by the principal conflicts with much of the evidence on effective schools highlighting the pivotal role of principals as instructional leaders' (Dimmock and Wildy, 1995, p. 319).

Stoll and Fink (1996) and Bowring-Carr and West-Burnham (1997) both question the need for principals at all, suggesting teamwork as an alternative. Dimmock and Wildy (1995) point out that there has been insufficient investigation of the link between the work of department or teams and effective learning. Whether it is accepted that principals are redundant or not, what is encouraging in this debate is the implied optimism that all those with a responsibility for managing teaching and learning can have a real impact on the quality of learning, either working with or without the direct involvement of senior staff.

## MACRO AND MICRO SYSTEMS

Influencing approaches to learning within institutions can be achieved by means of establishing 'deep' systems which are to some degree hidden, as each individual will have a differing interpretation of their nature, including:

- culture
- alliances
- strategy,

and by systems which are more overt such as:

- organisation and subunit structure of roles and responsibilities
- mode of resource distribution including configuration of use of space and time
- systems to support development of inputs such as teaching and work experience
- monitoring and evaluation.

Managers will differ in the weight of relative importance given to each of these elements and will also differ in the degree to which they believe existing systems are appropriate and need maintenance or development, or are inappropriate and require radical change. The differing elements can be reduced to a number of principles of curriculum management:

1) The organisation's culture must be focused on learners and learning.
2) The approach must be holistic with a diminution of internal and external boundaries.
3) Resources must be shaped to support learning.
4) The school or college itself must be a learning organisation, that is constantly monitoring, reviewing, and on this foundation, developing.

Examples of school and colleges acting in accordance with these principles are given in the following sections.

## CULTURE

A study of the intentions and experience of managers in further education colleges in England discovered that managers were quite deliberately setting out to change the culture of their organisation and that the purpose of the intended change was to bring the thinking and actions of all into line with the new paradigm of learning (see the Preface), that the focus must be on the learner and learning:

> It's a cultural thing isn't it really? There is this notion that there is a business culture and an education culture and they are different. I

think the more I do what I do, I am sure the cultures are different, there is no doubt about that, but the central notion of responding to the client, if you want to call them that, the customer, the student, whoever, that notion actually needs to be central whatever you are doing, whether it is a public service or the proverbial selling baked beans. (Marketing Manager 1)

(Lumby, 2001)

This manager was concerned to overcome what he saw as the professional perspective which gave pre-eminence to the views of teachers, a product-driven approach, and to replace it with a student-centred approach. The determination to change the perspective of the organisation, so that it is managed with the perspective of the learner as the driver rather than the perspective of the teacher, is the foundation stone of cultural change to underpin teaching and learning.

## A HOLISTIC APPROACH

An example of trying to achieve internal synergy, obliterating some of the divisions that exist between different types of staff, is exemplified by William Shrewsbury Primary School in England. On joining the school the headteacher had a vision of a school which could become a genuine team of all staff. His perception was that this was not the case at first: 'When you introduce the idea that we are all one staff, everyone goes "Oh yes. Of course" . . . how people themselves see it, the dinner ladies, the assistants, welfare workers, they see it in a very different way' (The Headteacher) (Lumby, 1999a, p. 71). The headteacher had worked with all the staff and by a series of sometimes quite small practical steps had begun to destroy internal divisions and to create a culture of one staff. This had a direct impact on teaching and learning. Classroom assistants who were included in curriculum planning and training events felt they understood learning goals better and, consequently, could support each child more fully. Dismantling internal barriers was matched by an effort to dissolve barriers between the school and the community. The headteacher was developing a holistic approach to people and community by conceiving the school as a centre for learning for the whole community, not just young children, so that all staff, pupils, their families and the wider community could see the school as a centre for lifelong learning. A parallel vision is embodied in a case example given by Siraj-Blatchford who describes a community-based approach to curriculum management in New Zealand, named Te Whariki based on a Maori metaphor of the woven mat:

Te Whariki (woven mat) has been used to describe a curriculum framework in which each early years centre weaves its own curriculum and creates their own pattern from features and contexts unique to them, their children and their Community (Carr & May, 1993). The curriculum framework includes four principles: empowerment: holistic development; family and community; and relationships.

(Siraj-Blatchford, 1999, p. 34)

In both the English primary school and the New Zealand early years centres, the learning of the children is seen as part of a continuum in two senses: first, there was continuity through time, in that it was assumed that learning related to previous experience and culture, and would continue throughout life. The small child who sat in the classroom bore shadow figures of the smaller child they had been and the adult they would become. Second, there was continuity in space, in that learning was seen to happen in the whole of the child's physical environment of which school was only a part. The metaphor of a woven mat is a powerful image of the thread of formal education interwoven with other strands. This is not to diminish its contribution but to strengthen it by binding it tightly and permanently to the whole of a learner's life.

## FOCUSING RESOURCES ON LEARNING

Throughout education, resources are still largely focused on inputs (see Chapter 13 for further exposition). In most educational situations, budgets tend to be committed to staff costs, with apparently little room for manoeuvre. Budgeting for staff, for maintaining the building(s), for providing books and materials is not resourcing learning but funding teaching. However, the Holy Grail of a method of resourcing learning has not been achieved and it is hard to see how it could be. Some states have linked funding to outputs, that is the achievement of specified test scores or qualifications. Funding which is related to outcomes actually funds the assessment process, not learning as defined in this chapter. If resources are tied to achievement of results, then the focus of teachers will be on getting the results, which is not the same thing as helping individuals to learn. Ironically, it may be that committing resources to inputs, that is, teachers and other needs, releases staff to focus on achieving the new paradigm of learning, whereas outcomes-based funding, with the stated aim of encouraging a focus on learning, actually undermines a more holistic and longer-term view of learning. Whatever the funding system, it may be that the imagination and creativity which is used to distribute resources internally is the truly important factor.

Stoll and Fink (1996) and Dimmock (2000) both question whether an adequate response to the individual learner's needs can be encompassed in traditional school structures. Dimmock provides case studies from schools in Tasmania and Germany of innovative groupings of the resource of staff to ensure that students are not trammelled by being placed in a class and working at a pace which may not be appropriate. These schools have also reconsidered their use of time. In similar fashion, Loughborough College in

England reshaped General National Vocational Qualification (GNVQ) students' time to give six of the 16 hours available for a tutor to work on learning management, rather than traditional teaching of the subject. Results improved (Lumby, 1999b). Pitcher (1995) describes the transformation of a building as one tool to change the culture of a further education college to focus on learning. The use of space became a radical statement, the removal of walls signalling the removal of inter-staff and inter-curriculum barriers. All these case examples highlight the power of staff to work with the resources they have to reshape an approach to teaching and learning. The implication is that the barriers to progress may be not only the lack of funds, as is constantly argued by educators, but the need for greater creativity, courage and skill to manage change (see Chapter 13 for a full discussion).

## THE LEARNING ORGANISATION

If schools and colleges are to offer effective learning to their students, then the staff and organisation as a whole must present a convincing role model. It has been argued that teachers are not necessarily effective learners (Boud, 1995; Lumby, 1997; Senge, 1993). They have, after all, largely been a product of the old paradigm of teaching and, consequently, often have little personal experience of the means of achieving 'deep' learning. The international trend to use quantitative data and performance indicators has further embedded the predilection towards single-loop learning in educational organisation; that is, the measurement of activity and comparison against set targets, rather than double-loop learning which questions and reconsiders the targets themselves, adjusting accordingly. The plethora of government initiatives raining down on schools and colleges has, in the most effective of them, encouraged the adoption of a more strategic approach to professional development with an implicit assumption of the need for continuous learning.

This chapter opened by suggesting that all staff involved in supporting learning needed to consider how they conceived the learner and learning. Whatever the conception of the learner, it must be applied to staff as well as students. If lifelong learning is to be more than rhetorical, then staff must not just 'deliver' learning to others, but embody that conception in their working lives. Southworth (1994) and Ralph (1995) provide case examples of a primary school and further education college respectively striving to put learning at the centre of the organisation for all, staff and students, first by acknowledging that a strategy is needed to help staff to learn and, second, by developing a range of initiatives to achieve this end.

## MOVING THROUGH THE TWENTY-FIRST CENTURY

Up to the 1990s there was overwhelming evidence that classroom practice was relatively homogeneous and unchanging. Schools were organised similarly throughout the world, with children divided largely by age and taught a similar range of subjects in a classroom by a teacher. Despite attempts to enforce change, the experience of learners remained much the same as ever. It was still possible for 'determined teachers in the privacy of their own classrooms [to] manage to violate numerous regulations and traditions' (Beattie, 1990, p. 29). Much of what teachers did and achieved was appreciated by learners, their parents and the wider community. But for all the reasons argued in this chapter, it may no longer be enough.

The twenty-first century demands a different approach. The role of education managers is to help teachers achieve this change. Beattie reminds us that most cannot be too ambitious. What is important to managers may have little importance to teachers. Parents, employers, the state and learners may be firmly located in the current culture and subscribe to the current assessment-driven process of education. There are, therefore, political and cultural barriers to change. Schools and staff may also be genuinely trapped by insufficient resources and state systems which inhibit development. There is, however, always the possibility of some change, some improvement, some progress. Additionally, the revolution in technology is enforcing change with a power which easily dwarfs that of states or individual organisations. The technological revolution is changing power relations, through opening knowledge and communications and changing the way society and the economy functions. The twenty-first century will exact change from the willing and unwilling in all spheres, including education. Those who manage teaching and learning have the ability and responsibility to help shape its direction.

# REFERENCES

Beattie, N. (1990) The wider context: are curricula manageable? in Brighouse, T. and Moon, B. (eds.) *Managing the National Curriculum: Some Critical Perspectives*, London, Longman in association with BEMAS.

Boud, D. (1995) Meeting the challenges, in Brew, A, (ed.) *Directions in Staff Development*, Buckingham, Society for Research into Higher Education and the Open University Press.

Bowring-Carr, C. and West-Burnham, J. (1997) *Effective Learning in Schools*, London, Pitman.

Chan, Y. and Watkins, D. (1994) Classroom environment and approaches to learning: an investigation of the actual and preferred perceptions of Hong Kong secondary school students, *Instructional Science*, Vol. 22, pp. 233–46.

Clark, D. (1996) *Schools as Learning Communities: Transforming Education*, London, Cassell.

Cordingley, P. (1999) Pedagogy, educational management and the TTA research agenda, in Bush, T., Bell, L., Bolam, R., Glatter, R. and Ribbins,

P. (eds.) *Educational Management: Redefining Theory, Policy and Practice*, London, Paul Chapman.

Devoogd, G. (1998) Primary schooling: a US perspective, in Moyles, J. and Hargreaves, L. (eds.) *The Primary Curriculum: Learning from International Perspectives*, London, Routledge.

Dimmock, C. (2000) *Designing the Learning-Centred School: A Cross-Cultural Perspective*, London, Falmer.

Dimmock, C. and Walker, A. (1998) Comparative educational administration: developing a cross-cultural conceptual framework, *Educational Administration Quarterly*, Vol. 34, no. 4, October, pp. 558–95.

Dimmock, C. and Wildy, H. (1995) Conceptualising curriculum management in an effective secondary school: a Western Australian case study, *Curriculum Journal*, Vol. 6, no. 3, Autumn, pp. 297–323.

Galton, M. (1996) Teaching, learning and the co-ordinator, in O'Neill, J. and Kitson, N. (eds.) *Effective Curriculum Management: Co-ordinating Learning in the Primary School*, London, Routledge.

Gardner, H. (1983) *Frames of Mind*, London: Fontana.

Goleman, M. (1996) *Emotional Intelligence*, London: Bloomsbury.

Handy, C. (1994) *The Empty Raincoat*, London, Hutchinson.

Harrison, G. (1997) The management of teaching and learning at Queen Elizabeth's Grammar School, in Bowring-Carr, C. and West-Burnham, J. (eds.) *Managing Learning for Achievement*, London, Pitman.

Lumby, J. (1997) The learning organisation, in Bush, T. and Middlewood, D. (eds.) *Managing People in Education*, London, Paul Chapman.

Lumby, J. (1999a) Transforming structures and cultures, in Middlewood, D., Coleman, M. and Lumby, J. *Practitioner Research in Education: Making a Difference*, London, Paul Chapman.

Lumby, J. (1999b) Influencing the management of the curriculum, in Middlewood, D., Coleman, M. and Lumby, J. *Practitioner Research in Education: Making a Difference*, London, Paul Chapman.

Lumby, J. (2001) *Managing Further Education: Learning Enterprise*, London, Paul Chapman.

Organisation for Economic Co-operation and Development (OECD) (1996) *Information Technology and the Future of Post-Secondary Education*, Paris, CERI.

Pell, A. (1998) Primary schooling in rural South Africa, in Moyles, J. and Hargreaves, L. (eds.) *The Primary Curriculum: Learning from International Perspectives*, London, Routledge.

Pitcher, T. (1995) Building blocks to transform learning, *Innovations in FE*, Spring, pp. 10–19.

Randle, K. and Brady, N. (1997) Further education and the new managerialism, *Journal of Further and Higher Education*, Vol. 21, no. 2, pp. 229–39.

Ralph, M. (1995) Developing the college as a learning organisation, *Coombe Lodge Report*, Vol. 24, nos. 7 and 8.

Regan, L. (1998) Primary schooling: an Australian perspective, in Moyles, J. and Hargreaves, L. (eds.) *The Primary Curriculum: Learning from International Perspectives*, London, Routledge.

Satow, T. and Wang, Z. (1994) Cultural and organizational factors in human resource management in China and Japan, *Journal of Managerial Psychology*, Vol. 9, no. 4, pp. 3–11.

Senge, P. (1993) *The Fifth Discipline*, London, Century Business.

Siraj-Blatchford, I. (1999) Early childhood pedagogy: practice, principles and research, in Mortimore, P. (ed.) *Understanding Pedagogy and its Impact on Learning*, London, Paul Chapman.

Southworth, G. (1994) The learning school, in Ribbins, R. and Burridge, E. (eds.) *Improving Education: Promoting Quality in Schools*, London, Cassell.

Sugimine, H. (1998) Primary schooling in Japan, in Moyles, J. and Hargreaves, L. (eds.) *The Primary Curriculum: Learning from International Perspectives*, London, Routledge.

Stoll, L. and Fink, D. (1996) *Changing our Schools*, Buckingham, Open University Press.

Wang, J. and Mao, S. (1996) Culture and the kindergarten curriculum in the People's Republic of China, *Early Childhood Development and Care*, Vol. 123, pp. 143–56.

Watkins, C. and Mortimore, P. (1999) Pedagogy: what do we know? in Mortimore, P. (ed.) *Understanding Pedagogy and its Impact on Learning*, London, Paul Chapman.

# 2

# MODELS OF CURRICULUM ORGANISATION

## Neil Burton and David Middlewood, with Roy Blatchford

The organisation of the curriculum is dependent upon many different pressures acting upon the educational institution, both internal and external. The relative importance of these various tensions, as perceived by the key curriculum decision-makers in the school or college (see Section C), will manifest as the learning and teaching culture within the organisation. Systems and structures will be developed or evolve to service this approach. The way that these influential factors are identified, and as a consequence managed, can be generalised through the development of simplistic models. These models reflect the different theories of learning and teaching, social and political perspectives of the role of education and the practical parameters and logistics of the educational establishments that they are delivered in. They represent, to some extent, the degree of ownership that stakeholders, in particular students and teachers, have on the curriculum. The management implications of these models will be addressed in Chapter 3 of this book.

Once we move beyond the perception of the curriculum purely being defined in terms of the content that is being taught (Chapter 1), then we come to a wider perspective of what is actually being learnt in educational organisations. Wragg (1997) proposes the concept of a 'cubic curriculum', whereby each axis of the cube offers a different aspect of the curriculum. The three dimensions that he offers are:

1) The subject being taught (i.e. *what* is being learned and taught).
2) Cross-curricular themes (i.e. *what* makes separate components into a whole).
3) The forms of teaching and learning employed (i.e. *how* everything is communicated) (Wragg, 1997, p. 3).

For an effective structure for learning and teaching it is imperative that all three aspects be acknowledged and approached in a balanced way.

Although this model is useful in terms of identifying a position from which to evaluate and describe the curriculum, it is perhaps less helpful in providing a way to view the management of the curriculum. Offered here is a variation on this three-dimensional model, this time focusing upon three distinct management levels that are apparent in many educational organisations (see also Figure 2.1):

- Visionary – the 'learnt curriculum' (the skills, knowledge and attitudes that provide a focus for the *discrete* educational experience at the school or college).
- Strategic – the 'taught curriculum' (the pedagogy, subjects and organisational culture/learning environment that will be employed to deliver the learnt curriculum).
- Structural – the 'enabled curriculum' (the identification, deployment and management of teachers (or teaching materials), resources and organisational systems to enable the taught curriculum to be delivered).

Given this view of the curriculum, it is apparent from a rational perspective that there is a hierarchy. First, a vision of the purpose of education in terms of the skills, knowledge and attitudes that are to be developed needs to be agreed and communicated. Only then can strategies be devised with these overarching goals in mind. It is at this point that decisions concerning the operational management can be taken. Implicit in this framework is the imperative for clarity of vision, but there is a range of ways in which this vision can be expressed – from the abstract and philosophical to the highly practical and quantitative. For example, it is often the way that the vision is expressed and who it is expressed by, that is a strong determinant of the nature of the model to be developed and employed.

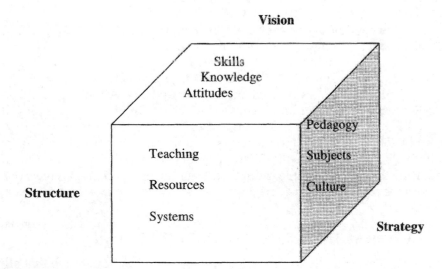

**Figure 2.1**  A three-dimensional view of curriculum management

Increasingly, varying degrees of state control over the curriculum offered in state schools and colleges, are providing frameworks for a curriculum to be taught, isolated from a clear vision expressing the purpose of the curriculum. To some extent, the local leadership, either at district or at the level of individual schools and colleges, is being required to 'work backwards' from this framework and set it within a meaningful and purposeful vision. 'The positive organisation is one where the constraints are defined and accepted but which tries to redefine and fulfil its purpose within these constraints' (Everard and Morris, 1996, p. 175). These external pressures or constraints are noted and acknowledged within the models described below. It does need to be recognised that the freedom and quality of the local leadership will be a prime enabler (or constraint) on the extent to which the local vision is balanced against the requirements of the state framework.

## THE IMPORTANCE OF LEADERSHIP

In any model of the curriculum, ownership of the vision by all those involved in the delivery and reception, is crucial to the level of success. Much of that ownership comes from the ability of the leader to align the vision with the needs, hopes and aspirations of the stakeholders. This ability of the leader to effectively evaluate and assess the environment is highlighted in the work of West-Burnham (1997), Morrison (1998), Pettigrew and Whipp (1993) and MacBeath (1998) among others. This vision will be an attempt to encapsulate the position that the school or college wants to be in, with respect to the curriculum, based on a clear understanding of the reality of where it currently is – the 'head in the clouds with feet firmly on the ground' approach, which is dealt with more fully in Chapter 7.

For the successful identification of the current state of the curriculum, it will be necessary to employ a range of evaluation tools, including measures of academic achievement. It is also necessary to gain insight into the perceptions of various stakeholder groups in respect of curriculum processes and curriculum outcomes beyond examination results. Although qualifications are a transferable and marketable outcome of an effectively deployed curriculum, there is often a richness of experience that can only be expressed in other terms. Chapter 6 of this volume discusses the key elements of curriculum evaluation while Waring (1999) takes a wider perspective of evaluating the outcomes of learning and teaching by seeking the views of a wider range of stakeholders.

## CHARACTERISTICS OF CURRICULUM MODELS

Models of the curriculum cannot be developed or imposed in isolation from other influential factors. To an extent any model of the curriculum, as it exists in the educational establishment, will be a compromise between these various pressures; a reflection of reality and the vision that is being worked towards. Some of these pressures can be seen as extremes on a continuum, though differences can be more perceived than actual (see Figure 2.2).

These driving forces are reflected in the ways in which the 'important elements' of the curriculum are perceived or the level of ownership and control of curriculum change. None of the points are necessarily mutually exclusive, but clearly the more influences that the curriculum is being encouraged to satisfy the more complicated (or possibly even confused) the vision will be. These cannot be seen as ten distinct curriculum models, simply as ideals that form reference points for further examination of the curriculum. Some of these pressures, such as the level of state control, are currently being placed under a greater level of scrutiny than others. Each pressure will now be described and exemplified.

## Student centred versus subject focused

Placing the student at the heart of the curriculum offers an important message in respect of the focus of the teaching and learning. The needs of the individual become paramount in the educational process. Programmes of study are directed towards the 'interests, attitudes and previous experience' (Galton, 1998, p. 77) of the student. This is often regarded as the 'traditional' model of primary education, which can still be seen in the organisation of primary or elementary schools in many parts of the world such as Japan (Yamamoto, 1998, p. 128), Hong Kong (Morris and Adamson, 1998, p. 196) and the component countries of the UK. The student-centred approach is deemed to be particularly appropriate for the younger student owing to the very localised world view that children are perceived to enter formal education with. Clearly this 'world-view' reasoning cannot be at the root of the rise of this model in post-compulsory education. These students may seek additional educational development with particular and specific aims in mind. This will require the school or college to offer learning opportunities specific to these needs. In doing so, particular teaching or

| | | |
|---|---|---|
| Student centred | ⟷ | Subject focused |
| Process | ⟷ | Content |
| Classroom led | ⟷ | State controlled |
| Open ended | ⟷ | Target driven |

**Figure 2.2**  Continuum of pressures on the curriculum

pedagogic approaches may be employed, such as distance or networked learning, or the offer of a unique timetable of courses.

There is a growing understanding, presented through recent literature focusing upon educational psychology and learning, that individuals have different learning styles. These differences can be identified in terms of how students receive information, analyse and construct concepts, and represent it. Because of these learning differences, for students to operate most effectively, information needs to be presented in a format and assessed in a style that is most suitable for their individual needs. Riding and Rayner (1998) discuss cognitive style in terms of two dimensions: organisation and representation. The organisational (holist-analytic) dimension refers to the way that an individual arranges information and has an impact on presentation of teaching and the curriculum – some students prefer to focus on the 'larger picture', others on the details. Representation (verbal-imagery) refers to the way that students analyse information (do they think in words or mental pictures?) and this has a significant impact on the preferred assessment format (some will more effectively demonstrate their understanding through an essay, others through a practical activity). Preedy (in Brundrett and Burton, 2000), working in primary education, confirms that acknowledging the preferred learning style of the student through the curriculum leads to significant improvements in overall educational performance.

A student-centred approach to education is a key feature of many target-driven models. Individual needs and learning styles are matched to teaching styles to enable individual (and thus class and school) learning targets to be met. This has been a particular feature of the current trend in the UK, the USA, Australia and Hong Kong, among others, towards the ideal of 'self-managing' schools (Caldwell and Spinks, 1998), focusing on the work of Dimmock (2000). Designing the curriculum around the needs of individuals has also been a feature of special needs education, which is now becoming a formal element of mainstream curriculum planning. These individual education plans (IEPs) (DfEE, 2000) are designed to focus the efforts of individuals towards personal achievable targets. Clearly, the question of 'who sets the targets?' is an important one that will be addressed below.

Traditionally this approach implies a secure educational development across a range of learning areas but will often require well-defined lines of communication and co-operation to ensure progression and development over the longer timescale.

## Subject focused

The difference between student- and subject-focused curriculum organisation has traditionally been seen as being the distinction between primary and secondary education in the UK, at least until the introduction of the

National Curriculum to England and Wales in the late 1980s. This approach concentrates upon the conceptual development of the subject, sometimes quite narrowly defined, and often in isolation from the development of other subject areas. While being an effective means of employing the subject specialisms of academically focused teaching staff, it has been the basis of the organisation of state-sponsored curricula (England, Japan, Canada, Switzerland and Germany). Many within the teaching profession have expressed doubts over the desirability or potential of such an approach to deliver a broad and balanced learning experience. Lawton sums this up by saying: 'Subjects might be useful for 'delivering' certain aspects of the curriculum, but they (are) most unsatisfactory as a basic structure' (1996 pp. 72–3).

In many educational systems (UK, Eastern Europe, among others) a subject-focused approach to the development of a curriculum has been the result of an assessment system which concentrates upon academic achievement in a limited range of subject areas. Once widely recognised qualifications (such as the English A-level, or the single honours degree) had become established, the curriculum became purely a means of achieving a narrowly defined subject aim.

Many nationally defined curricula will attempt to find a compromise position between these foci. The French Framework Law on Education (French Education Ministry, 1989) places an emphasis on outcomes and targets: 'to educate an entire age group to at least the level of the vocational aptitude certificate or vocational studies certificate and 80 per cent of the group to *Baccalaureate* level within ten years', while at the same time confirming that the public sector education service is 'designed and organised around students and aims to contribute to equality of opportunity'. Canada, a culturally and ethnically diverse country, focuses upon the needs of the individual but places these within the context of encouraging multicultural harmony. According to an international comparative review of curricula published on the World Wide Web (WWW) by the Qualifications and Curriculum Authority (QCA). 'Education in Singapore "aims to develop the potential and ability of school children to the fullest". To this end, the "curriculum is broad-based and places emphasis on high academic standards and moral, physical and cultural studies" ' (INCA, 1998). The balance between the needs of the individual and the needs of the subject are evident in the curricula of many different public state education systems.

## Process versus content

To prepare for the upcoming 21st century, Korean education has established humanisation, refinement, informativeness, human welfare and open-mindedness as its ultimate goals. Various efforts are being made to raise a self-reliant individual equipped with a distinct

sense of independence, a creative individual with a sense of orig-
inality and an ethical individual with sound morality and democratic
citizenship.

(Republic of Korea, 1997, online)

Certainly there is a knowledge base that is at the heart of all learning styles.
For learning to take place it is necessary to be able to communicate effectively and, for this, knowledge of language is essential. The teaching of a
learning process can never be completely free of subject matter or content.
Similarly, knowledge cannot be delivered in isolation from a learning process. It is the balance of emphasis between these two in terms of actual
classroom practices that is a determinant of the curriculum model.

A curriculum that focuses upon content can be seen as an 'academic'
approach to learning. For example, teaching methodology will concentrate
on the effective delivery of knowledge and will be best served by assessment techniques that emphasise recall, interpretation and analysis. Students are more likely to be the recipients of learning rather than playing a
particularly active role in the learning process. In order to be recipients of
knowledge, students will need to develop at least some learning styles,
though in practice these tend to be the more passive ones such as listening
(as in a lecture format) and reading (usually under direction).

A 'process' approach uses content as a means of developing particular
learning skills which can then be employed for independent, focused
study. The assessment of this form of learning will need to concentrate on
the demonstration of these skills through application and task completion.
It is very unlikely that some content knowledge will not be learnt as a
consequence of developing the skills; in fact the processes are being learnt
to enable the student to gain access to a wider range of subject content.

By comparing the two approaches in general terms significant distinctions can be made apparent in order for strategic decisions to be made
(Figure 2.3). Process-led curricula notoriously require significantly greater
input of teacher time and learning resources at the initial stage but usually,

| Process | Content |
|---|---|
| Initially very heavy resource and teacher demands as processes are learnt | Moderate resource and teacher demands throughout |
| Active learning style | Passive learning style |
| Encourages individual learning needs to be addressed | Encourages class learning needs to be addressed |
| Slow development of knowledge base | Rapid development of knowledge base |
| Secure understanding demonstrated through application | Secure understanding demonstrated through interpretation |
| Potentially time-consuming assessment | Potentially time-efficient assessment |
| Leads to independent learning | Continued teacher/resource-dependent learning |

**Figure 2.3**  Distinction between process and content approaches

as skills are developed, allow for a more student-centred focus later. A content-led curriculum tends to be dependent upon the teacher and/or specified resources throughout. Clearly a balance between the two is desirable to ensure the rapid development of content knowledge, with simple assessment procedures, alongside active learning to encourage understanding and the development of a more independent approach to learning.

The management implications of such decisions focus on the use and distribution of resources, particularly teaching and learning support staff. A process model should deliver long-term educational gains for the students, but this may be at the expense of clearly identifiable short-term gains. Clearly it would be necessary for the senior management to ensure that students (and parents in the case of schools) are aware of the potential for slow academic growth in the initial stages while the processes become embedded.

## Classroom led versus state controlled

Where the curriculum arises out of the practice within the classroom or school or college as whole, the ownership of the curriculum in terms of professional engagement can very secure. The curriculum is developed on the basis of 'best practice' within the institution and can take into account the specific needs and aspirations of local stakeholders. A state-controlled or state-determined curriculum ensures that there is a consistent entitlement across all schools under its jurisdiction. The development of the curriculum, though potentially open to political expediencies, can take into account a much wider range of 'best practice' over a much wider range of teaching and learning situations, working towards national, as opposed to local, educational priorities.

There are now numerous examples of 'national' or state curricula in the world at various levels of prescription. Several nations, including England and South Korea, or states such as Victoria, in Australia, have introduced curricula in order to retain educational control after passing responsibility for the effective provision of educational entitlement to the schools. The prescribed curriculum, alongside testing and inspection, is seen as a balance to the delegation of funding.

## Open ended versus target driven

A curriculum which has no specified aims in mind is rightly described as 'open ended'. Such an approach suggests a particular educational philosophy where the purpose of education is purely altruistic, learning for the joy of learning. In a curriculum model based upon this approach the direction that learning and teaching takes will either be by negotiation between students and teacher, or dependent upon the interests and whims of the teacher.

It is likely that progression and continuity will not be addressed either within or between courses. Under such circumstances, unless students have a particularly clear appreciation of their own needs (thus setting their own informal targets), learning may lack direction. Where informal and open-ended goals are identified it may be possible for significant learning to take place as particular themes or interests are followed.

Given the level of accountability within most educational systems, it would appear unlikely that this will form the basis of a curriculum structure favoured by governments. It is important to acknowledge this as a potential curricular model in order to act as a balance to a narrowly defined target-driven model that does not allow the informal educational interests of students and teaching staff to be followed. In this way, the open-endedness of this model encourages a more flexible approach to incorporate spontaneous educational developments.

## Target driven

Most countries have an 'official' curriculum, which lays down a list of aims frequently alongside an outline of the content to be taught. Unfortunately not all of these curricula contain a rationale or a statement of educational philosophy to place the curriculum into clear context. This will give the curriculum an operational parameter in isolation from a strategic direction. For this reason the curriculum becomes driven by a series of operational targets which, by and large, tend to focus on the performance of the school or college rather than the needs of the individual student.

## These targets can be expressed in a variety of ways

1) *Time* (number of subject days, hours or lessons). In Japan (DES, 1992), the Ministry of Education stipulates the number of hours, per subject per grade per year, regardless of whether the school is state run or private. In England there is pressure from the national inspection process (Ofsted) for primary schools to ensure that students receive an hour of literacy and numeracy activities per day. In higher education, English initial teacher training requires students to have a prescribed number of days in school per year of training. The implication of this model for the management of the curriculum can be satisfied by the teaching timetable – as long as it indicated that the specified subjects are being taught for the prescribed lengths of time.

2) *Curriculum content* (what is to be taught). Several national curricula (including France and the countries of the UK) prescribe the content to be covered in each taught subject, either by year or educational phase. In post-compulsory vocational education, where stakeholder groups have a particularly significant influence over the curriculum, to gain the

validation of professional or trades bodies, courses may have to be developed to meet these targets. Clearly, like the time target above, this is purely in terms of educational input rather than output – the focus is on the teaching rather than the learning. Here the targets are met through medium- and long-term planning documents (see Chapter 4) which should indicate how and when the different elements of the prescribed curriculum would be delivered.

3) *Curriculum assessment* (what is achieved). This is a clear focus on the output as a result of the curriculum – learning. There are two main ways in which the achievements can be expressed: in aggregated terms (by class or school/college) or on an individual basis (by student or by student for each subject). There are many countries, including the UK, Israel and Hong Kong, where aggregated examination results are used as a measure of the success of the school – even being published as 'league tables' in England. The focus of assessment, if it is to be used for these purposes, is entirely as a measure of attainment rather than for diagnostic or formative use. If this is to be the only measure of success, then the curriculum becomes assessment led – the form and focus of the assessment tool drive teaching and learning. Examination technique may become as important as the understanding of the content of the curriculum, with the risk of impoverishment of learning as a process.

The ways that the targets are expressed have significant implications for the management of the curriculum. Individual student targets imply individual learning programmes and the imposition of systems to monitor individual progress (see Chapter 5). Resources must be employed for this purpose and appropriate recording systems developed. Where aggregated data is used to set targets moral and ethical considerations come into play. In England, where aggregated school examination results have been used for some years to indicate school performance, two morally questionable trends were noted:

- The increased likelihood of 'less able' students to be excluded (thus taking them out of the calculations).
- The concentrating of educational resources on those students at the threshold of meeting targets (increasing support for students on the C/D grade boundary in 16+ examinations to attain a 'C' at the expense of those students deemed to be 'safe 'B's). O'Neill (2000) notes an almost identical trend in New Zealand.

## TURNING MODELS INTO REALITY

With these theoretical models in mind as a framework to make reference to, we now give three examples of how educational models have been turned into reality with examples from primary, tertiary and secondary education in the UK. These examples are offered simply *as* examples of how particular leaders and staffs have attempted to give their communities an effective curriculum through a specific approach, based on their own philosophy.

## KINGSHURST JUNIOR AND KNOWLE CHURCH OF ENGLAND PRIMARY SCHOOLS, SOLIHULL

The social contexts of the schools are very different, one in the middle of a large urban rented-housing estate, the other in a prosperous semi-rural situation. Both headteachers, Jeff Derby and Pat Preedy, were seeking to enhance the learning within their schools; Kingshurst because it had recently failed an external inspection owing to low standards of pupil achievement in English and maths, and Knowle because it was felt there was untapped potential among the children.

In both cases it was apparent that the curriculum, as it was currently being delivered, was not entirely meeting the needs of the students. With additional funding, made possible by Knowle achieving 'Beacon School' status (one given by the government, with funding, to help spread good practice), the schools were able to implement a programme of 'accelerated learning'. This approach to learning paid a great deal of attention to the way that children learn, and acknowledged that learning itself was a skill that could be taught. With a greater awareness of these skills, the children could become more effective students and the teachers more effective in their role. Central to their approach is ensuring that the child is in the right state to learn. These are:

- *Intellectual state* – focus on the educational goals (start with the 'big picture' and visualise the outcomes).
- *Emotional state* – success oriented based upon the positive self-image of the children.
- *Biological state* – reinforcement through success.
- *Physical state* – an appropriate environment (temperature, ventilation, etc.) that encourages alertness.
- *Dependency state* – having a positive role model to aspire to.
- *Social state* – ensuring that everyone in the school has a positive attitude towards learning.
- *Activity state* – ensuring that learning is broken down into manageable 'chunks'.

Teaching is differentiated to take into account not only different abilities but also different learning styles. By ensuring that they employ an appropriate balance of visual, auditory and kinaesthetic forms to their presentations and the responses they request for the children, the teaching allows a greater number to access the content of the learning. By concentrating on how they teach and having a much greater awareness of how children learn, this has had a significant effect on the rate and the security with which the children are now learning. In both schools the children have become much more successful as students, both in terms of their depth of understanding and their examination results – those of Kingshurst in particular showing significant improvement.

## OLDHAM COLLEGE

This medium-sized further education college has 7,500 students pursuing courses on a full- or part-time basis. Courses at A-level (16–19 years), which are offered in the daytime at local schools, are only offered in the evening at the college with only about a third of the 'normal' time available. The college is committed to inclusive learning practices and differentiation of teaching and learning, with a requirement therefore to consider students as individuals and review curriculum 'delivery'. With a heavy commitment to and investment in ICT, the college explored the teaching and learning of A-level biology through a multimedia approach which, while attaining comparable standards, would also:

- give students the chance to use alternative learning strategies
- enable them to take responsibility for their own learning
- allow them to work at their own pace
- enable them to develop transferable skills beneficial to further study of work.

The results of the study by Joy (2000) showed:

- higher satisfaction by students with the multimedia approach
- lower satisfaction by students with conventional approaches.

*But* in the need to prepare for external examinations, students expressed a preference for conventional methods and wanted ideally a mixture of both.

The project highlighted for the college the need to address urgently the issue of independent learners and the relevance of multimedia technology, and to recognise the individuality of learners so that they can learn in a way that is best for them within a context of delivering a curriculum with a vast array of influences upon it (see Figure 2.4).

Our third example is given in detail since it considers elements already identified in this volume as being key to the new emphasis on learning in the twenty-first century, including 'cradle to grave' learning and increasing flexibility of schools and colleges to support this. Those fortunate enough to have the opportunity to open a brand new school at the turn of the century have both a real and symbolic opportunity to turn vision into reality. In the words of Roy Blatchford, principal of Walton High in Milton Keynes, England, this new reality had to offer 'some kind of golden bridge between the safe, the recognisable, the radical and the pioneering'. Walton High was opened in the autumn of 1999 as a leading learning centre and school for the twenty-first century. Roy Blatchford's 'model' is presented here in his own words.

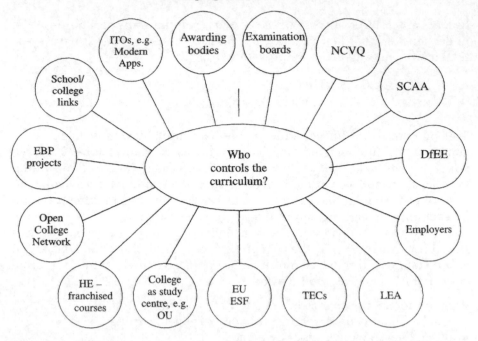

**Figure 2.4** Influences on curriculum design in further education in the UK
*Source:* Joy, 2000.

## WALTON HIGH, MILTON KEYNES – PRINCIPAL: ROY BLATCHFORD
© ROY BLATCHFORD

Walton High was launched by its governing body and staff in the knowledge that those we serve have clear views about what a *school* means. Families look back to their own experience, they compare notes with others in their family and with their friends, they go by reputation and often examination results. In the end, we each wish for a child an environment which matches our own family values and expectations of what formal education should provide.

Trawling through the literature of the past 25 years on comprehensive education, one might identify six core (and evolving) ideals upon which the system has been built and developed:

- entitlement
- equal valuing
- empowerment
- community
- participation
- excellence.

Further, the world of education has drawn much in recent years from international business trends. Pundits talk of 'zero defects' and 'total quality management' (not to mention 'performance thresholds'), and you cannot attend a conference about schools today which does not in some shape or form focus on the culture of high quality learning.

Clean slates do not exist. Orthodoxies are powerful. It is a brave group of people opening a new learning community that dares to step far outside the prevailing mood of the times.

We are daily reminded that change is a constant. Yet is it not the case, as the American poet Robert Frost wrote, that most of the change we think we see in life 'Is due to truths being in and out of favour'? There are five fundamental 'truths' which underpin any flourishing school, and which should serve as the starting points for curriculum and organisational planning.

FIRST – we know that schools matter, that the provision of a well-ordered, stimulating learning environment is a common right for all our children. Truly, each child has one chance.

SECOND – we know that schools matter more and more as the family unit is less constant for so many children. Whatever else they do, schools need to redefine, refine and articulate social and moral values and respect for others, irrespective of their class, sex, race, religion or heritage tongue.

THIRD – we believe that schools must promote the highest achievement in youngsters, *irrespective* of their abilities or aspirations. Competition and collaboration must play equally in learning.

FOURTH – we celebrate, in a climate of equal opportunity and access to that opportunity, a broad range of achievements. We challenge fixed notions of ability. We value and reward children's oral, practical, academic, sporting, artistic and yes, leadership skills.

FIFTH – we believe that an effective and flourishing school should be 'public' rather than 'private', explaining to parents what is being taught and how the curriculum is being interpreted. It should be open to praise and criticism (not blame) in a genuine spirit of partnership while at the same time reasonably affirming that judgments about pedagogy rest with the professionals.

How then do these fundamental of values help build this golden bridge? Let us suppose for one moment that on one side of the bridge lies the familiar post-1944 school curriculum; grafted on to that is the National Curriculum, in turn inspected by the Ofsted framework and, tellingly, enshrined in performance management frameworks. There is a controllable, classroom-based, academic subject focus to all that which central government of any persuasion is not willingly going to release. What lies on the other side of the bridge? There are four key points to be made here:

- The current organisation of the school day and year reinforces the idea that education takes place in strictly defined circumstances.

- The heavy public investment in schools' physical facilities is vastly under-exploited.
- Equipment in schools – particularly ICT – is looking distinctly old-fashioned by comparison with the external worlds of work and leisure.
- Teaching and learning methods used in schools have yet to catch up with the understanding scientists now have of how the human brain works.

In creating a curriculum model for Walton High and its business partner, Walton Learning Centre, year-round learning in and beyond classrooms is at the heart of our quest to make lifelong learning a local reality for families (see Figure 2.5).

Translating this model into practice, Walton High staff roundly embrace much of what has been learnt in recent years about school improvement techniques: standardising best practice, target-setting, monitoring, audit and self-review. (No school planner should underestimate the enormous value of a termly tutorial for each student with his or her tutor.) Teaching and support staff work smart to challenge under-expectations and under-achievement of any kind, while remembering that learning is about both fun and fundamentals.

- The 'learning day' operates 'Eight till late', with Session 1 (8 a.m. – 8.30 a.m.) and Session 9 (3.30 p.m. – 5.30 p.m.) not viewed by students as extracurricular but rather as an integral part of their day.
- Short Courses (Wednesdays 1.40 p.m. – 3.20 p.m.) bring outside tutors to work with students in small, mixed-age groups for an extended block of time, enjoying anything from Politics, First Aid, Line Dancing and Fencing to Batik and Powerpoint.

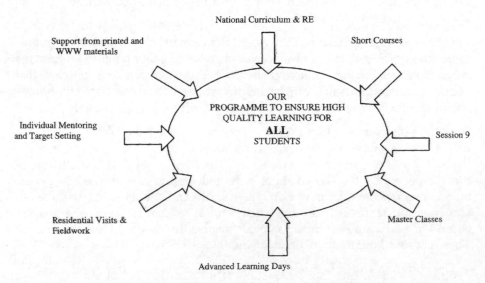

**Figure 2.5** The Walton High model

- Master Classes operate during weekends, evenings and (historical term!) school holidays in Maths, Literacy, Music, Sailing – whatever students express an interest in and staff expertise/visiting tutors can match. The Yamaha Music School runs four evenings a week and at weekends to provide family music-making of the highest order.
- Advanced Learning Days serve to highlight that each of us learns in various ways, using different intelligences days when the normal timetable is suspended in favour of 'The Chemistry of Air' (Science) or 'On the Lake' (Outward Bound) or 'Choosing the Future' (Citizenship), during which youngsters and adults alike can work in small groups with visiting tutors and experience the challenge, fun and excitement of learning something new.
- In an e-age, curriculum schemes of work, guides for parents on how to help their children, homework schedules and the rest are readily accessible online. These are areas of our work which will surely expand to serve the connected community of 3,000+ families in the Walton Partnership of schools.

We are still in early days, and will continue to push the boundaries in shaping the above model. Learning in the classroom is our core business. Thinking through how we can best stimulate – for students and families alike – learning *beyond* the classroom is a natural next step. One thing is certain: the rapid advances in information technology (not the *whole* story of the future of schooling it should be remembered) are set to challenge and redefine our current ways of working.

A key part of Walton Learning Centre's work in the coming decade will be to find practical and innovative solutions to building that golden bridge between learning and teaching practices that are past, passing and to come.

In the first year of our growth we have glimpsed the 'world-class education' much quoted by UK government and advisers. The 'cocktail' is not rocket science: regular students, a whizzy group of motivated staff, flexible working conditions, high-quality environment, lots of new resources and reasonable class sizes. Crucially, confidence, self-esteem and motivation among our student body are high because we have time and space to see them each as individuals with potential. The staffroom is a place where animated conversations about styles of learning are the norm.

Sustaining what we have begun is our core and invigorating challenge. To realise our ambitions to lead learning in Milton Keynes and beyond, we shall not be afraid to take some quiet steps into the twenty-first century which challenge historical assumptions of what schools are all about. What we develop locally in the context of lifelong learning may then have national resonance.

---

All three examples above, of many that could have been given, demonstrate the importance of clarity in the curriculum model for a school or college. A confused model, one that lacks support, or one that is not shared between teachers and learners will be less effective.

# REFERENCES

Brundrett, M. and Burton, N. (2000) *Case Studies in Excellence: the Beacon Schools Experience*, Dereham, Peter Francis.

Caldwell, B. and Spinks, J. (1998) *Beyond the Self-Managing School*, London, Falmer.

Department for Education and Employment (DfEE) (2000) http://www.dfee.gov.uk/sen/sensupp.htm (accessed 14 March 2000).

Department of Education and Science (DES) (1992) *Teaching and Learning in Japanese Elementary Schools*, London, HMSO.

Dimmock, C. (2000) *Designing the Learning-Centred School*, London, Falmer.

Everard, K. B. and Morris, G. (1996) *Effective School Management*, London, Paul Chapman.

French Education Ministry (1989) *Loi d'orientation*, no. 89–486 of 10 July.

Galton, M. (1998) Principles of curriculum building, in Moyles, J. and Hargreaves, L. (eds.) *The Primary Curriculum: Learning from International Perspectives*, London, Routledge.

INCA (1998) *Singapore: 1 Context and principles of education*, www.inca.org.uk (accessed June 2000).

Joy, P. (2000) Evaluation of independent/multimedia learning materials for part-time A-Level students, University of Leicester (unpublished).

Lawton, D. (1996) *Beyond the National Curriculum*, London, Hodder and Stoughton.

MacBeath, J. (ed.) (1998) *Effective School Leadership: Responding to Change*, London, Paul Chapman.

Morris, P. and Adamson, B. (1998) Primary schooling in Hong Kong, in Moyles, J. and Hargreaves, L. (eds.) *The Primary Curriculum: Learning from International Perspectives*, London, Routledge.

Morrison, K. (1998) *Management Theories for Educational Change*, London, Paul Chapman.

O'Neill, J. (2000) Headship: the missing standards, *Headship Matters*, Vol. 1. no. 5, Cambridge, Optimus.

Pettigrew, A. and Whipp, R. (1993) Understanding the environment, in Mabey, C. and Mayon-White, B. (eds.) *Managing Change*, London, Paul Chapman.

Republic of Korea, Ministry of Education (1996) *Education in Korea 1996–1997: A Brief Outline*, Seoul, Ministry of Education.

Riding, R. and Rayner, S. (1998) *Cognitive Styles and Learning Strategies*, London, David Fulton.

Waring, S. (1999) Finding your place: sensing the external environment, in Lumby, J. and Foskett, N. (eds.) *Managing External Relations in Schools and Colleges*, London, Paul Chapman.

West-Burnham, J. (1997) *Managing Quality in Schools*, London, Longman.

Wragg, E. (1997) *The Cubic Curriculum*, London, Routledge.

Yamamoto, K. (1998) Primary schooling in Japan, in Moyles J. and Hargreaves, L. (eds.) *The Primary Curriculum: Learning from International Perspectives*, London, Routledge.

## 3

# THE MANAGEMENT CONSEQUENCES OF DIFFERENT MODELS OF TEACHING AND LEARNING

## *Peter Silcock and Mark Brundrett*

### INTRODUCTION: THREE MODELS OF TEACHING AND LEARNING

There are many different stances that curriculum managers and teachers may take when organising curricular programmes (see Chapter 2) but these will tend to cluster around three possibilities or 'ideal types', referring to three modal relationships between the two pedagogic activities, teaching and learning. They are:

- A teacher- or subject-centred ('top down') approach – where a predetermined curriculum is delivered.
- A learner-centred ('bottom up' approach) – where the curriculum manager determines or designs the curriculum on the basis of student needs.
- A 'partnership' approach which seeks to bind teacher and learners to a common enterprise combining external expectations and individual needs.

### TEACHER-CENTRED APPROACHES

Teacher-centred approaches comprise all those methods deploying a firm control of learner behaviour to achieve prescribed ends. They are therefore likely to be chosen where curricular coverage is at a premium. Enshrined values are sometimes called 'traditional', being pre-specified on the basis of what has previously been found worthwhile. Procedures will include not only teaching methods, but also assessment techniques geared to measuring outputs (to check curricular delivery). Where forms of assessment are a main criterion for standards, it is often these which provide the surest guide for teachers. Teacher-centred approaches are, for these reasons, usually subject oriented and assessment led.

There are sound practical and theoretical reasons why teachers might wish to take firm charge of learner behaviour.

## Practical reasons

It may be that closely prescribed curricula can only be realised successfully through a tightly controlled pedagogy. This likelihood explains why the implementing of common curricula in English and Welsh state schools over recent years has been accompanied by 'reforms' increasing teacher accountability for learning outcomes, making it imperative for curriculum managers to plan for progression within their subjects. It also explains why the implementing of common (national) curricula for initial teacher education courses has followed on the heels of school reform, since such direct, bureaucratic control ensures teachers are prepared, during initial training, to focus on delivering pre-specified knowledge and skills. Increases in accountability (for example, through standard assessment tasks (SATs) testing for school pupils and the setting of 'competency' targets for adult trainees) have forced curriculum managers to concentrate on the goals politicians identify for them.

More broadly, any teaching 'model of good practice' which involves strict target-setting overrides differences between institutions and learners in favour of using procedures best able to shape students' test performances. Student achievements are inflated so as to raise an institution's examination performance, and educational standards (at least those measured through testing) rise commensurately. This model can be described as that of a 'skilled traditionalist' (Lee and Fitz, 1997). It is equivalent to the one embodied in current Ofsted school inspection frameworks (ibid.). Her Majesty's Chief Inspector of Schools publicly endorses methodologies geared to subject coverage (Ofsted, 1996). Politically speaking, teachers might expect tangible rewards to spring from following the lead of their own school inspectors. Yet teacher-centred approaches are not confined to schools. In any organisation where curricular coverage is linked to set targets, managers are likely to adopt a subject- or teacher-oriented approach. For this reason, teacher-oriented management practices are also found in colleges, universities and other post-compulsory institutions.

As it happens, there are more humane 'top-down' strategies which can ameliorate the didacticism implied by strict target-setting. Teaching staff, who see themselves as craftspersons or technicians, may fulfil their professional briefs within supportive, less rigid frameworks than any governed by strict obedience to formal guidelines. For indirect methods to remain teacher centred, they need only conform to the connected criteria of – in practice – directing students' learning (albeit tacitly) while, thereby, dictating curricular outcomes. It is easiest to grasp this difference between separate sorts of teacher-directed work by saying something about theoretical reasons for managing a curriculum in this way.

## Theoretical reasons

The control of learners' performance outcomes (meeting targets) implies the management of learner behaviour. Behaviour-management techniques used in educational and other contexts are underwritten by Skinnerian Behaviourism built on 'laws' of conditioning (summarised in Atkinson *et al.*, 1990). The best-known law – the 'law of effect' – states that 'behaviour which is rewarded will tend to be repeated'; and, by rewarding (positively reinforcing) or not rewarding (negatively reinforcing) student responses to tasks, teachers can 'shape' quite complex skills (ibid.). A major limitation of relying exclusively on this controlling system is that (as Chomsky, 1959, helped to draw to our attention) complex 'higher order' skills (such as critical thinking) cannot be directly conditioned simply because they are mentally organised, not behaviourally structured. What we know about higher-order capabilities suggests that a single-minded focus on transmission cannot at the same time achieve goals of knowledge application and transfer (Davis, 1998; Kelly, 1994, 1995). Fortunately, recent work in developmental psychology has generated theories which suppose that complex learning occurs when people 'internalise' the interactive or modelled processes they meet in group situations. From a 'socio-cultural' perspective (see, for example, Pollard, 1999), the establishing and promoting of an institutional culture valuing prescribed knowledge and skills can, itself, create a framework within which curricular outcomes are to a significant degree predetermined.

## Management implications

In order to achieve narrowly defined goals, curriculum managers have to ensure that teachers influence learner behaviour more surely than they may have formerly. They can, as argued, require teachers to use fairly strict management techniques (derived from Behaviourism), where 'correct' responses are rewarded and incorrect ignored, or broader strategies connected to group motivations and pressures, working – for instance – through peer tuition and collaborative teamwork as well as through teachers' dexterity. The degree of 'control' exerted by educators in teaching situations is mimicked by that managerial control of teacher behaviour often expressed in the form of 'criteria' by which performance is judged (see DfEE, 1998). The probability is that a mix of direct and indirect management strategies will prove most effective in reaching goals set by standard curricula. In fact, this is what research discovers. In observational research, piloting ways of implementing the National Literacy Strategy in primary schools in England, Sylva *et al.* (1999) found the best teaching methods (measured by improvements in reading age) did rely on forms of instruction much more than were used in parallel classrooms. But they were not used the whole time. For reasonable periods, pupils were engaged (and were encouraged to engage) in independent, individual and group activity.

There has, lately, been a move towards encouraging teachers to adopt more formulaic guidelines devised by empirical researchers into institutional 'effectiveness' (see, for example, Brophy and Good, 1986; Caldwell and Spinks, 1988; Creemers, 1994; Gipps, 1992; Sammons, Hillman and Mortimore, 1995). The whole tenor of these projects implies that teaching success boils down to an up-to-the-minute familiarity with what the best research tells us: context-specific factors (such as learner ability and background, resource constraints, value orientation and so on) are minor irritants to be overcome by conscientiously keeping to whatever is prescribed. Unfortunately, there is a bewildering number of lists of criteria (reviewers often find themselves reviewing reviews, see, for example, Hallam and Ireson, 1999), all set at a high level of generality. Anyone looking for a package of measures to improve teaching skill usually needs to transcend the very general. Indeed effectiveness conditions discovered by research often do no more than pin down what is essential to the job anyhow. To illustrate with Hallam and Ireson's (1999) review for secondary school teachers: 'It appears important that teachers pay attention to the quantity and pace of instruction, giving information, questioning the students, handling seatwork and homework and also take account of the learning context. They also need to have clear intentions and convey these to their pupils' (pp. 82–3). With advice such as this, it is instructive to reflect on the conditions which would have to apply for it to be different.

What makes for an effective teacher is to a considerable extent built into the expectations we already have about the nature and purposes of teaching. None the less, the enhanced focus on teacher-centred approaches has, quite rightly, led to calls for improved teacher knowledge and enhanced management training for school senior managers who are required to supervise curriculum construction and development. The concomitant emphasis on continuing professional development (see, for instance, Tomlinson, 1997; West-Burnham and O'Sullivan, 1998) in the UK is being met though the developing 'national programmes' such as the National Professional Qualification for Headship (NPQH), the Headteachers Leadership and Management Programme (HEADLAMP), and the Leadership Programme for Serving Headteachers (LPSH). All such leadership programmes are underpinned by the *National Standards for Headteachers* (TTA, 1998), which defines a knowledge of 'Teaching and Learning' as one of the 'key areas' for headship. Programmes with similar aims have been introduced in many other countries, such as Australia, New Zealand, California in the USA,

Israel and Hong Kong. There is, however, a growing call for the 'ownership' of school development to emphasise the needs of an individual school (MacBeath, 1999). It is therefore entirely appropriate that the professional development of teaching staff is (at least in part) school based and designed to meet targeted priorities as defined in schools' development plans for teaching and learning (West-Burnham, 1998).

# LEARNER-CENTRED APPROACHES

Learner-centred approaches are those where top-down control is relaxed such that learners can to a degree determine educational means and ends. The qualifier ('to a degree') is significant since most learner-centred work does not deny teachers' or lecturers' authority, it simply gives them a facilitating and guiding role (for example, clarifying which goals are and are not of intrinsic value – Silcock, 1999), rather than a controlling one. Teachers will rarely adopt 'pure' learner-centred forms of curricular management. They will, however, as far as is practicable, orient themselves towards values distinct from the teacher-centred – a belief, for example, in helping students develop attitudes which they need as autonomous lifelong learners, and an acceptance that outcomes can be worth achieving though not pre-specified (in terms of content). Students entering further and higher education, especially, often have educational aims and needs beyond those specified by a 'course' and these can be addressed by means of a learner-centred form of curriculum management. Where learner outcomes are pre-specified as 'processes' (ibid.; Kelly, 1994, 1995), these indicate students' profitable relationships with knowledge and with the various activities involved in learning. Knowledge which has process features is sometimes called 'transformative' (Young, 1999).

Again, it is worth discussing practical and theoretical reasons for teachers adopting a learner-centred approach.

## Practical reasons

One difficulty for anyone teaching a standard or common curriculum is that a detailing of outcomes which pretends to be at all comprehensive will be conceptually heavy. The first English/Welsh National Curriculum was notoriously unmanageable due to the weight of subject matter it contained (Campbell, 1993), and attempts to slim it down have been only patchily successful. In this context, teachers who take a learner-centred approach delegate to students some responsibility for learning and also ease their own managerial workloads. Curricular selection procedures should operate routinely, according to students' developing commitments and interests. In short, where learners work independently and set their own targets, curriculum managers are freed to provide a more subtle 'scaffolding' of help for slow learners, set 'challenges' for the more able and work on the organisational and resource frameworks which learner-centred approaches demand.

Such an approach thus has major implications in terms of resource management for anyone who wishes learners to take charge of their learning. For example, through devolved funding, the leaders of schools and colleges can target resources on priority issues, allowing teachers and students (via curriculum managers) to become 'involved' in the purchasing priorities of the organisation. Some commentators have advocated an 'open systems approach' to institutional financing (Levacic, 1996) whereby organisations are depicted as living organisms, interacting with and responding to their environments (Hanna, 1997; Morgan, 1986). Such 'living entities' produce outputs in exchange for resources and support (Levačić, 1996 p. 128), tracing linkages between increased flexibility in deploying resources and the intended desirable effects on educational processes.

Given that teachers in learner-centred systems guide as well as facilitate, there is no reason in theory why this guidance should not occur as part of the management of a common curriculum. What is required is an interpretation of common programmes as 'frameworks of possibilities' rather than as sets of non-negotiable prescriptions. If we accept that it is *in principle* impossible to arrange the wholesale delivery of any large-scale curriculum (which has to be translated into teachable programmes), we must also see that even the most learner-governed system will need containing within some agreed framework. The curriculum manager will need to acknowledge a 'trade-off' between improved depth of learning and degree of curriculum coverage. Adey and Shayer (1996), reviewing their application of developmental theory to the teaching of secondary school science, found that their pupils not only learned a set science curriculum but were able to apply their learning to other subject areas. Teachers who stress 'process' rather than content or product will believe that in-depth learning helps students compete over the long term with more formally taught peers. Such students may, however, lose out in the short term when their progress is measured through standardised tests which, by their nature, are sensitive to surface (memorised) improvements rather than developmental (structural) gains.

Within the educational system generally, it is no accident that learner-centred approaches commonly give way to the teacher-centred approaches as pupils pass from childhood to adolescence, before returning to a rather different sort of learner-centredness as students become adult. The first transition (accompanying children's entry to secondary education, though beginning during late childhood) probably happens because of the rather obvious fact that older pupils are more amenable to influence than younger ones. It may be extremely difficult (impossible in some cases one suspects) for those managing an early years' curriculum to exert that top-down control required by rigorous target-setting. With the youngest learners, a thin line divides education from childcare: to assume one can abandon the former to achieve the latter is to risk damaging not only the emotional climate of classrooms but the fledgling self-concepts of the pupils themselves. For this reason, early childhood educators may always remain 'child centred' in the ways they teach.

However, turning to the second transition (accompanying students' entry to further education – FE – or higher education – HE), FE and HE tutors who manage 'student-centred' courses, 'distance-learning' or 'flexible-learning' programmes, usually expect students to work independently (to a degree) and so to benefit motivationally and organisationally from being delegated key responsibilities. Having effective control over their work, students can organise it to suit themselves. This situation contrasts sharply with that of early childhood education, since adult students should, theoretically, be amenable to any rational form of curricular organisation. The learner-centred system in this latter case is most likely preferred because of the practical benefits flowing from it, rather than its being chosen because of its developmental suitability.

## Theoretical reasons

Theoretical foundations of learner-centred work are those developmental and humanistic ideals asserting that learners are active constructors of their own minds (developmental), consciously 'actualising' their own identities (humanistic philosophy and psychology). Between them, these two bodies of theory compose the cognitive and affective grounds for the approach (though 'phenomenographic' studies, construing the many qualitatively separate ways human learners experience the world, complement these – Marton, 1981).

'Constructivism', born from the writings of Piaget (see, for example, 1954), is the notion that human mental advance is accomplished by individual learners working from a given experiential base. Human beings progress intellectually by applying lessons learned from past experiences to new ones. Teaching which ignores individual learners' prior and occurrent experiences will be superficial and not lead to the qualitative changes letting learners apply a 'richly textured' knowledge to their lives (Davis, 1998). Put another way, the transformative capabilities theorists like Young (1999) claim will underwrite the 'curriculum of the future' (p. 469) are transforming because they are constructed by the learners themselves 'from the inside'. Pollard (1990) points out that reflective teachers, sensitive to learner needs, provide the group impetus which helps in the construction of school knowledge. This 'social constructivist' option is popular with many (see, for example, Gipps, 1992; Gipps and Macgilchrist, 1999; Gipps, McCallum and Brown, 1999). Humanistic writers such as Rogers (1983) insist that giving learners charge of their own learning leads to their 'self-actualisation' – that self-concept transformation which turns learners into fulfilled individuals.

## Management issues

Learner-centred approaches require skilled management of curricular content, general methodology and educational resource.

Broad, integrated topic work and interdisciplinary forms of enquiry are linked to learner-centred teaching because they provide open-ended menus of options from which students of varying backgrounds and abilities can choose. Standard curricular topics can be so treated if teachers abandon any attempt at 'delivering' them. In other words, it is not the nature of a topic or interdisciplinary study which makes it learner centred, it is the way the topic is treated. On adult education courses, forms of curricular organisation may be more complex than those used in schools, acknowledging most adults' capability for designing programmes, from sub-programmes or modular units, to suit their own career pathways. But some breadth of possibility in terms of curricular content remains intrinsic to most learner-centred courses.

Depending on the nature of students' choices, curriculum managers normally monitor these to check that socially as well as personally valued goals are implicit in them, as are step-by-step increases in task difficulty which produce subject-related advance. The degree of topic differentiation encouraged will vary with learner interest, capability and according to the topic's own conceptual richness. Even where it is claimed that progression can only be accomplished by individuals (that is, all learners will have different achievement profiles at any one time), this claim implies, none the less, a tight monitoring by curriculum managers of learner activity. Popular jibes against 'progressivist' curricula that learners too often waste time on activities chosen because these are unchallenging, or endlessly repeat 'fun' exercises (see Silcock and Wyness, 1997), represent dangers which can only be guarded against by tight monitoring.

Similarly, Galton's (1989) warning that curricular choice confuses learners who try to 'second guess' what teachers themselves wish marks another danger for learner-centred work. For learners to be truly independent, curricula need designing so that taught skills, concepts and attendant procedures are included within foundation studies. Thus pupils become 'empowered' within their working environments and do not flounder, uncertain of what is expected of them. This requirement is just as important for adult as child learners, since any course programme needs to be accessed via core skills and procedures related to course demands. Core learning skills will include those generic to academic work (how to access resources, check errors, research topics, take field notes, adapt institutional technologies for specialised uses and so on).

Such skill-learning is 'learner centred' because it is a means to a valued end, not (usually) set as an end in itself. For example, literacy and other study skills are essential for much independent learning, but will often be taught as part and parcel of learner-centred curricula not as discretely assessed skills (arousing in students attendant fears of failing at the skill

*per se*). In circumstances where learners' needs are such that it is impractical for them to gain required skills except through instruction (for example,
where students' first language is not English), these may well be taught as a
formal preliminary to the learner-centred course. However, in such circumstances, achievement targets will be geared to students' accessing of the
parent course (and may well be set as minimal targets for that reason),
rather than being geared to standards determined by the skills themselves.

Less obviously, in order to harness learners' own personal energies to academic work, they will not only learn study skills (as they require them) but
will probably become familiar with the political and academic contexts of
their studies. They will realise to an extent the nature of the courses they take
(thus gaining some curricular 'ownership'). What evidence we have suggests
learners do make some sense of the political framework governing their institutional lives (see Davies, 1995, 1999). Even the youngest can assess their
own work and evaluate their own progress when they are helped to grasp
criteria they need to use (Emery, 1996). It is nevertheless hard for primary
school managers to delegate decision-making powers to learners, even where
pupils can realistically participate, just because of the difficulties such pupils
will have grasping the context of the decisions they have to make (Davies,
1999). Adolescent pupils, on the other hand, are unlikely ever to be wholly
ignorant of changing educational policies, and their citizenship education
should be one beneficiary of teachers arranging an open forum for educational
debate. With adults, one would expect a learner-centred course to make explicit, somewhere, basic reasons for the particular form the course takes.

The resource implications for learner-centred work can be inhibiting for
institutions, since diversity of learning implies a diversity of resource.
Schools and colleges which opt for student-centred learning as a *modus
operandi* should have a flexible system of resource organisation, with
(mainly in secondary, further and higher education) delegated study areas
and course-related, pastoral and learning-support systems. Nevertheless,
resource constraints apply in any institution and can set parameters with
which all curriculum managers learn to live. What is helpful with individualised work is that students who follow a line of personal interest may
well resource themselves, through visits to libraries, museums, personally
organised field work and exploratory research.

Practical problems may arise associated, for example, with the management of space, noise levels (where one activity is more 'active' than another) and record-keeping. At primary level, as Mortimore *et al.* (1988)
discovered in London, poor attainments sometimes result where a curriculum is organised around a variety of disparate activities, rather than around
a single theme. Imaginative curriculum managers can bypass resource limitations when activities are arranged to complement each other –
contributing perhaps to a common goal. Many students working independently, including adults on 'flexible-' or distance-learning courses, may feel
isolated or uncertain of standards being reached, when selecting courses
from a variety of options. This situation often demands careful attention

from curriculum managers, who may (where practicable) take appropriate preventative action – perhaps helping students build up networks of 'critical friends' to support each other and share scarce resources. Finally, it is worth noting that, in many countries, such as South Korea, France and the UK, curricular values require learner-centred teaching. Guidance for curriculum managers in England, for example (QCA, 1999), suggests: 'The School Curriculum should develop pupils' enjoyment of, and commitment to, learning . . .' (p. 11). Logically, 'a commitment to learning' is something learners *can* only manage for themselves. If education is successful, students will, over a period, make commitments for their own reasons (we usually talk about 'personal' commitments). Anyone committed to a pursuit or activity must, first, evaluate it. We accordingly become committed in circumstances where we voluntarily assess an activity's demands and rewards, and take that step which ties us emotionally to the object of our commitment. In circumstances where learners have no choice but to comply with whatever subject fare is presented to them, it is hard to see how they can make real commitments. It follows that for curriculum managers who judge process-values (such as personal commitment) as key to lifelong learning, the learner-centred option is the one tailor-made for their task.

## PARTNERSHIP APPROACHES

Partnership approaches are approaches to the management of teaching and learning which recognise the complementary roles of teachers and learners. If the essential role for curriculum managers in teacher-centred curricula is that of *managerial control*, and of *guidance and facilitation* in a learner-centred context, those practising partnership policies will find themselves engaged in *negotiation*, seeking to establish a *democratic* form of course or classroom social organisation. Discussion, debate, co-operation and collaboration, compromise, and the pragmatic resolving of disagreements arising between individual students and groups, and between students and those more formally responsible for making managerial decisions, are cornerstones of partnership activities. Needless to say, the introduction of such a system can extend democratic policies to include parental and other community commitments to an institution's welfare. Core values of partnership (within democratic) systems are knowledge advancement through conflict resolution (cognitive and social), multiple-perspective taking and a celebration of differences.

Once more, the practical and theoretical reasons for teachers selecting such an approach help us grasp more overt management issues.

### Practical reasons

Two factors, especially, might guide curriculum managers towards partnership policies. One is the increasingly pluralist nature of many societies.

The second is the way democratic classroom policies strike some flexible position between thoroughgoing learner-centred and teacher-centred approaches, without resorting to a 'pick and mix' eclecticism, or a rather *ad hoc* pragmatism.

First, an accelerating computer revolution has given educators access to world cultures, which supplement indigenous provision as well as being sources of enlightenment in themselves. The same access helps curriculum managers cope with (potentially) diverse cultural differences among those they may teach. Democratic processes, by nature, explore in their operation issues thought by participants to be relevant to any study, while seeking to establish parity between views, regardless of background. That is, in an educational democracy, teaching staff show, through a willingness to negotiate differences and compromise on important decisions, their commitment to equality of opportunities' policies and their openness to influences from world cultures and alternative lifestyles. This conception shares similarities with both approaches introduced, though especially with modern learner-centred approaches which also seek to adapt to the pluralist conditions of modern societies (see Kelly, 1995; Silcock, 1999). It separates most from other approaches in curriculum managers' obligation to embrace conflict as an essential feature of modern educational settings. Students have to learn social and intellectual skills of conflict resolution which help them mature not simply academically but socio-politically. According to some commentators (Crawford and Jones, 1998; Crick, 1999; Friel and Fagan, 1998) these are conditions required for promoting important 'citizenship' themes included now, at school level, in the curricula of many countries.

Second, the great virtue of partnership approaches is their recognition that successful education demands a fruitful collaboration between the teachers and learners, where each has complementary roles, rather than one being subsidiary to the other. Although (due to the generally prescribed nature of curricula at all educational levels) some subjects have to be studied and some lessons have to be learned, there is agreement that learners need to be agents for their own learning (by right as well as on socio-psychological grounds), students being free to assert their own ideas for consideration by the wider group. Learners will habitually question their curricula for bias and any institutionalised rules for procedural injustices, expecting objections they raise to be debated, perhaps via student representatives on institutional or departmental councils.

## Theoretical reasons

Areas of study connected with partnership approaches are socio-political theory and aspects of cognitive developmental psychology. A substantial body of literature sets out the principles of democratic schooling (Brown, 1997; Davies, 1995, 1999; Harber, 1997; Jensen and Walker, 1989; Kelly,

1995; Silcock, 1999). In America, schemes devised by people such as Deutsch (1994) for turning competing into co-operating groups, associated with ideas about integrative bargaining refined by writers such as Rubin (1980), have stimulated interest in the concept of co-operative learning (Johnson and Johnson, 1994; Silcock and Stacey, 1997). Those who oppose teacher-centred approaches, yet see the individualism of learner-centredness as resistant to the legitimate demands communities make upon learners, take refuge in a 'third way' alternative to the 'traditional' and 'progressive' ideologies that Sugrue (1997, p. 1) calls 'ideological cyclops' (also Brehony, 1992; Jones, 1983; Lawton, 1992).

## Management issues

Chief management issues for those adopting this approach concern the organisational and methodological strategies required to make it succeed.

Organisationally, setting up rule-governed democracies where forms of decision-making and conflict resolution are respected by all, is a first step towards a social system which, once in place, should be self-perpetuating. Davies (1999) reflects on what she believes can be generally agreed as the core 'decisions and rules' operating in a democratic organisation. All are underpinned by 'voice: the ability to articulate one's views and have them heard' (ibid., p. 40). People will always:

1. Understand that power must be held and operated legitimately, and have a clear picture of how power operated.
2. Participate in decisions that affect them.
3. Agree the procedures and rules that govern day-to-day behaviour.
                                                         (Davies, 1999, p. 40)

As with learner-centredness, by the framing and implementing of such rules learners become politically 'empowered' within institutions, part of that empowerment requiring them to become familiar with the organisation of a school in which they work along with its curricula. How curricula are interpreted depends on actual group negotiations, though a curriculum manager's authority as a representative of a parent society (the educational institution) is more explicit than in an out-and-out learner-centred system. It is ostensibly a teacher's job to ensure that values built into democratic decision-making are internalised by learners, and that socially worthwhile ends are recognised as such in order that these can be achieved. As well as having the chance, daily, to bring home to learners the virtues of sharing, co-operation and so forth, teachers become gatekeepers for the whole classroom/school (and often wider) community, allowing its members to contribute to standard-setting, policy construction and curricular prioritisation.

Although Davies (1999) finds young school pupils have relatively poor notions of their own powers of influence, Kelly (1995) believes democratic schools can give to learners a sense of their own rightful powers, as well as help them acquire those social and moral qualities we prize as citizens. He explains how, in a democratic system, curricula are not transmitted from the group which 'owns' the knowledge to one that doesn't, but are explored imaginatively and critically by teachers and students alike, as singular cultural forms – sets of possibilities – chosen from a potentially infinite set.

Methodologically speaking, educationists who have tried to synthesise a 'top-down' with a 'bottom-up' approach have provided paradigms for the types of activity which teachers organise. Adey and Shayer's (1994, 1996) research with young adolescents, Resnick, Bill and Lesgold (1992) with pupils of infant age and Osborne (1997) teaching science, suggest strategies which cater equally for the individual and group needs of learners. Characteristically, a three-phase programme is followed:

- A base mode for teaching is experiential, in that learners bring to a course of study diverse background experiences and explore these from whatever course perspectives can be used for the purpose.
- New knowledge is introduced quite quickly, in a way which challenges learners' existing preconceptions. It may be introduced in a variety of guises, using different types of media, but it will usually be framed in ways respecting the experience-rooted perspectives contained within a group. That is, the new knowledge will be assimilated as far as is possible to what is already known.
- Finally, through debate and discussion learners are invited to defend their positions – adjusted in the light of new knowledge – against those of peers (and teachers), gaining confidence, understanding and 'higher-order' cognitive skills (for example, critical thinking, abstract forms of analysis, various types of evaluation and appraisal) in the process.

The stresses of having to debate and justify positions and the benefits resulting from their resolution are well stated by Osborne (1997). A dominant strategy (highlighted by Adey and Shayer, 1994, 1996) is the organising of group discussion such that students learn, through challenging and defending positions, why their views are or are not viable. This 'highroad to metacognition' (learners retaining a controlling overview of their own learning), as Adey and Shayer call it, is in their terms also a high road to subject mastery.

This partnership approach also requires great skills in planning and co-ordinating the learning experiences of students, and the growing adoption of such systems has been a contributory factor to an increasing emphasis on planned organisational change (see, for instance, Fullan, 1997). Moreover the advocacy of more democratic approaches to teaching and learning, which integrate the teacher's professional responsibility to manage the curriculum with a commitment to pupil engagement in learning, can aid the inculcation of appropriate value systems in students (Halstead and Taylor, 1996). Schools and colleges seeking to develop in this way are wise to take an overall view of curriculum development that links vision, mission and values into a systematic and measured notion of strategic development (Middlewood and Lumby, 1998).

## CONCLUSIONS

Three value-orientations detailing different managerial roles for teachers have been discussed. Teacher-centred, learner-centred and partnership approaches seek distinct, although sometimes overlapping, ends through different stances taken towards curricular organisation. Curriculum managers have little choice but to explore their own value positions with colleagues to decide the dominant approach their curriculum decision-making should take. Yet education is by nature a value-driven process, which tells us that priorities among aims have to be set before priorities among curricular technologies can be chosen. This does not mean that any group of teachers will ever teach in a 'pure' subject-centred, learner-centred or democratic fashion. All curricula compromise to an extent the beliefs of those who teach them. What is important is that within any one institution, teachers not only know what means will best achieve particular ends, but reach some agreement about the ends themselves. They can, then, work unflinchingly together towards these ends.

## REFERENCES

Adey, P. and Shayer, M. (1994) *Really Raising Standards*, London, Routledge.

Adey, P. and Shayer, M. (1996) An exploration of long-term far-transfer effects following an extended intervention program in the high school science curriculum, in Smith, L. (ed.) *Critical Readings in Piaget*, London, Routledge.

Atkinson, R. L., Atkinson, R. C., Smith, E. E., Bem, D. J. and Hilgard, E. R. (1990) *Introduction to Psychology*, 10th edn, New York, Harcourt Brace Jovanovich.

Brehony, K. J. (1992) What's left of progressive primary education?, in Rattansi, A. and Reeder, D. (eds.) *Rethinking Radical Education: Essays in Honour of Brian Simon*, London, Lawrence and Wishart.

Brophy, J. and Good, T. L. (1986) Teacher behaviour and student achievement, in Witrock, C. M. (ed.) *Handbook of Research in Teaching*, 3rd edn, New York, Macmillan.

Brown, L. (1997) A democratic classroom, in Davies, L. (ed.) *Democratic Discipline, Democratic Lives, Proceedings of Education Now/Institute for Democracy in Education conference*, Conference Papers, Loughborough, Loughborough University.

Caldwell, B. and Spinks, J. (1988) *The Self-Managing School*, London, Falmer Press.

Campbell, R. J. (1993) A dream at conception: a nightmare at delivery, in Campbell, R. J. (ed.) *Breadth and Balance in the Primary School Curriculum*, Bristol, Falmer Press.

Chomsky, N. (1959) Review of 'Verbal Behaviour' by B. F. Skinner, *Language*, Vol. 35, p. 226.

Crawford, K. and Jones, M. (1998) National identity: a question of choice?, *Children's Social and Economics Education*, Vol. 3, no. 1, pp. 1–16.

Creemers, B. (1994) *The Effective Classroom*, London, Cassell.

Crick, B. (1999) The presuppositions of citizenship education, *Journal of Philosophy of Education*, Vol. 33, no. 3, pp. 337–52.

Davies, L. (1995) International indicators of democratic schools, in Harber, C. (ed.), *Developing Democratic Education*, Ticknall, Education Now.

Davies, L. (1999) Researching democratic understanding in primary school, *Research in Education*, Vol. 61, p. 48.

Davis, A. (1998) The limits of educational assessment, *Journal of the Philosophy of Education*, special issue, Vol. 32, no. 1.

Department for Education and Employment (DfEE) (1998) *Standards for the Award of Qualified Teacher Status (Circular 4/98)*, London, HMSO (online at http://www.dfee.gov.uk/circulars/4–98/annexa.htm 7 August 2000).

Deutsch, M. (1994) Constructive conflict resolution: principles, training and research, *Journal of Social Issues*, Vol. 50, no. 1, pp. 13–32.

Emery, H. (1996) Children evaluating and assessing their progress in learning, in Webb, R. (ed.). *Primary Practice: Taking a Leadership Role*, Bristol, Falmer Press.

Friel, V. and Fagan, C. (1998) Citizenship: a challenge to teacher education, *Children's Social and Economics Education*, Vol. 3, no. 1, pp. 17–27.

Fullan, M. G. (1997) Planning, doing and coping with change, in Harris, A., Bennett, N. and Preedy, M., *Organizational Effectiveness and Improvement in Education*, Buckingham, Open University Press, pp. 205–15.

Galton, M. (1989) Negotiating learning, negotiating control, in Bourne, J. (ed.) *Thinking through Primary Practice*, London, Routledge and Open University Press.

Gipps, C. (1992) *What We Know about Effective Primary Teaching*, London, Tufnell Press.

Gipps, C. and Macgilchrist, B. (1999) Primary school learners, in Mortimore, P. (ed.) *Understanding Pedagogy and its Impact on Learning*, London, Paul Chapman.

Gipps, C., McCallum, G. and Brown, M. (1999) Primary teachers' beliefs about teaching and learning, *Curriculum Journal*, Vol. 10, no. 1, pp. 123–34.

Hallam, S. and Ireson, J. (1999) Pedagogy in the secondary school, in Mortimore, P. (ed.) *Understanding Pedagogy and its Impact on Learning*, London, Paul Chapman.

Halstead, J. M. and Taylor, M. J. (1996) *Values in Education and Education in Values*, London, Falmer Press.

Hanna, D. (1997) The organization as an open system, in Harris, A., Bennett, N. and Preedy, M. *Organizational Effectiveness and Improvement in Education*, Buckingham, Open University Press, pp. 13–21.

Harber, C. (1997) International developments and the rise of education for democracy, *Compare*, Vol. 27, no. 2, pp. 178–91.

Jensen, K. and Walker, S. (1989) *Towards Democratic Schooling: European Experiences*, Buckingham, Open University Press.

Johnson, D. W. and Johnson, R. T. (1994) Constructive conflict in the schools, *Journal of Social Issues*, Vol. 50, no. 1, pp. 117–37.

Jones, K. (1983) *Beyond Progressive Education*, London, Methuen.

Kelly, A. V. (1994) *The National Curriculum: A Critical Review*, London, Paul Chapman.

Kelly, A. V. (1995) *Education and Democracy, Principles and Practices*, London, Paul Chapman.

Lawton, D. (1992) *Education and Politics in the 1990s: Conflict or Consensus?*, London, Falmer Press.

Lee, J. and Fitz, J. (1997) HMI and OFSTED: evolution or revolution in school inspections?, *British Journal of Educational Studies*, Vol. 45, no. 1, pp. 155–65.

Levačić, R. (1996) Managing resources in educational institutions: an open systems approach, in Preedy, M., Glatter, R. and Levacic, R. (eds.) *Educational Management: Strategy, Quality and Resources*, Buckingham, Open University Press, pp. 127–36.

MacBeath, J. (1999) *Schools Must Speak for Themselves*, London, Routledge.

Marton, F. (1981) Phenomenography – describing conceptions of the world around us, *Instructional Science*, Vol. 10, pp. 177–200.

Middlewood, D. and Lumby, J. (1998) *Strategic Management in Schools and Colleges*, London, Paul Chapman.

Morgan, G. (1986) *Images of Organisation*, London, Sage.

Mortimore, P., Sammons, P., Stoll, L., Lewis, D. and Ecob, R. (1988) *School Matters: The Junior Years*, London, Open Books.

Office for Standards in Education (Ofsted) (1996) *The Annual Report of Her Majesty's Chief Inspector of Schools*, London, HMSO.

Osborne, J. (1997) Practical alternatives, *School Science Review*, Vol. 78, no. 285, pp. 61–6.

Piaget, J. (1954) *The Construction of Reality in the Child*, New York, Basic Books.

Pollard, A. (1990) *Learning in Primary Schools*, London, Cassell.

Pollard, A. (1999) 'Towards a new perspective on children's learning?', *Education 3–13*, vol. 27, no. 3, pp 56–60.

QCA (1999) *The National Curriculum*, London, HMSO.

Resnick, L. B., Bill, V. and Lesgold, S. (1992) Developing thinking abilities in arithmetic class, in Demitriou, A., Shayer, M. and Efklides, A. E. (eds.) *Neo-Piagetian Theories of Cognitive Development: Implications and Applications for Education*, London, Routledge.

Rogers, C. (1983) *Freedom to Learn in the '80s*, revd edn, Columbia, SC, Merrill.

Rubin, J. (1980) Experimental research on third-party intervention in conflict: towards some generalization, *Psychological Bulletin*, Vol. 87, pp. 379–91.

Sammons, P., Hillman. J. and Mortimore, P. (1995) *Key Characteristics of Effective Schools*, London, Institute of Education, for Ofsted.

Silcock, P. J. (1999) *New Progressivism*, London, Falmer Press.

Silcock, P. J. and Stacey, H. (1997) Peer mediation and the cooperative school, *Education 3–13*, Vol. 25, no. 2, pp. 3–8.

Silcock, P. J. and Wyness, M. (1997) Dilemma and resolution: primary school teachers look beyond Dearing, *Curriculum Journal*, Vol. 8, no. 1, pp. 125–48.

Sugrue, C. (1997) *Complexities of Teaching: Child-Centred Perspectives*, London, Heinemann Educational.

Sylva, K., Harry, J., Mirelman, H., Brusell, A. and Riley, J. (1999) Evaluation of a focused literacy programme in Reception and Year 1 classes: classroom observations, *British Journal of Educational Research*, Vol. 25, no. 5.

Teacher Training Agency (TTA) (1998) *National Standards for Headteachers*, London, TTA.

Tomlinson, H. (1997) *Managing Continuing Professional Development in Schools*, London, Paul Chapman.

West-Burnham, J. (1998) Leading and managing school-based development, in West-Burnham, J. and O'Sullivan, F., *Leadership and Professional Development in Schools*, London, Pitman, pp. 107–20.

West-Burnham, J. and O'Sullivan, F. (1998) *Leadership and Professional Development in Schools*, London, Pitman.

Young, M. (1999) Knowledge, learning and the curriculum of the future, *British Educational Research Journal*, Vol. 25, no. 4, pp. 463–78.

# Section B: Operational management of the curriculum

Following the strategic perspective that was taken in Section A, this section examines the practical consequences of implementation at various levels within the educational hierarchy. Once the theoretical perspective and philosophical framework have been established, communicated and agreed, then secure and positive steps can be taken towards making the vision a reality. It is only following the setting of these higher-level goals that the curriculum, as it is taught and learnt within educational organisations, can be given shape and direction. For the operational elements to be effective there is a need, according to Kelly (1999, p. 96), for educational honesty: 'Since it requires that we analyse and make quite explicit what our educational ideology is rather than pretend that we don't have one.' Clearly the contextual and conceptual elements must be fully acknowledged before operational issues are addressed.

The operational issues of planning, monitoring and evaluating the curriculum, addressed by Neil Burton, Brian Hardie and Maggie Preedy respectively, offer both a practical insight and also a theoretical rationale. While it is not possible to address all eventualities, these chapters do offer guidance on the cyclical processes. As well as addressing the needs of curriculum managers within the educational organisation, they also take into account the external pressures that need to be enveloped within the operational processes.

## REFERENCE

Kelly, A. (1999) *The Curriculum: Theory and Practice*, London, Paul Chapman.

# 4

# MANAGING THE PLANNING OF LEARNING AND TEACHING

## Neil Burton

## INTRODUCTION

This chapter focuses on the operational issues concerned with putting policy decisions into practice. Planning is, by nature, a compromise activity of tempering ideals with logistical constraints.

Three key issues to be addressed are:

- *Resource issues* – total financial allocations, time, personnel.
- *Management issues* – structures (planning cycles), accountability, responsibility.
- *Expectation and progression issues* – developmental, consistency, matched to internally or externally devised norms.

Each of these issues can be seen as being both enablers and constraints on transforming the curriculum ideals into operational reality. It is the management perceptions, and in particular the *relevant* leadership qualities of the headteacher or principal, of these issues at the planning stage that will determine whether they will be positive or negative forces. Clearly the key to effective planning is to ensure that the vision for the institution subsumes constraints and establishes a clear set of priorities.

Each issue can and, it will be argued, should be addressed at a number of levels. Two of these levels are very much dependent upon the nature of the educational system the school or college is operating in. National and local curriculum planning requirements may have to be adhered to and these will clearly have a significant impact on the extent to which the curriculum can be planned and managed within the organisation. The impact of this is usually a set of constraints that the school or college needs to work within, such as the National Curriculum (England), religious doctrine (Israel) or school boards (USA). If these external constraints are taken as being part of the context that the education must be planned within, then four distinct levels are possible within the educational organisation. The curriculum needs to be planned and managed at:

- *Organisational level* – 'graduateness' at a university, the overall curricular aims at a school or college.
- *Curriculum area, course or 'phase'* – the linear development of a particular subject or group of subjects over a number of years, or the development of a cohort of students, across a range of subjects, over a period of time (usually relating to a particular educational stage within the school or college).
- *Class or group* – relating the planning to the development of a specific group of students (either within a subject or across all subject areas being taught to them).
- *Individual student* – 'to engage *students* in taking responsibility for their own learning by articulating what they have to do to meet learning and other developmental targets' (Davies and Ellison, 1999, p. 131).

Therefore a grid is possible on which to identify and record how the issues are addressed at each level (Figure 4.1). In a school or college with a comprehensive curriculum management policy, each of the cells should contain a statement, understood by all teaching staff, to provide the essential elements of a common management framework.

| | Resource | Management Structures | Expectations/ Progression |
|---|---|---|---|
| Institutional | | | |
| Subject/Phase | | | |
| Class/Group | | | |
| Individual | | | |

**Figure 4.1** Grid to identify and record how issues are addressed

A further parameter that needs to be considered is the degree of dynamism within the curriculum, where the distinction between curriculum design and curriculum planning can usefully be made. The design of the curriculum is the first stage of institutional or subject/phase planning. It is where the curriculum aims (the ideology) are converted into a framework to support more detailed planning and it provides an initial check point to match operational considerations against ideals. Increasingly detailed planning can then take place through a 'sequence of stages from general outcomes, as expressed in the framework, to detailed lesson outcomes' (Dimmock, 2000, p. 95). The design parameters may be in a state of continual flux due to external influences requiring the constant realignment of the detailed planning. It is possible, therefore, that the overall process is more one of strategic intent – 'a process of coping with turbulence through direct, intuitive understanding' (Boisot, 1995, p. 36) – than strategic planning which is more 'effective in an environment in which the rate of change is slower than the rate that the organisation can understand and adapt to' (Davies and Ellison, 1997, p. 17).

Most of the curriculum planning models currently employed in education, such as Figure 4.2, are derivative of the seminal work of Ralph Tyler (1949) who based planning on four key principles.

It is possible to apply the Tyler cycle, or any later development, to any cell of Figure 4.1 (above) to ensure a level of dynamism that matches changing needs to changing provision. Figure 4.3 is one such diagram which represents the planning cycle attributed to local education authorities (LEAs) in England as a format to follow to ensure a positive and constructive impact of pupil achievement through a focus on improved curriculum provision within schools. Similar cycles can be developed to incorporate the processes explored in this and the following two chapters.

The cyclical approach is not the only one proposed in the literature. Walker (1971) suggests a linear process based upon a conscious move from one curriculum position to another. As Marsh compares: 'Whereas Tyler's starting point is identifying the linear logic of rational planning, Walker's starting point is studying what people actually do when planning curricula' (1997, p. 129). In the Walker model the starting point is a *platform* of beliefs encompassing the educational theories and procedures held by the individuals involved in the planning process. These are the foundation for *deliberations* where alternative curricula approaches are generated, debated and compared, with the favoured ('most defensible') approach used as a basis of the curriculum *design*. The increasing emphasis on formal processes has seen a resurgence of the Tyler approach as a defensible practice, away from the once perceived realities of Walker.

The following sections of this chapter will address issues pertinent to the different cells in Figure 4.1. The approach taken here, to start at the institutional level and work towards the student, is purely arbitrary and, given the educational philosophy espoused by the institution, the issues may be more appropriately considered in the reverse order. It should also be recognised that curriculum planning cannot be managed in isolation from decisions concerned with approaches to monitoring and evaluation. Indeed it is

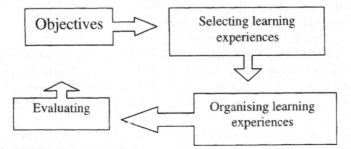

**Figure 4.2**  Tyler's principles

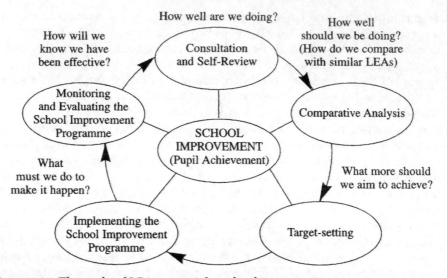

How well are we doing?

How will we know we have been effective?

How well should we be doing? (How do we compare with similar LEAs)

Consultation and Self-Review

Monitoring and Evaluating the School Improvement Programme

Comparative Analysis

SCHOOL IMPROVEMENT (Pupil Achievement)

What must we do to make it happen?

What more should we aim to achieve?

Implementing the School Improvement Programme

Target-setting

**Figure 4.3** The cycle of LEA support for school improvement
*Source:* DfEE, 2000.

likely, since the institution will already exist, that the process will start with an evaluation phase – an audit of current practice and procedures.

# INSTITUTIONAL PLANNING

## Resources

The extent to which the institutional management has the freedom to manage resources is determined by its relationship with external bodies, in particular, the state. Foreman (1999, p. 68) suggests that there are three trends: self-management (budgetary control), centralisation (policy and practice of curriculum and assessment) and competition and consumer preference (enrolment). The self-management allows greater control over how resources are to be used to meet educational aims through curriculum provision, the centralisation sets constraints on what that curriculum provision might be, and the 'market culture' ensures that educational provision is responsive to stakeholder groups.

Responsiveness to the state or other funding body (often parents, employers or the students themselves) will result in a curriculum which is planned, at an institutional level, to meet particular externally set criteria. These criteria are frequently enforced through external monitoring and evaluation of the curriculum. Schools in England, for example, are subject to regular visits from Ofsted who provide: 'Regular and systematic inspections . . . to appraise and evaluate the quality and standards of education in the school in an objective manner' (Earley, 1998, p. 2). Issues concerned with monitoring and evaluation of the curriculum will be addressed in subsequent chapters.

Where funding is delegated to the school or college to resource educational provision it is more normally done so on a per capita basis. This may be achieved through state funding based upon student enrolment (possibly with some age, subject or location-based formula element) or through direct fees (paid by students, parents or employers). Additional funds may be obtained for specific, often predefined, purposes from a range of sources. Private schools might raise funds from former pupils to improve curricula provision by refurbishing science laboratories. Employers may donate equipment to a college to ensure training provision. Schools, particularly state schools in England, may 'bid' for additional funding from the state for specific purposes, such as computer education provision. Further discussion of sources of funding can be found in Anderson (2000).

Acquiring resources is the first step, deploying them effectively is the key function of senior managers. The strategic vision of the curriculum of senior managers needs to be turned into operational reality at the institutional level. The strategic vision is addressed in Chapter 7, while deployment will be explored here. At the greatest level of flexibility, the institution will have an amount of money that can be converted into any educational resource at the discretion of the senior manager. In reality the institution is likely to have a number of existing resources that will restrict the flexibility of provision. The curriculum that the institution is able to offer will be constrained by the existence of 'fixed' resources such as buildings, equipment and current staffing. In the long term it will be possible to change even these resources to effect curriculum change. Infrequently it may be possible for the institution to start 'afresh', either because a new course is being devised and currently held resources are fully employed, or because a new school or college is being instituted. This provides the opportunity to make significant curricula decisions – not just the what (the content), but the how (large lecture, seminar, class, distance learning), the where (classroom type – if any; location (for example, work-based); and when (fluidity of the provision). The funding for the provision of the curriculum can potentially be converted into buildings, equipment or personnel.

Restrictions on educational resources may affect the curricular provision that the institution is able to offer. Institutional plans for the curriculum will need to be constructed within the constraints of resource availability. If a school or college is unable to employ a teacher of Spanish as a foreign language, it will have to reconsider its institutional planning. It can plan not to offer Spanish as a subject, or it can commit resources to either develop non-teacher based resources (for example, interactive computer packages) or to retrain existing teachers to fill the need or possibly even pay for the students to study elsewhere.

Different personnel working within the educational environment have different costs attached to them. At an institutional level it is important to make use of staff, teaching and non-teaching, in the most cost-effective way. As Knight (1983, p. 15) rationalises: 'let no-one deride the word "cheaper". There is no advantage in education being more expensive than it has to be.' The more efficiently resources can be used, the greater the curriculum provision can be. The time given over to particular duties by teaching staff in England is examined in detail by Campbell and Neill (1997, p. 101) who found that primary teachers spent less than 19 hours, of an average 60-hour working week, teaching. From an institutional planning perspective, senior mangers need to ensure that staff are appropriately deployed to ensure best use of available talents. The appointment of non-teaching support staff could improve curriculum provision by reallocating administrative duties to allow teaching staff to concentrate on their professional responsibilities. It is frequently the case in education that the best teachers are promoted to positions where they teach less!

At the institutional level it is not only the provision of curricular resources in absolute terms that need to be managed but also how they interact and mix. These resources need to be combined in such a way as to support and enhance the educational philosophy and learning psychology that the institution has chosen as a basis for its curriculum. This curricular provision needs to be planned so that students who wish to study science, for example, are provided with laboratory time which corresponds with the availability of appropriate science teaching staff supported by suitable non-teaching staff (laboratory technicians) and equipment in a format most conducive to the desired learning style. The curriculum timetable, ideally, needs to be determined, both in the long and short terms (the construction of courses and the construction of the 'learning week'), by the strategic rather than operational concerns. Although it is necessary to acknowledge the constraints imposed by the operational parameters, these can be further complicated, for example, by the availability of part-time staff, staff who teach more than one subject or in a number of buildings (or, even, campuses), the preferences that staff may have for particular time slots and numerous other details. Such logistical planning, once all of the parameters have been defined, is now the domain of specialised computer software packages in larger organisations. It may even be necessary to divide the curriculum into more manageable units (by subject or department, phase or campus) to make this aspect of institutional planning feasible. In reality the course or weekly timetable must be regarded as both the means by which curricular goals can be delivered and a key constraint on realising that reality.

Giving further consideration to the practical provision of the curriculum at the institutional level it is worthy of note that the relative availability of resources will potentially subvert the strategic curricular aims. These aims will be written in the context of the resources that are known to be available – the nature of the school or college buildings, the existing staffing and equipment, will almost inevitably have a significant impact on the expectations of the strategic vision for the curriculum. This force for change has been recognised by the UK government which is encouraging schools and colleges (in England and Wales) to commit themselves to particular curricular initiatives through a process of bidding for additional funds which are 'ring fenced' for a specific purpose. An emphasis on developing ICT within the curriculum has been financed in this way by ensuring that only those institutions willing to make the commitment, in curriculum terms, would receive the funding.

## Management issues

The structures that the institution sets in place to support curriculum provision and development should be seen as enabling factors. The management structures, which are examined in Section C of this book, need to be developed and installed as a unifying force to ensure a consistent approach to devolved resource allocation, curriculum planning formats and processes, delegation of responsibilities and lines of accountability. Such structures will provide, among others, a clearly defined format for the process of developing new courses, translating institutional curricular aims into medium-term objectives within schemes and individual lesson or activity plans. An additional element of these enabling structures and processes will be the identification of roles and accompanying responsibilities. The particular issues surrounding the implication of role management within education is taken up by Hall (1997) who examines the changing nature of management roles in education.

As suggested above, a dynamic planning cycle based upon the Tyler model (Figure 4.2) is necessary to ensure that institutions develop a reflective and professionally informed curriculum matched to the changing needs of students and other key stakeholders. Although the process, once completed at institutional level, may establish a curriculum that remains intact and coherent, the cycle will still be employed at other levels to ensure that individual student and subject needs are met. Procedures involved in the planning process, including internal resource allocation and mid/short-term planning and evaluation, need to be communicated and shared between staff, as an operational embodiment of a shared vision for the curriculum and institution as a whole.

The format of the operational planning system needs to provide clear guidance to staff on how they are to translate the curriculum vision of the institution into learning objectives for individual students (or groups, depending upon the educational philosophy that is being followed). Effectively there needs to be a planning format that identifies a series of steps for students (and their teachers) to follow in order for the students to progress from where they (educationally) are, to where they (or their institution) wants them to be (Figure 4.4). The direction of the arrows can be seen as a reflection of stakeholder influences on the learning and teaching process – external influences coming through the institutionally defined curriculum vision, the influence of individual educational needs from student-centred learning objectives.

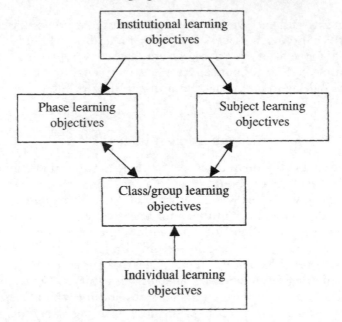

**Figure 4.4**  Planning hierarchy

## Expectation and progression issues

At the institutional level it is important to demonstrate how policies and targets for learning will be put into effect. This will usually be achieved in one of two ways. In the case of schools, where the students progress through a relatively standard set of courses or experiences over a number of years, this may be presented as a 'map', providing an overview of the expected progression from entry to the attainment of the school's stated goals. In a primary school, operating on a cross-curricular basis, this will probably include a list of the topics to be 'covered' in each of the year groups with the predicted skill and content focus. In a secondary school, operating a separate subject approach, the development towards the over-all curriculum goals will probably be identified in each year group for each subject. In colleges, where students are more likely to enrol for particular courses, the responsibility will normally be devolved to course managers to demonstrate how their courses intend to meet institutional learning aims.

The institutional curriculum manager needs to ensure that the students receive a coherent curriculum which is consistent, between year groups and courses, across the whole of the school or college. To make this possible, whether it is communication skills between nursery and reception classes or research skills across a modularised undergraduate degree course, an institution-wide plan needs to be agreed and adopted as a basis to work from in order to avoid gaps and overlaps. This is often achieved by a clear statement of 'core skills' which are central to the educational development of the student. This level of planning does not dismiss the need to address individual learning needs but it does provide a template to confidently develop course or phase plans.

Within this overall plan for the curriculum, the school or college also needs to plan for the procedures that enable the progression in student learning to be assessed, monitored and communicated. Clearly these procedures need to meet a variety of needs, both institutional and individual. The variety of assessment styles employed needs to reflect the overall learning philosophy within the institution, individual needs and any external requirements and pressures (England – 'league tables' of examination results; Israel – matriculation success). Systems for monitoring the curriculum need to be commonly understood and applied to ensure that there is a consistency and comparability throughout the school or college. There needs to be a common format for registering curricula concerns and achievements of individual students and the curriculum as a whole to simplify communication of these issues.

Institutional ethos and the overall learning environment are key factors that need to be planned for and developed as a coherent approach – part of a corporate identity that confirms the distinctiveness of the institution. In fact these elements will not be so much planned as embedded, a formative part of the corporate culture and the basis for the image that is presented both internally and externally, the marketing element of which is explored by Foskett and Hemsley-Brown (1999).

Once these issues have been addressed at an institutional level, more detailed curriculum planning can take place with a greater degree of confidence that students will be receiving a coherent curriculum.

## CURRICULUM AREA, COURSE OR 'PHASE' PLANNING

Planning at this level provides a very important indication of the main organisational structures of the institution.

- Planning by phase (one or more year groups across all subjects) is indicative of a generalist teacher approach, where a class or group of students will have the same teacher for the majority of the time that they are taught (this teacher will also tend to manage the balance of the curriculum that is delivered to the students). Traditionally, this form of planning is more likely to be found in primary education.
- Planning by curriculum area or subject, where the linear progression of subject content in the basic planning format, is considered to be a 'secondary' education approach. Here, the majority of the time, students will receive subject-specialist teaching, with a planned emphasis on progression through the subject, rather than the educational development of the student across all subjects.

- Course planning is more frequently the preserve of post-compulsory education, where students elect to attend particular courses rather than receive a legal entitlement to a range of subjects.

Each of these approaches have implications for the effective planning of the curriculum, particularly in terms of communicating intent and achievements to ensure institutional consistency. Baines (2000, p. 200) notes the increased importance of ICT in the effective management of this communication.

## Resource issues

Where schools plan by age phase there still needs to be an element of subject-based planning to ensure that subject-specific resources, such as those for science or mathematics, are effectively managed and maintained and their use is planned to avoid clashes. Centralised planning and booking procedures will often have to be instigated. In some small schools, it may even be extremely inefficient for the school to purchase specialist equipment owing to the infrequency of its use, so entitlement becomes an issue. The use of specialist teaching areas, such as the school hall or gym for physical education, will need to be planned at an institutional level in many cases. Subject development will need to be planned at an operational level to ensure that equipment–specific curricular activities are spread throughout the school year. The deployment of teaching staff also needs to be sensitive to subject specialisms and expertise. Even though they may not be specifically employed to teach their subject specialism they will have a curriculum-monitoring role to play within the age phase. It would be expedient to ensure an even distribution, where logistically possible, of specialist staff throughout the age phases. Time allocations for the different subject areas will also need to be planned for carefully, though it is necessary to recognise that quantity is no direct measure of quality. The planned use of learning support staff is often achieved much more effectively, especially where the support is focused on individual students, as this form of organisation encourages a much more holistic approach to student-centred planning.

Although curriculum- or course-focused planning allows for a much more effective allocation of subject- (or course-) specific resources, there will still need to be an institution-wide agreement on which curriculum resources are to be managed centrally. The time allocations for planned courses or subjects need to be agreed at the institutional level along with the resourcing of cross-curricular aims (such as research skills) before subject plans and progression can be finalised.

## Management issues

The main management issues at this level are ones concerning the communication and co-ordination of the planning. Within phases there needs to be an acknowledged responsibility for monitoring discrete subjects within the institutional plans (see Chapter 9). Within subject-planning teams, there needs to be responsibility to co-ordinate the progression of core skills with other subject teams (see Chapter 10) and also to ensure that a coherent curriculum, taking into account the input of other subjects, is being delivered to particular cohorts of students (see Chapter 8).

The structures that are put in place to assist middle managers in the performance of their duties also have a human resource cost – it takes time to perform management duties. Institutional management needs to take these factors into account (see Chapter 12).

## Expectation and progression issues

Once again there is a distinction between the different approaches. Phase planning tends to favour the planned progression of the individual over a given time span, while a subject focus tends to emphasise subject progression. The planning implications are that for the former there needs to be an emphasis on subject continuity between phases, and for the latter the co-ordination of student progression across subjects. Such lines of communication require careful consideration and an appropriate means of recording planning.

# CLASS OR GROUP PLANNING

The class or group as a taught unit is often considered as a convenient means of organising planning within a school or college. Irrespective of the organisational distinctions referred to in the previous section, in most traditional educational settings, the 'class' is the basic recipient of a taught session and so planning is constructed around this. In England, newly qualified teachers (NQTs) are expected to demonstrate competence in planning on different timescales, in that they should: 'provide clear structures for lessons, and for sequences of lessons, in the short, medium and longer term, which maintain pace, motivation and challenge for pupils' (DfEE, 1998).

Such a level of planning, to ensure that institutional curricula aims are translated into a series of clear learning objectives for the day-to-day progression of groups of students, clearly has management implications. Many of these are already addressed in previous sections of this chapter: the provision of organisational structures, learning resources, planning information and lines of communication. Other points need to be addressed at the class level.

## Resource issues

At the class level the arrangement of the physical learning environment, the classroom and the equipment and associate staff that it contains, becomes a key determinant in the operational planning process. Many learning resources, particularly in primary and especially nursery education, are provided on a cross-subject classroom basis. At the phase or institutional level, structures need to be established to ensure that teaching staff responsible for planning the curriculum of class groups are fully aware of the potential of these resources and plan effectively for them.

The proportion of the 'working week' spent by teachers in England and Wales undertaking lesson planning and preparation duties has been subject to a rigorous study by Campbell and Neill (1994a, 1994b) and reported further in Campbell and Neill (1997). They found that primary teachers spent, on average, 10.5 hours per week planning lessons (out of a 52.6 hour working week), while secondary teachers used 5.8 hours of their working week of 54.4 hours for the same purpose. Planning systems need to minimise the bureaucracy while maintaining the professional rigour since Dunham and Varma (1998) found this to be one of the key causes of stress in teachers. Clearly the human resource element, as part of the planning process, requires careful management and appropriate training and support (another resource cost that must be planned for) for it to be employed successfully in the long term.

## Management issues

Those who teach have a crucial role in the management of teaching and learning and there are numerous texts which focus on the management of student learning. The issue here is one of managing the structures to support the learning and teaching, specifically how teaching staff can enhance the curriculum through the planned use of learning support or associate staff. There will be a need to develop structures that are consistent with those of the institution as a whole, an issue developed in Chapter 12.

It must also be recognised in the planning process that there is a 'first line' responsibility in terms of the setting of appropriate learning expectations and accountability for progression that lies with the professional in the teaching room. Ideally the management structure and use of resources will all be focused within the institution on ensuring that these professionals are as effective as they possibly can be to enhance the learning of students.

## CURRICULUM PLANNING AT THE LEVEL OF THE INDIVIDUAL STUDENT

By definition, for learning to be effective, teaching must be effective – whether this is as a direct result of conscious teacher action is another matter. It would seem appropriate that the student be placed at the centre of the curriculum. All measures of educational effectiveness must ultimately be based upon the strength of student learning. A deficit model based upon individual student progress has been developed to support special educational needs (SEN) students. These IEPs (DfEE, 1999) are designed to enable professional educators to plan curricula around individual needs. In England, this approach is moving into mainstream education on the back of traditional recording and reporting procedures. Individual students (or their parents) are being advised by teaching staff on the setting of educational targets to increase the student's responsibility for their own learning development. Generally this may be seen as a form of educational contract, a curriculum plan, with responsibilities and obligations for both the student and the teaching staff. A move towards a student-centred approach to curriculum planning does have significant implications. Although individual needs are planned to be addressed, this must be within the constraints of the learning programme that is already in existence (the curriculum of the course, subject or class).

## Resource issues

Top-down planning of the curriculum is still eminently possible, indeed necessary in order for the institution to retain its distinctiveness, but now the key stakeholder in the determination of the curriculum is the student. With a student/learning-centred approach, the work of Dimmock (2000) suggests that a much more flexible approach to curriculum planning will be a necessity – which actually implies that curriculum management structures will need to be much more secure and firmly embedded within the organisational culture. Time and appropriately qualified and informed personnel are required to manage the individual planning agreements, and the monitoring and assessing of progress.

## Management issues

The flow of information, both about students and about curriculum resources, will become the key issue for the manager (see Chapter 10). Matching student needs to learning resources or opportunities might require a complete reassessment of the nature of the curriculum management structure. For example, a tighter control of physical resources is necessary to ensure that they can be targeted to support individual needs in addition to the needs of the many – instead of curriculum resource planning being based upon courses or set groups, individuals may now become the variable.

## Expectation and progression issues

The information recording, management and reporting systems become the core enabling process. The planning process, from a management perspective, will focus on matching curriculum availability (through whatever learning resources are possible) to the curriculum needs of individuals and groups. The use of ICT for such purposes may well see the eventual demise of the traditional school or college as we know it.

## CONCLUSIONS

The key element of curriculum planning is to match resources to learning needs in a coherent and justifiable way. This will necessitate the establishment of management structures and procedures to ensure an equitable distribution in line with educational goals of the organisation. The planning process will include a cyclical process of renewal and reformation in line with the changing educational environment, and will operate at different levels within the organisation with senior management acting as an enabling factor.

## REFERENCES

Anderson, L. (2000) The move towards entrepreneurialism, in Coleman, M. and Anderson, L. (eds.) *Managing Finance and Resources in Education*, London, Paul Chapman.

Baines, E. (2000) Managing information as a resource, in Coleman, M. and Anderson, L. (eds.) *Managing Finance and Resources in Education*, London, Paul Chapman.

Boisot, M. (1995) Preparing for turbulence: the changing relationship between strategy and management development in the learning organisation, in Garratt, B. (ed.) *Developing Strategic Thought*, Maidenhead, McGraw-Hill.

Campbell, R. and Neill, S. (1994a) *Primary Teachers at Work*, London, Routledge.

Campbell, R. and Neill, S. (1994b) *Secondary Teachers at Work*, London, Routledge.

Campbell, J. and Neill, S. (1997) Managing teachers' time under systematic reform, in Bush, T. and Middlewood, D. (eds.) *Managing People in Education*, London, Paul Chapman.

Davies, B. and Ellison, L. (1997) *Strategic Marketing for Schools*, London, Pitman.

Davies, B. and Ellison, L. (1999) *Strategic Development and Direction of the School*, London, Routledge.

DfEE (1998) http://www.dfee.gov.uk/circulars/4_98/annexa.htm (accessed 6 July 2000).

DfEE (1999) http://www.dfee.gov.uk/sen/sensupp.htm (accessed 6 July 2000).

DfEE (2000) www.standards.dfee.gov.uk/otherresources/publications/development (accessed 28 June 2000).

Dimmock, C. (2000) *Designing the Learning Centred School*, London, Falmer Press.

Dunham, J. and Varma, V. (eds.) (1998) *Stress in Teachers: Past, Present and Future*, London, Whurr.

Earley, P. (ed.) (1998) *School Improvement After Inspection?*, London, Paul Chapman.

Foreman, K. (1999) Schools and the state, in Lumby, J. and Foskett, N. (eds.) *Managing External Relations in Schools and Colleges*, London, Paul Chapman.

Foskett, N. and Hemsley-Brown, J. (1999) Communicating the organisation, in Lumby, J. and Foskett, N. (eds.) *Managing External Relations in Schools and Colleges*, London, Paul Chapman.

Hall, V. (1997) Management roles in education, in Bush, T. and Middlewood, D. (eds.) *Managing People in Education*, London, Paul Chapman.

Knight, B. (1983) *Managing School Finance*, London, Heinemann.

Marsh, C. (1997) *Planning, Management and Ideology: Key Concepts for Understanding the Curriculum (Volume 2)*, London, Falmer Press.

Tyler, R. (1949) *Basic Principles of Curriculum and Instruction*, Chicago, Chicago University Press.

Walker, D. (1971) A naturalistic model for curriculum development, *School Review*, Vol. 80, no. 1, pp. 51–65.

# 5

# MANAGING MONITORING OF THE CURRICULUM

## Brian Hardie

## INTRODUCTION

The focus of this chapter is on the management of curriculum monitoring at school or college level. Monitoring is a process with clear aims, and a number of basic questions about monitoring are explored initially, followed by attention being paid to some of the problems and difficulties encountered by managers at institutional level.

I have noted previously (Hardie, 1998) that monitoring and evaluation are sometimes used as if they were synonymous, or even as the description of a single process. However, it is worth trying to clarify differences. While planning is about looking forward and evaluation about looking back, monitoring may be seen as continuously looking in both directions to track progress from one point to another. Monitoring attempts to answer the ongoing question 'Are we getting there?' Evaluation, which partly asks 'Did we get there?' is considered in the next chapter of this book.

Monitoring can best be seen by managers as a *questioning* activity. As well as answering the question 'How *are* we getting on?', according to Holy Family College, a Catholic secondary school in Walthamstow, London, monitoring answers the basic question: 'Do we do what we say we do?' In addition, according to the principal of Longsands College, St Neots, monitoring is 'Asking questions that people don't want asked' but must always be linked back to the strategic vision of the school or college. Perhaps, more importantly, it is finding the answers to certain key questions.

## WHY MONITOR?

Five reasons may be suggested:

70

- It allows you to assess how well you are doing.
- It allows you to see where you are achieving targets and reaching standards.
- It allows you to see where you are *not* achieving targets and reaching standards.
- It shows where you need to improve.
- According to Torrington and Weightman (1985, p. 161), monitoring can 'prevent procedures becoming obsolete and inefficient'.

Additionally, monitoring should be part of a cycle of 'continuous improvement'. West-Burnham (1992, p. 37) suggests that there needs to be an obsession with enhancing and improving every process. This is where professional expertise and development are so important. It is the professional skills and knowledge of teachers and managers in schools that are the principal source of this process. West-Burnham argues that this is a natural process for professionals – 'never accepting the status-quo'. The crucial thing for managers is that there should be no complacency, no notion of a plateau of acceptability.

## WHAT IS MONITORING?

Adapting Stake's (1976) dimensions of education to monitoring *and* evaluation, it is possible to see them as shown in Figure 5.1.

Raffan and Ruthven (2000, p. 22) define monitoring as 'keeping in touch with your pupil's learning, including informal classroom processes . . . or more formal processes . . . such as the national system of tests and examinations'. While this definition keeps the focus firmly on learning, I suggest that a working definition of monitoring is 'the planned routine gathering of useful information in a regular continuous and systematic checking process against previously set targets in order to take any necessary action'. If key words are noted from this definition, the essential elements of the management of monitoring may be emphasised.

| FORMATIVE | SUMMATIVE |
|---|---|
| Development | At the end |
| Diagnostic | Evaluative |
| Continuous assessment | Examinations |
| Professional development | Accountability |

**Figure 5.1** Monitoring and evaluation dimensions
*Source:* based on Stake, 1976.

## Planned

Monitoring is an activity planned by those who manage in an organisation, department or classroom. It is not an *ad hoc*, haphazard process which happens occasionally or 'when I happen to think about it'.

## Routine

Monitoring is the routine collecting and organising of factual data, some-thing which all those in schools and colleges should expect to happen and one in which they should expect to be involved.

## Gathering information

Mintzberg (1979) suggests that gathering information is part of the information-processing role of a manager. This may mean seeking out informa-tion and is certainly concerned with looking, observing and listening. It is not, however, just the gathering of information for the sake of it, rather it is gather-ing information which is useful. It is, for example, about observing students and producing a good analysis, or about the results that teachers obtain.

Gathering useful information is certainly likely to include listening to pupils, to students, to staff, indeed to anybody who has useful information. Monitoring, therefore, is finding out what is really happening, not what man-agers might think is happening or what managers would like to be happening.

## Regular

Monitoring is a process that takes place at regular intervals, for example, yearly, termly, every half-term or even monthly, weekly or daily – whichever is most appropriate. It may even be planned to be irregular, if that is not a contradiction in terms.

## Continuous

Monitoring is not a 'one-off' process but, rather, a continuous and continu-ing process until a target or targets have been reached. This important aspect was mentioned in the introduction to this chapter and is critical.

## Checking

Monitoring involves checking without necessarily making value judge-ments. It therefore means having an open mind. It may involve any or all of, for example, checking progress, checking commitment and checking success or successes.

Holy Family College suggest that their aim is to check the match between the intended curriculum, as set down in schemes of work, lesson plans, etc. and the curriculum as it is implemented by individual teachers. It is done through observing students and producing an effective analysis.

## Previously set targets

Target-setting has now become a mandatory activity in schools and colleges in the UK. It is against such targets, whether major or minor, that monitoring takes place.

Hardie (1995) has used the acronym MACFEWOI! related to targets:

| MACFEWOI! | |
| --- | --- |
| **M**easurable within **A**ny **C**onstraints (often, but not always time) **A**chievable **C**hallenging | A balance between these two |
| **FEW** in number **F**lexible | A balance between flexible and 'written in stone' |
| **E**asily read, but not easily written **W**ritten | |
| **OI!** Do it now! **O**rganisation **I**ndividual | A balance between these two |

Certainly, if targets have been developed in this way, it should make monitoring easier for managers.

## Action

Having found out what is really happening, then managers can make the decision whether to take any action . . . or not.

## Adjustments to the plan

Monitoring is about making adjustments to original plans, during the implementation process.

# WHAT IS THE PURPOSE OF MONITORING?

Combining the questions of Hardie (1995) and Aspinwall *et al.* (1992), a relevant list for managers preparing to undertake monitoring might be:

- What is the purpose of the monitoring?
- What has caused the monitoring to be needed?
- Why are we carrying out the monitoring?
- How will we know when the monitoring has been completed?
- What are the measurable objectives of the monitoring?
- Are these objectives shared by all?
- What needs to be done for these objectives to be shared by all those involved in the monitoring?
- To whom is it necessary to communicate these objectives?
- Have they been communicated to all who need to know about them?

Holy Family College (1998) in their policy document suggest that, whatever monitoring methods are used, it is important to be clear about:

- the purpose
- how the monitoring will take place
- who will do it
- how long that process will take
- what use will be made of the results
- what we expect to see
- how feedback will be provided to colleagues
- how the monitoring will be evaluated.

# WHAT KIND OF PROCESS IS MONITORING?

Although there is more literature related to evaluation than to monitoring and also although these two processes are perceived to be different, I think it is reasonable to apply Stake's (1976) dimensions of education to monitoring processes (see Figure 5.2). Some of these dimensions are worth commenting on in more detail, as they seem to place monitoring at the left-hand side with evaluation on the right.

### Formative/summative

Stake (1976) uses the example of tasting soup. He suggests that the cook tastes the soup in order to make any adjustments to the flavour, that is, during the process, and for developmental reasons. When the guests taste the soup it is after the cooking has been completed, at the end of the process. Thus all they are able to do is evaluate; they cannot make any changes, other than, perhaps, the minor ones of adding salt and pepper.

| INFORMAL | FORMAL |
|---|---|
| Personal | Impersonal |
| Internal | External |
| | Accurate |
| | Valid |
| | Credible |
| **CASE PARTICULAR** | **GENERALISATION** |
| Fixed ultimate target | Representative of others |
| Worth of particular | Worth of general approach |
| **PROCESS** | **PRODUCT** |
| Transactions | Outcomes |
| Intrinsic value | Payoff value |
| **DESCRIPTIVE** | **JUDGEMENTAL** |
| | |
| **RESPONSIVE** | **PREORDINATE** |
| Subjective | Objective |
| | Hypotheses |
| No prior expectations | Prior expectations |
| **HOLISTIC** | **ANALYTIC** |
| Whole | Key characteristics |
| Case study | |
| **INTERNAL** | **EXTERNAL** |
| Insiders | Outsiders |

**Figure 5.2**  Dimensions of monitoring
*Source:* adapted from Stake, 1976.

Stake (1976) says that the key is not so much *when?* during the process or at the end, as *why?*

Using his dimensions, monitoring is likely to be more concerned with developmental, diagnostic, continuous assessment and professional development processes. The end result may be concerned with evaluative, examinations and accountability reasons. Monitoring, therefore, may be seen as largely formative, in that the feedback from it may provide an institution with the opportunity either to reinforce good practice, or to make improvements to existing practice. Evaluation may be more summative, particularly when it is initiated by bodies external to the school or college.

## Informal/formal

Monitoring is more likely to be involved with the personal rather than the impersonal and the internal rather than the external. Consequently, it may be that monitoring for managers in schools and colleges may tend towards the informal, rather than the formal, although it might be both. Monitoring may be part of the process of curriculum development, leading to professional reflection and development. Schools and colleges, at least those that are willing to look critically at their own practice, may build monitoring into the cycle of development and improvement.

## Case particular/generalisation

Monitoring may be more likely in school or college to concentrate on a specific issue or practice on a particular case, such as examining the worth of a particular programme, rather than generalisation, representative of others and the worth of general approaches.

## Internal/external

Monitoring may be more internal, conducted by insiders, rather than external conducted by outsiders. This may be the opposite of evaluation as evaluation may be more likely to be initiated externally, operated by those external to the institution and the outcomes owned externally. In this case, evaluation is often to be linked with public accountability. In the UK, for example, schools are held accountable in law for the delivery of the National Curriculum, and subject to a four-yearly cycle of inspection. Inspection reports are the outcomes of an evaluative process. The whole inspection process in a country may be seen as the means by which a government monitors the effectiveness of its educational system, while each individual inspection of a school or college is an evaluation of the institution's performance at that particular time.

## WHO SHOULD MONITOR?

Based on Hardie (1995), questions that might be adapted and asked by the manager preparing to undertake any monitoring include:

- Who wants the monitoring to be carried out and what are their reasons for this?
- Who wants the information the monitoring will provide and what are their reasons for this?
- On whose initiative will the monitoring take place?
- Is there agreement about the purpose? What is needed to get this agreement?

Schools committed to monitoring, such as Holy Family College, London, maintain that everyone at the college has a role in monitoring and evaluation: classroom teachers, governors, heads of departments, heads of years/ tutors, senior management, headteacher, parents (and their equivalents in other phases). Monitoring is likely to be built into a number of these persons' specific roles and responsibilities.

The governors and senior management team of schools and colleges in the UK have a responsibility to put a whole organisation monitoring and evaluation policy and process in place. The senior management in a school will need to take account of the Ofsted publication on school evaluation matters, *School Evaluation Matters* and use relevant information as an aid to school evaluation and target-setting. They will identify areas of whole-school experience and extracurricular activities and will be responsible for developing monitoring and evaluation strategies. They should carry out an annual review of the impact of training and development at the college.

As far as governors are concerned, Martin (2000) suggests that governors only have to ensure monitoring takes place, not do it themselves. Much will be covered in the headteacher's report or discussed in committee. Governors need to ensure delegation and reporting systems are in place. Nevertheless, monitoring systems should help governors develop a working knowledge of the school, via links with school staff and planned school visits.

A head of department has overall responsibility for monitoring and evaluation within the department, with the support of their line manager from the senior management team. Monitoring is carried out by the head of department as part of his or her responsibility and in line with the school or college development or business plan.

In secondary schools in the UK, as the traditional academic/pastoral divide began to be challenged, the issue of monitoring the performance of the 'whole child' became part of the relevant reshaping of roles in the staffing structures of these schools. The form tutor began to be seen as having the potential to have an overview of pupil performance, both academic *and* pastoral. 'Some tutorial staff were beginning to see their role as being concerned with oversight, monitoring and support for the total educational experience of their tutees' (James, 1998, p. 225). Writers such as James (1998) and Newman (1998) thus advocate the use of key personnel such as form tutors to monitor this aspect of pupils' work. This aspect of cross-curriculum monitoring is to some extent further explored in Chapter 9 by Les Bell and in Chapter 10 by Daniela Sommefeldt.

## WHEN TO MONITOR?

Martin (2000) suggests that summer is a good time to ensure appropriate monitoring systems for governors. This may be so for governors, but as it is suggested here that monitoring is a continuous process, it is likely to take place throughout the year. It may involve the collection therefore of data, or reviewing data that has been collected already, data that may have been collected, perhaps, for another purpose.

Academic progress of individual children or students is likely to be monitored by regular subject assessments, every five to six weeks for example. In this way, students, parents and staff are aware of the progress being made in all courses and of the need, if it arises, for guidance and support to improve academic performance.

Formal reports to parents are required to be issued as a part of the monitoring process in all schools in the UK. In addition there are also likely to be parents' evenings or similar consultation occasions to give parents the opportunity to discuss their son's or daughter's progress with staff.

## WHAT TO MONITOR?

Ofsted (1997) include in their key characteristics of well-managed subject departments the systematic monitoring of the quality of teaching and observation of lessons accompanied by debate about good practice; regular monitoring of the assessment of pupils and moderation of assessments to maintain consistency; systematic monitoring of the achievement and progress of individual pupils and classes, linked to target-setting and the evaluation of teaching. Studies of effective departments (Harris, Jamieson and Russ, 1995; Sammons, Thomas and Mortimore, 1997) also found that monitoring of these issues played a key role in effectiveness, and the absence of monitoring contributed to pupils having less confidence in departments where it occurred less. It is worth noting that such studies showed a variation in practice among departments within the same school. However, what is to be monitored clearly depends upon the nature of identified targets.

## THE FOCUS AND EMPHASIS OF THE MONITORING

The following questions might be considered by managers in order to establish the focus of the monitoring. Which aspects of school life are to be monitored? Is it, for example, curriculum areas, teaching, learning, administration, etc.? Is the monitoring concerned with the whole school, a part of the school or an individual? Are all the teachers to be involved, or just individuals or groups? Is the monitoring concerned with the teacher or the pupils? Is the monitoring concerned with curriculum or management? Is the monitoring classroom based? Such questions as these, posed by Hardie (1995), enable managers to ensure focus.

What is to be the *emphasis*? Is it to be on inputs, such as staff, resources or planning? Aspinwall *et al.* (1992) suggest that anyone managing a programme of any kind will be concerned to ensure that money, time and other resources have been expended according to budget. This may be required by an external party, but it should be considered a matter of good practice in any case. Monitoring here typically involves the regular reporting and analysis of expenditure against budget.

Or should the emphasis be on outputs such as the quality of pupils' work, that is, children's learning, pupil self-assessment of learning, teacher self-assessment of learning, levels of attainment in tests or examinations or number of children at level 3? Aspinwall *et al.* (1992) suggest there is a limit to the amount of information about outcomes which can usefully be collected through routine monitoring as opposed to more rigorous investigations. They point out that outcomes are important, first, because we need to be sure that we are 'on course' in the periods between more substantial evaluations and, second, because information about key aspects of implementation which has been regularly and systematically collected will be an important source for the evaluation process itself. As Preedy points out in Chapter 6 the current context concerns itself primarily with measurable outputs or outcomes.

It is impossible to monitor everything so the advice of Rogers and Badham (1992), originally directed to evaluation, may be applicable here. They advise limiting monitoring to specific focuses and to target priority objectives which are achievable in the short term and are readily measured.

## WHAT IS TO BE DONE WITH THE MONITORING?

This is often anecdotally referred to as the 'So what?' question, and refers to what action should be taken by managers as a result of the monitoring. Obviously, to a large extent this is encapsulated in having a clear purpose in the first place (see above).

## HOW CAN THE MONITORING BE REVIEWED?

Harlen and Elliott (1982) present some questions for managers at school or college level. They include:

- Was the monitoring task interpreted and carried through consistently as intended?
- What steps were taken to allow for bias, unrepresentativeness and low reliability in the information gathered?
- Did those involved in supplying the information approve of the methods used for collecting it?
- What were the side effects, positive and negative, of the monitoring process?
- Were satisfactory procedures used to protect the interests of those who supplied information?
- Was the monitoring reported in a way which communicated effectively with the intended audience?
- What reactions did the report provoke in the participants and the decision-makers?

As Harlen and Elliott (1982) point out, answers to such questions enable managers to elicit feedback about the conditions which facilitate effective monitoring. They also, therefore, help to develop an appropriate ethos within which it will occur in future.

## HOW IS MONITORING BEST DONE?

Ultimately, for school or college managers, this is the key question and here a number of methods are commented upon, with actual examples from schools visited.

Many schools and colleges now have management information systems in place. These may be particularly useful for obtaining statistics on, for example, attendance, number of students on a course, etc. Rogers and Badham (1992) advise collecting essential information only, as it is all too easy to be carried away by enthusiasm and to try to collect everything about the chosen topic when a much more limited exercise would suffice.

Data may be collected by a variety of methods including: questionnaires, by teachers or from pupils; interviews; observation, including observing teaching in action, that is, monitoring teachers' work, and also observing learning in action, that is, monitoring students' work; tests; official statistics; documents; meetings; tracking and target-setting – defining short-term goals; effective use of time – walking the talk and finally, management by walking about (MBWA).

Those who are monitoring might use this last technique, MBWA, where they can observe, listen, comment and encourage. It is certainly one where they should try to catch people – students and teachers – *doing things right* and then praise them for it rather than to catch people doing things wrong and then having to correct or reprimand them.

Rogers and Badham (1992) advise making the maximum use of information already available. Before rushing into designing questionnaires, interview schedules and classroom observation checklists, they suggest that managers scan existing sources of information such as attendance registers, room/equipment-usage logs, published statistics and other data collected recently by the school. Also they suggest making maximum use of any evaluation data about the school, for example, inspection reports. In the twenty-first century, there is a considerable and increasing risk of information overload. Crucial for managers is to demonstrate to staff that use is made of data collected, including that already in existence.

One secondary school lists the following wide variety of ways used to monitor what is happening in the school: classroom/lesson observation; looking at documentation, for example, policies, development plans, curriculum plans, handbooks and pupil records; looking at students' work; performance data analysis – GCSE, Key Stage tests, teacher assessments, post-16 results; talking to students, other teachers, parents, governors; interviews; pupil tracking; questionnaires to pupils; moderation/agreement trialling; spot checks.

A primary school perspective comes from St Brendan's Roman Catholic Junior School, in Corby, Northamptonshire, who suggest that the following evidence is available for monitoring a subject:

- Results in standard tests at 7 and 11.
- Results in optional tests in other years, LEA and national averages.
- End of year assessments by teachers, standardised tests, for example, reading tests.
- School- or class-based tests devised by teacher.
- Baseline assessment indicators.
- The latest Ofsted report.
- Link inspector joint evaluation reports.
- PANDA benchmark comparisons.
- LEA family school comparisons.
- Classroom observations by headteacher or co-ordinator.
- Tracking of individual pupils YR to Y2 to Y4 to Y6.
- Proportions of pupils in each year group who are on special educational needs register.
- Targets and evidence of progress towards targets in individual education plans.
- Analyses of samples of work: more able, average, less able.
- Work on display or shown in assemblies.
- Teachers' plans and records.
- Children's evaluative commentaries through discussions or questionnaires.
- Status of subject in school development plan.
- Feedback from governors' visits.
- Feedback from parents.

The key element for managers is, of course, the *appropriateness* of the method of monitoring to the aims and the object. Observation will be wholly unsuitable in some circumstances. The basic research principle applies – methodology must be appropriate.

## ASSESSING CRITERIA FOR JUDGEMENTS

Rogers and Badham (1992) suggest that the uses of the data – who has access to the information and why – also need to be agreed. Similarly, the credibility of the monitoring system within a school has to be established by ensuring that the outcomes are valuable to all the parties concerned. The judgements made must be valid, that is, they must be supported by evidence. The process should be verifiable, that is, reasons for the judgements should be specific with the supporting evidence presented. The process should be viable, that is, cost-effective in terms of time and resources and, therefore, sustainable.

## ACCEPTABILITY

There may be a number of issues for managers concerned with the acceptability of the monitoring process to those being monitored.

Kemmis and McTaggart (1981) give some ethical guidelines, which although intended for action research, are nevertheless applicable to monitoring in schools or colleges (see Figure 5.3). It may be that those who are managing monitoring may feel that they need not consider all of these ethical issues, although Hopkins (1989) suggests that action researchers must pay attention to the ethical principles guiding their work because their actions are deeply embedded in an existing social organisation and the failure to work within the general procedures of that organisation may jeopardise not only the process of improvement but also existing valuable work.

## REPORTING AND CONTROLLING THE MONITORING

Having completed the monitoring, it will need to be *reported*. Relevant questions, according to Hardie (1995), include:

- What form will the report of the monitoring take? (Will it be verbal, written, multimedia?)
- Who will actually compile and make the report?
- Who is the report for and what is the intended audience?
- Will the report be at different levels for different people, e.g., governors, parents, inspectors?
- Will the report include *all* the findings?
- Does there need to be balance between description and monitoring data and opinion?
- How much analysis and reflection are needed?
- Are there references to teacher performance?
- Are individuals named or is it anonymous?
- Is there reference to children and their performance or outcomes?

The issues too for managers, of who sees reports and what agreements are needed, are important, described by Hardie (1995) as 'the control and availability of the information'.

## PROBLEMS AND DIFFICULTIES

### Overload

Institution-wide monitoring can only succeed if it does not take up disproportionate amounts of time, effort and resources. Constraints on schools include shortage of time, lack of expertise in monitoring and reluctance of staff to embrace monitoring as an integral part of normal practice (Rogers

Observe protocol: take care to ensure that the relevant persons, committees and authorities have been consulted, informed and that the necessary permission and approval have been obtained

Involve participants: encourage others who have a stake in the improvement you envisage to shape the form of the work

Negotiate with those affected: not everyone will want to be directly involved; your work should take account of the responsibilities and wishes of others

Report progress: keep the work visible and remain open to suggestions so that unforeseen and unseen ramifications can be taken account of; colleagues must have the opportunity to lodge a protest to you

Obtain explicit authorisation before you observe: for the purposes of recording the activities of professional colleagues or others (the observation of your own students falls outside this imperative provided that your aim is the improvement of teaching and learning)

Obtain explicit authorisation before you examine files, correspondence or other documentation: take copies only if specific authority to do this is obtained

Negotiate descriptions of people's work: always allow those described to challenge your accounts on the grounds of fairness, relevance and accuracy

Negotiate accounts of others' points of view (e.g. in accounts of communication): Always allow those involved in interviews, meetings and written exchanges to require amendments which enhance fairness, relevance and accuracy

Obtain explicit authorisation before using quotations: verbatim transcripts, attributed observations, excerpts of audio and video recordings, judgements, conclusions or recommendations in reports (written or to meetings)

Negotiate reports for various levels of release: remember that different audiences demand different kinds of reports; what is appropriate for an informal verbal report to a faculty meeting may not be appropriate for a staff meeting, a report to council, a journal article, a newspaper, a newsletter to parents; be conservative if you cannot control distribution

Accept responsibility for maintaining confidentiality and retain the right to report your work: provided that those involved are satisfied with the fairness, accuracy and relevance of accounts which pertain to them, and that the accounts do not unnecessarily expose or embarrass those involved, then accounts should not be subject to veto or be sheltered by prohibitions of confidentiality

Make your principles of procedure binding and known: all of the people involved in your action research project must agree to the principles before the work begins; others must be aware of their rights in the process.

**Figure 5.3**   Ethical guidelines
*Source:* Kemmis and McTaggart, 1981.

and Badham, 1992). Coleman (1999) agrees that teachers collecting data in their own institution may have to be particularly sensitive to issues such as taking the time of their colleagues in the investigation process.

Fullan and Hargreaves (1991, p. 8) point out that teachers are keenly aware that their job has changed immensely in the last decade or so. Expectations have intensified. Obligations have become more diffuse. Advisorship, consultancy and curriculum leadership at the school level are beginning to emerge as alternative solutions to the expertise problem. Finally, and ironically, they say:

> innovations-as-solutions exacerbate the overload problem. As if adding insult to injury, fragmented solutions, faddism and other bandwagon shifts, massive multi-faceted, unwieldy reform, all drive the teacher downward. The solution becomes the problem. Innovations in curriculum, testing and other areas are not making the teacher's job more manageable. They are making it worse. Overload of expectations and fragmented solutions remain the number one problem.
>                                (Fullan and Hargreaves, 1991, p. 10)

As teachers face up to rising and widening expectations in their work and to the increasing overload of innovations and reforms, it is important that they work and plan more with their colleagues, sharing and developing their expertise together, instead of trying to cope alone with the demands. In this emerging conception of the teacher's role, leadership and consultancy are part of the job for all teachers, not just a privilege allocated to and exercised by a few. This conception has gained strength at the level of theoretical discussion but it remains underdeveloped in practice. In the meantime, the problem of overload worsens.

## Avoiding undue intrusion

Johnson's (1994) points about carrying out research are applicable to monitoring, I believe. She reminds those involved to remember that they are embarking on monitoring, not investigative journalism! Monitoring a management or other issue may not of itself be intrusive, but individuals' self-image and self-esteem are often closely bound up with their work role.

Johnson's (ibid.) point about the aims of research are also valid here. Access should be negotiated with sensitivity, so the impression is not given that the aims of the monitoring are covert rather than declared.

## Maintaining confidentiality

Johnson (1994) suggests that confidentiality is a relative concept, but for managers it can on occasions be an issue when monitoring in schools and colleges. When monitoring on a whole school or college issue, concealing individual identity may be important but difficult. Coleman (1999) suggests that maintaining anonymity when disseminating the data outcomes may be particularly difficult in a small institution. The insensitive or unscrupulous use of findings on the part of the 'researcher', or potentially on the part of the senior management team, indicates the possibility of using data for micro-political ends. Equally, in a small team (such as a department in a school or college) the identity of individuals may often be obvious.

No matter how collaborative and shared the monitoring process is, it is still essential to ensure that individuals are not damaged, but this does not mean that difficult matters are not addressed. For example, it may be possible to describe the teaching styles and approaches that are proving most useful in the context of a new curriculum development without identifying who is, or is not, using them. Steps may need to be taken to help individuals who are experiencing difficulties, but these need not be made public in any way. It is important to remember that pupils also have rights to privacy and confidentiality. Reporting includes what is said as much as what is written, and the same ethical code applies. Both written and verbal reports should focus on issues not individuals (Aspinwall *et al.*, 1992).

## Bias

If small samples are used, for example the monitoring of accidents or exclusions, there is clearly potential for bias in interpretation as these small numbers may not be 'typical'. Other areas of potential bias are where those undertaking the monitoring have a particular axe to grind and may therefore present the monitoring with this bias in mind. Interviews, considered below, are mentioned as a specific area of potential bias.

## Problems and strengths of specific monitoring tools

The problems of using specific tools for the collection of data for monitoring, which I think might be seen as a particular type of research, are now considered briefly.

### Questionnaires

The disadvantages of questionnaires include the following issues. Designing questionnaires is difficult but crucial (Aspinwall *et al.*, 1992). You will only be given the answers you ask for (ibid.). Important issues may be missed or obscured, even if you add 'Is there anything else you would like to say?' as the final question (Aspinwall *et al.*, 1992; Rogers and Badham, 1992). Analysis of the data can be difficult and time-consuming (Aspinwall *et al.*, 1992; Rogers and Badham, 1992). The choice of a response scale may lead to an averaging of responses and the broader the scale, the more likely this is (Aspinwall *et al.*, 1992). Because questionnaires are impersonal, we may lack information that sets responses into context (ibid.). Recipients may feel that questionnaires are an imposition, a bore or difficult to fill in, and this may affect the response rate (ibid.). Questions can be misinterpreted by respondents (Rogers and Badham, 1992). Responses may be superficial (ibid.). In-depth questioning may be difficult (ibid.). Questions may miss some important facets (ibid.).

## *Interviews and conversations (one to one or group)*

The disadvantages of interviews include the following issues. Interviews are time-consuming to plan, administer, write up and analyse (Aspinwall *et al.*, 1992; Coleman, 1999; Rogers and Badham, 1992). The breadth and amount of data may make interpretation and analysis difficult (Aspinwall *et al.*, 1992). Difficulties with interviews arose from the danger of manipulation by either the interviewer or the interviewee (Aspinwall *et al.*, 1992; Coleman, 1999; Rogers and Badham, 1992). There is a danger of bias, both in the way that the interview is conducted and in the way that comments are recorded (Aspinwall *et al.*, 1992). The interview itself cannot be anonymous. If quotations are used in a report they may be identifiable, even if the speaker is not named, particularly within a group who know each other well (ibid.).

## *Documentary sources (including reported assessment of pupils' work)*

Because documentation may be partial, or part of the writer's desire to influence rather than record, it may distort or conceal aspects of a development (Aspinwall *et al.*, 1992). Letters, diaries and journals may be confidential documents and therefore not available to others (ibid. ). Reports, materials and minutes may be rather do-it-yourself, 'safe' documents which contain no hint of important aspects of a development such as the feelings generated or the intensity of the debate (ibid.). There may be a large amount of documentation available which may be tedious and difficult to analyse (ibid.). Records may be incomplete, inaccurate or out of date (Rogers and Badham, 1992). They may be difficult to collect, collate or analyse data presented in an inappropriate form (ibid.). They may have limited applicability (ibid.).

## *Observation*

The disadvantages include the following issues. Observation and analysis are time-consuming (Rogers and Badham, 1992). Observation provides a 'snapshot' of an event. It is hard to establish how typical this is (Aspinwall *et al.*, 1992; Rogers and Badham, 1992). The presence of an observer often influences what happens (Aspinwall *et al.*, 1992). It is impossible to observe everything all of the time. Open observation can be confusing and closed, checklist observation may limit what is seen (ibid.). Observation may alter learning environment, inhibiting both staff and pupils (Rogers and Badham, 1992). There is a risk of subjective judgements (ibid.).

Students' work is time-consuming to monitor for a statistically valid sample (Aspinwall *et al.*, 1992). In addition, application of objective evaluation criteria is made difficult by the variability of the material (ibid.).

## Over sensitivity

It must be acknowledged that, however collaborative a school or college wishes to be, monitoring (as evaluation) may often need to identify precisely where a problem is and that may be with an individual person. It is pointless monitoring a process if in the end no one can recognise how improvement can be made if that needs to be through a person.

## TO SUMMARISE

Effective monitoring offers an answer to the question 'Are we getting there?' and is a questioning activity. It also asks, 'Do we do what we say we do?'

Monitoring allows managers to assess how well the institutions are performing, whether targets are being worked towards nor not. It allows you to see where you are not progressing towards targets or standards. It shows where the institution needs to improve and can 'prevent procedures becoming obsolete and inefficient' and, finally, monitoring should be part of a cycle of 'continuous improvement'.

Monitoring is a process that is crucial for organisational effectiveness. It might be carried out by a variety of people at a variety of times as appropriate to a particular school or college. The emphasis might be on the inputs, outputs or the process itself. A variety of methods might be used, with different perspectives for different colleges or schools. There may be issues concerning checking the criteria for the judgement of monitoring, acceptability and also the reporting and control of the monitoring. Since monitoring carries within it an idea of 'checking', managers need to develop systems and procedures which are sensitive as well as efficient.

## REFERENCES

Aspinwall, K., Simkins, T., Wilkinson, J. F. and McAuley, M. J. (1992) *Managing Evaluation in Education*, London, Routledge.

Coleman, M. (1999) What makes for effective research in a school or college? in Middlewood, D., Coleman, M. and Lumby, J. (1999) *Practitioner Research in Education: Making a Difference*, London, Paul Chapman.

Fullan, M. and Hargreaves, A. (1991) *What's Worth Fighting for in Your School?* Milton Keynes, Open University Press.

Hardie, B. L. (1995) *Evaluating the Primary School*, Plymouth, Northcote House.

Hardie, B. L. (1998) Managing monitoring and evaluation, in Middlewood, D. and Lumby, J. *Strategic Management in Schools and Colleges*, London, Paul Chapman.

Harlen, W. and Elliott, J. (1982) A checklist for planning or reviewing an evaluation, in McCormick, R., Bynner, J., Clift, P., James, M. and Brown, C.M. (eds.) *Calling Education to Account*, London, Heinemann in association with the Open University Press.

Harris, A., Jamieson, I. and Russ, J. (1995) A study of effective departments in secondary schools, *School Organisation*, Vol. 15, no. 3, pp. 283–99.

Holy Family College (1998) *Monitoring and Evaluation*, Walthamstow, Holy Family College.

Hopkins, D. (1989) *A Teacher's Guide to Classroom Research*, Milton Keynes, Open University Press.

James, M. (1998) *Using Assessment for School Improvement*, Oxford, Heinemann.

Johnson, D. (1994) *Research Methods in Educational Management*, Harlow, Longman.

Kemmis, S. and McTaggart, R. (1981) *The Action Research Planner*, Victoria, Deakin University Press, pp. 43–4.

Martin, J. (2000) Governors only have to ensure that monitoring takes place, not do it themselves, *Times Educational Supplement*, 16 June.

Mintzberg, H. (1979) *The Nature of Managerial Work*, 2nd edn, Englewood Cliffs, NJ, Prentice-Hall.

Newman, G. (1998) Rethinking the pupil-teacher band, *Managing Schools Today*, Vol 7, no. 5, pp. 25–6.

Ofsted (1997) *Subject Management in Secondary Schools; Aspects of Good Practice: 93/97/NS*, London, Ofsted.

Raffan, J. and Ruthven, K (2000) Monitoring, assessment, recording, reporting and accountability, in Beck, J. and Earl, M. (eds.) *Key Issues in Secondary Education*, London, Cassell.

Rogers, G. and Badham, L. (1992) *Evaluation in Schools*, London, Routledge.

Sammons, P., Thomas, S. and Mortimore, P. (1997) *Forging Links: Effective Schools and Effective Departments*, London, Paul Chapman.

Stake, R. E. (1976) *Evaluating Educational Programmes*, Paris, OECD.

Torrington, D. and Weightman, J. (1985) *The Business of Management*, London, Prentice-Hall.

West-Burnham, J. (1992) *Managing Quality in Schools*, Harlow, Longman.

# 6

# CURRICULUM EVALUATION: MEASURING WHAT WE VALUE

## Margaret Preedy

This chapter looks first at some of the main components of curriculum evaluation, and the impact of external evaluation requirements on schools and colleges. Two main approaches to evaluation and their strengths and limitations are discussed. It is argued that, notwithstanding external pressures, schools and colleges need to set their own evaluation agendas, clearly focused on internal priorities. There are, it is suggested, three important issues in setting this agenda: recognising the centrality of values, developing a community of enquiry among the staff and involving stakeholders, especially students, in the evaluation process.

Curriculum evaluation is concerned with gathering evidence to describe and make judgements about the value or worth of curriculum plans, processes and outcomes, as a basis for developing and improving them. As this definition suggests, curriculum evaluation is a complex process, which, since it involves values and judgements, is likely to be subject to very fundamental ideological and political differences about the purposes of the curriculum. It is also important to emphasise the second part of the definition above – that is, the link to development and ongoing change. This element is often neglected – too many evaluation reports lie on the shelves gathering dust rather than forming a basis for action. Evaluation should be used to provide the evidence to inform decision-making.

Evaluation is often discussed in connection with the related process of monitoring. The distinction between the terms is not clear-cut and they are often used as if they were synonymous. Monitoring is usually seen as a more specific and tightly defined activity than evaluation; it is an ongoing and systematic process, which answers the question: are we doing what we intended to do? Evaluation is concerned with the question: is what we are doing worthwhile? Monitoring data is often used as part of the evidence for an evaluation. Thus for example monitoring a scheme for the development of teachers' repertoire of teaching methods would entail routine checking that the scheme was being implemented as planned. This information might be used in an evaluation of the success of the scheme in improving teaching and pupil learning.

Evaluating the curriculum takes place at various levels within the education system – nationally, by regional bodies such as local education authorities (LEAs), at whole-school/college level, within departments/subunits, and by individual teachers and students within the classroom. Here we shall be concerned with the whole school/college perspective and the management issues that arise. The evaluation process forms part of the cycle for the management of pupil learning: reviewing/auditing → planning → implementing → monitoring/evaluating → reviewing, and so on. While it is useful to distinguish these stages in analysing management tasks, in practice they are, of course, very much interrelated and overlapping. Thus, for example, monitoring and evaluation are important at the implementation stage to check on the progress and success of putting plans into practice. Evaluation should be concerned with all three main dimensions of the curriculum:

- The *intended* curriculum – what is planned.
- The *offered* curriculum – what teachers teach.
- The *received* curriculum – what pupils actually experience.

An important evaluation activity is assessing the degree of match between these three elements – how far is what we intend incorporated in teaching, and actually evident in pupils' experience in the classroom?

A useful distinction can be made between two broad purposes for curriculum evaluation:

1) Evaluation for justification and accountability – that is, the need to render an account of the curriculum to agencies, whether external or internal to the school/college, which have authority over it (for example, by teachers or the school to an external inspector, or by a department to the senior management team as part of a review of the distribution of curricular resources across departments).
2) Evaluation for improvement – that is, designed to enhance or develop a particular aspect of curricular provision (for example, appraising the contents, teaching and learning and assessment methods of a course in order to improve its quality from the perspectives of teachers and students).

In practice, many evaluation activities are likely to include elements of both purposes, though these may well be in tension, especially where external agencies are concerned. Thus, for example, if I am explaining my lesson planning to an external inspector, I am likely to focus on proving the quality of my work and justifying its effectiveness. If I am evaluating my work with trusted colleagues with a view to improving it, I am likely to look at areas of weakness and problems as well as strengths, asking for advice on how I could do better.

A distinction is also often made between *formative* evaluation, which enables adjustments to be made during the course of an activity or programme, and *summative* evaluation, which examines the activity in its entirety after it has been presented or finished. Thus, for example, a teacher might provide formative feedback on students' coursework in order to enable them to modify and improve it before it is presented for summative evaluation in the form of end-of-course assessment. In practice, given limitations of time and resources, much useful evaluation activity in schools and colleges is small-scale formative evaluation – providing evidence about the strengths and weaknesses of a course or activity so that ongoing adjustments can be made.

The discussion in this chapter focuses largely on the English and Welsh education system. However, the main components of curriculum evaluation mentioned above and the two broad evaluative approaches discussed later are generic and relevant to other education systems. There are, though, some differences between the English and Welsh arrangements and those of many other countries with respect to the degree of curricular autonomy of school/college managers *vis-à-vis* the two main external levels of control – the LEA or district level and the state or national level. These differences affect how curriculum evaluation is tackled. The balance of power and control of the curriculum between schools/colleges, local or regional bodies and national or state governments, differs from country to country and alters in response to changing national policies and priorities.

Recent years have seen increasingly centralised curriculum control in England and Wales, with a shift in the balance of power away from schools and LEAs in favour of central government. On the other hand, many European countries, especially the Nordic ones, and the USA, have experienced a contrary movement with increasing decentralisation of the curriculum (Maden, 2000; Peck and Ramsay, 1998). However, whether they have moved towards or away from central government curricular control, most European countries, including England and Wales, have seen the development of centralised educational standards, statistical and inspection agencies, which seek to monitor and enhance standards of pupils' performance across the educational system. The growth of these central agencies has been prompted largely by national concerns about maintaining and increasing educational standards in order to compete and survive in the global marketplace (Maden, 2000). Thus curriculum management, including evaluation, at school level is considerably circumscribed by the monitoring role of central agencies. As discussed below, external accountability pressures are particularly evident in England and Wales, but still present in other contexts, as are the other evaluation issues mentioned in the first paragraph of this chapter.

## EXTERNAL EVALUATION REQUIREMENTS

External requirements have a major impact on evaluation concerns within schools and colleges, so these are discussed first, before turning to internal considerations. The latter years of the twentieth century in England and Wales saw increasing centralised control of the curriculum and its evaluation, based on a centrally prescribed curriculum and associated testing arrangements, backed by regular inspections, the annual publication of comparative student performance data for schools, colleges and LEAs, and the setting of national, LEA and school/college targets for year on year improvements in student performance. This strong framework of external evaluation requirements places considerable emphasis on the accountability dimension of evaluation discussed above, for schools, departments and individual teachers, requiring them to justify and explain their performance and to demonstrate ongoing improvement in student test and examination results. Performance management arrangements for schools link teachers' and headteachers' pay and career development closely to improving these results. The evaluation role of Ofsted[1] is described as 'essential if schools are to be held accountable for the public funds they receive, and to provide an objective, external and expert view of their performance' (DfEE/ Ofsted, 1999). It is intended by the Department for Education and Employment (DfEE) that these external accountability pressures should act as an incentive to internal institutional improvement, and hence 'drive up' standards of student attainment (DfEE, 1997a).

This set of requirements also places considerable weight on one single indicator – student performance data – as a basis for making evaluative judgements about departments, schools/colleges and LEAs. Thus, for example, the Ofsted inspection model judges the school's effectiveness by assessing 'outcomes', defined as 'the standards achieved by pupils at the school'. The quality of teaching and leadership and management are treated in the model as contributory factors to these outcomes. The then DES (1989) asserted that the national curriculum assessment arrangements would serve a wide range of evaluative purposes at different levels, providing: formative and summative information for teachers on individual pupils, comparative aggregated data for teachers and schools, informative evidence on the performance of schools, and information contributing to the professional development of teachers. As many commentators have pointed out (see, for example, Gipps, 1990; Kelly, 1999) it is not clear that any assessment system can serve both formative and summative functions without the summative overwhelming the formative. Also, the fairly simple Key Stage (KS) standard assessment tasks ( SATs)[2] testing arrangements provide a somewhat limited and doubtful database for such a wide range of evaluation purposes, leaving aside the issue of the reliability and validity of these tests, which has also been questioned.

This external framework for assessing the work of educational institutions can be seen as an example of the rational objectives-based approach to curriculum evaluation. This approach stems from the work of Ralph Tyler in the 1930s and 1940s, which has had a very considerable influence on curriculum planning in the USA where it originated, the UK and elsewhere. Tyler argued that any curriculum plan must answer four fundamental questions:

1) What educational purposes should the school seek to attain?
2) What educational experiences can be provided that are likely to attain these purposes?
3) How can these educational experiences be effectively organised?
4) How can we determine whether these purposes are being attained? (Tyler, quoted in Kelly, 1999, p. 14).

This gives a simple linear model: objectives → content → learning experiences → evaluation (see Figure 4.2 in Chapter 4 of this book).

It was later acknowledged that the model needed to take account of changes in the curriculum, so planning is better seen as a cyclical and continuous process, with evaluation feeding back into the formulation of modified objectives. From this perspective, evaluation is a matter of determining how far objectives have been achieved, by comparing products or outputs with pre-specified purposes and objectives – that is, product evaluation.

## PRODUCT EVALUATION

This form of evaluation, based on the Tyler model, is extremely important in education. Back in the 1980s, Skilbeck (1984, p. 7) suggested that much evaluation focuses on a particular aspect: 'the immediate outcomes, usually in the form of student performance'. This is probably even more evident today than when this comment was made. Thus in the case of the National Curriculum, for each subject, the content and objectives, or attainment targets, for performance at each of the various attainment levels are specified. Pupil outcomes, in the form of KS test and public examination performance, are measured against these objectives. Aggregated assessment data are then used as evaluative evidence in making judgements about the performance of teachers, departments, schools and so on.

Product evaluation, using student performance data, has a number of advantages. It is logical and rational – clearly we need to make some assessment of student outcomes in the light of intended curriculum purposes. It uses relatively objective measures – though, of course, no test or examination can be entirely objective, reliable and valid. It is also straightforward to use, relatively economical and can be applied at any level of the educational system, from the teacher in the classroom, adjusting curriculum content and teaching approaches in response to the information provided by pupil assessment data, to national-level policy decisions in response to the overall performance of schools – for example, the DfEE's literacy and numeracy targets for LEAs.

Product evaluation approaches, however, have a number of disadvantages. They tend to focus attention on immediate and easily measurable outputs, such as test results and attendance rates, leading to a neglect of equally important but hard to measure outcomes such as students' moral, social and spiritual development, and the range of 'intelligences' discussed in the work of Howard Gardner (1993). Many of the most valuable outcomes of education are multidimensional, complex and long term, and cannot be represented by test scores. By focusing on measuring outcomes against pre-specified objectives, the product evaluation model ignores unplanned outcomes, and fails to explore the value and worth of the prescribed objectives and purposes. There is also a tendency to de-emphasise contextual factors, such as the school/college environment and the community in which it is located – student performance is only partly related to what has been achieved by means of the curriculum. Process factors, such as students' motivation and level of satisfaction with their courses of study, are also neglected.

Given the high stakes of student performance data as an evaluative measure at all levels of the education system, there is a very real danger of 'teaching to the test', and a focus on the performance of particular groups at the expense of others, raising equity issues. Thus for example, seeking to raise the percentage of A*–C grades at GCSE may lead to particular attention being given to raising the attainment of pupils performing at grade D level, with correspondingly less attention to the needs of higher and lower attaining pupils. There is also a risk of 'massaging the data'. For example, it was reported (TES, 2000) that one LEA had been allowing the removal of up to 7 per cent of truanting Year 11 pupils from school rolls, hence 'boosting' the GCSE results of the schools concerned and the authority as a whole. High stakes performance indicators are subject to corruption, and may well distort the activities they are designed to measure (Norris, 1998).

## PROCESS EVALUATION

A process model of evaluation provides a means of addressing some of the limitations of the product model discussed above. While product evaluation is important and necessary, it throws little light on what is arguably the essence of the curriculum: teaching and learning as they are experienced by teachers and students in the classroom – the offered and received curriculum. Process evaluation focuses on the perspectives and interpretations of participants, on qualitative rather than quantitative data, taking a subjective phenomenological stance, rather than a 'rational', quasi-scientific one. It acknowledges multiple realities – that different groups and individual stakeholders construct different meanings of the curriculum in the light of their own contexts, values and perspectives.

Process evaluation has been tackled in various ways. One approach is based on Stake's (1986) discussion of portrayal evaluation, which is responsive to the needs and interests of the immediate stakeholders and attempts to understand situations by use of a mixture of measurement techniques, to provide a picture of a course or programme as a whole, not solely in terms of pre-specified goals. Other perspectives are based on Parlett and Hamilton's (1975) illuminative evaluation, which is concerned with 'description and interpretation rather than measurement and prediction . . . to provide a comprehensive understanding of the complex reality or realities' surrounding curriculum activities. Such approaches seek to discover what a course, teaching method or curriculum decision-making process is like from the perspective of participants and what they see as the significant features, and strengths and weaknesses of the process. This will entail gathering the views of staff peers and subordinates as well as students, lateral and 'bottom-up' evaluation, and hence can be a potentially sensitive process.

Process evaluation is an important dimension of evaluation for school improvement, as will be argued later. However, it has a number of limitations which should be acknowledged. This approach draws largely on qualitative data, which tend to be more difficult and time-consuming to collect and assess than quantitative data, with implications for staff time and other resources. It is hard to devise performance indicators and success criteria for factors such as student satisfaction with their courses and staff/ student relationships. There are also issues of reliability – quantitative indicators tend to be more reliable. Qualitative data are specific to the context in which they are gathered and hence cannot be generalised. For this reason they tend to have less credibility than quantitative measures, especially with external agencies (Norris, 1998).

## SETTING THE AGENDA

Earlier sections of this chapter have examined external requirements, and the strengths and limitations of product and process approaches to evaluation. Internal evaluation for improvement purposes should build on and complement the external accountability dimension. Inspection reports (together with pre-inspection preparation and post-inspection action planning) and pupil performance data are important and useful forms of evidence in the school's own work in reviewing teaching and learning and seeking to enhance it. Similarly, national and LEA benchmark data provide useful comparative information for use in school self-evaluation. Internal evaluation also needs to draw on both product and process approaches; each provides a necessary, though partial, perspective. However, in the current context, there is a danger of focusing too much on external requirements to demonstrate rising standards and hence on a product-based approach, and a view of evaluation as a largely rational and straightforward process. This may lead to a neglect of equally important but harder to measure process factors. It is essential for schools to set their own evaluation agendas, clearly linked to the school's own core purposes, aims, values and priorities – to evaluate what is important, not just what is required and easy to measure. It also needs to be recognised that evaluation is a contested and problematic process.

The external accountability agenda impacts on schools in indirect, as well as direct, ways by prescribing a model for what counts as self-evaluation, and framing the ways and language in which it is approached and discussed. Thus for example the Ofsted (1999) handbook guidance on self-evaluation claims that 'it is advantageous to base school self-evaluation on the same criteria as those used in all schools by inspectors. A common language has developed about the work of schools, expressed through the criteria. Teachers and governors know that the criteria reflect things that matter' (p. 138). Much of the guidance on self-evaluation from the DfEE and other government agencies draws on an objectives-based, product-focused approach, where evaluation is seen as a relatively systematic and straightforward matter, ignoring issues of context, values and multiple stakeholder goals. Thus for example the DfEE (1997b) five-stage cycle for target-setting focuses on *how* to measure performance, omitting the important prior question of school values and aims – *what* should we be aiming for? Schools and teachers risk being 'colonised' (Jeffrey and Woods, 1998) by the official discourse of evaluation for accountability, unless they are very clear about their own agendas – measuring what they value.

Managing any internal evaluation activity entails addressing a number of key questions:

- What is the purpose and focus of the evaluation?
- What criteria are to be used to make judgements?
- What evidence is to be collected, and what data collection methods will be used?
- Which stakeholders will be consulted?
- Who is responsible for the evaluation and the judgements made?
- What timescale and resources will be allocated to it?
- What action is to be taken as a result of the evaluation findings?

In order for schools to be able to answer these questions in ways which give priority to measuring what is valued and important, and which are responsive to the needs of the central stakeholders – staff, students, parents and governors – I would argue that three main issues need to be addressed:

1) Recognising the importance of values.
2) Building a community of enquiry.
3) Involving stakeholders.

The remainder of this chapter briefly considers each of these issues.

## THE IMPORTANCE OF VALUES

Since evaluation is concerned with values and judgements, each of the questions listed above is likely to be contentious. It is a complex political activity, which, by making judgements and recommendations, threatens the status quo, and those who have a vested interest in it. Unless this is recognised, evaluation activities are likely to be focused either on areas of interest to powerful groups or individuals within the school or, where consensus is a priority, on superficial matters, rather than important ones. There may be tensions between what ought to be evaluated and what is feasible politically. Different participants will have differing views on the appropriate purposes and focus for evaluation and what counts as evidence, stemming from their own underlying sets of values, beliefs and assumptions, based on their upbringing, experiences and professional socialisation. These sets of values or ideologies will influence how people perceive the nature and purpose of the curriculum and its evaluation. Thus, for example, it might be agreed that major purposes for the school are to enable students to achieve their full potential and to prepare them for adult life. However, priorities and emphases will differ, based on people's values about the balance between meeting the needs of the individual learner and those of the group, between societal expectations and individual needs, and between the various forms of learning experience provided in schools. In evaluating curricular provision, what is the appropriate balance between the various teaching and learning purposes of the school, for example: students' academic, moral and social development, preparation for working life, responsibilities as a parent, citizen and so on?

It is therefore important to acknowledge that schools have multiple and often competing values and purposes for student learning and to review these regularly as part of ongoing professional dialogue within the school, and to ensure as part of this process that evaluation activities are linked to agreed school aims and school/college development plan priorities. It is also important to check that whole-school aims are enacted in the classroom – that the intended, offered and received curricula are in harmony. A frequent comment in Ofsted inspection reports is that school aims are not reflected in what happens in the classroom. Some schools have worked out specific, agreed strategies for how aims can be achieved in practice in work with pupils. Similarly, it is useful periodically to conduct an aims-tracking exercise to assess the ways in which each school aim is being achieved and supported (or not) in the teaching and learning activities across the school and individual subunits, including the allocation of resources and identifying areas where consistency between aims and practice needs further development.

## A COMMUNITY OF ENQUIRY

A second major factor in evaluating what is of importance is to develop a climate of enquiry and reflection on practice, where evaluation is seen not as a one-off or threatening activity, but as a routine and valuable part of professional life. This entails developing a collaborative climate of trust and openness, in which people feel able to admit weaknesses and mistakes and to seek advice from colleagues. It is based on a democratic model of evaluation which recognises a plurality of values and interests, where ongoing review of teaching and learning quality is an ongoing group activity involving all staff, rather than a 'top-down' activity which is 'done to' teachers.

This has implications for accountability relationships. Top-down evaluation within the school or college and external inspection are based on a public or managerial accountability model (Kogan, 1986), where teachers are held to be formally accountable to the head or principal, and to Ofsted inspectors, acting on behalf of the DfEE and, more broadly, to the public as taxpayers who provide the funds to support maintained schools and colleges. This is a 'hard' or coercive form of accountability, in that managers and external agencies with control over the curriculum have the authority to call teachers and schools to account, and to impose sanctions where they deem performance to be unsatisfactory.

Democratic approaches to evaluation reflect a professional or mutual culpability model (Adelman and Alexander, 1982) of accountability. Here, teachers are seen as having a responsibility as members of a profession to act in the interests of students as clients, and to uphold the values and ethical standards of the profession. This is a 'softer' form of accountability, based on moral responsibility and duty to colleagues and students, linked to professional standards of performance rather than coercion or sanctions. From this perspective, all teachers in a school or college are mutually responsible to each other for the quality of teaching and learning. Curriculum evaluation, therefore, forms the means by which teachers account to each other for their various contributions to the teaching and learning process. Evaluation activities are controlled democratically, and answers to the evaluation questions listed above are agreed collegially. In such a situation, evaluation is not an optional extra, but a shared whole-school enterprise, where all staff feel commitment to, and ownership of, an ongoing process of evaluation, reflection and development of practice.

## INVOLVING STUDENTS AS STAKEHOLDERS

The importance of involving staff as partners in the evaluation process has been discussed above. Parents and governors, as other immediate stakeholders, also have a part to play. However, given limitations of space, I focus here on student perspectives. I would argue that their views are a very important, but much neglected, dimension of internal evaluation, which should receive more attention than it does currently in many schools. The Ofsted inspection framework also provides remarkably little scope for including pupil perspectives on the work of the school. While inspectors observe pupil-learning in classrooms and examine samples of pupils' work, there is no significant place in inspection reports for consumer satisfaction as a measure of schools' quality. The further education inspection framework and the arrangements for self-evaluation by colleges give more prominence to student perspectives, perhaps partly because as young adults it is felt that they have a right to be consulted, and perhaps partly for more pragmatic reasons – post-compulsory students, as voluntary participants, can drop out or move to another college if they are dissatisfied, so colleges' success and survival is dependent on their continuing support.

It has been suggested (Gray, 1993) that there are three key performance indicators for schools – the proportion of pupils:

- who are making above average levels of academic progress
- who are satisfied with the education they are receiving
- who have formed a good or 'vital' relationship with one or more teachers.

Evaluation activities in relation to the first criterion above are likely to draw largely on a product approach (see above), using quantitative data from test and examination results. Thus, for example, one might conduct an evaluation of the relative progress of boys and girls in Year 9 by assessing their KS3 SATs results in relation to their KS2 results or Year 7 cognitive ability test (CAT) scores, and comparing these data with those for previous cohorts and with national and LEA benchmark data. Evaluation in relation to the second and third of Gray's criteria requires a process approach (see above), using qualitative data, collected by methods such as pupil questionnaires or interviews, or pupil shadowing. As discussed earlier, process evaluation is harder and more time-consuming to design, conduct and draw judgements from.

However, it is important to involve students more closely in the evaluation of schools' work, using a process approach, for a number of reasons. First, students are the main intended beneficiaries of what goes on in schools and colleges – their central task is to help students to learn. It is therefore important to explore what students consider to be the important features of their experiences in school. These may not be the same as those viewed as important by teachers and other stakeholders such as parents (MacBeath *et al.*, 1997). Second, only students can tell us what the *received* curriculum as they experience it is actually like. Third, there is considerable evidence (see, for example, MacBeath *et al.*, 1997; Rudduck, Chaplain and Wallace, 1996) that students can provide very helpful and constructive feedback on their experience in school, and do not tend to abuse the opportunity to give their opinions by making negative, destructive or personalised comments. Fourth, if we espouse a democratic approach to evaluation, as discussed earlier in relation to staff, there is a strong moral case for involving students as well. Fifth, seeking pupil views, taking them seriously and using them in curriculum development, demonstrates that pupil perspectives are valued, and helps to encourage pupil ownership of,

and commitment to, school norms and values, and to enhance pupil
motivation towards their own work.

Sixth, the last point is particularly important in the case of disaffected
pupils who have negative attitudes towards school. Quite apart from those
who actively truant, many pupils lack motivation in school, and are disen-
gaged for much of the time in the classroom, and hence underachieve. A
large-scale research study, for example, found that over 40 per cent of Year
7 and 9 students were bored in some lessons (Keys and Fernandez, 1993).
Drawing on pupil perspectives to explore the reasons for lack of motivation
is an important area for school self-evaluation. A small-scale, school-based
investigation (Williams, 1997), for example, used pupil interviews and
questionnaires, and found that among the main factors inhibiting pupil
motivation were poor communication between teachers and pupils, and
that interaction with teachers focused predominantly on negative aspects
of pupils' work with little perceived praise and support. Strategies developed in response to these findings included a student motivation checklist, which students discuss with staff and which is used by staff in
designing schemes of work. The school also identified areas where teachers
could try to maximise student motivation, for example, by strategies to
demonstrate that they valued each student's work and that they valued all
students as learners, actively helped students with their work and respected students' 'intellectual space' by encouraging them to use their own
methods to work things out.

A final and fundamental reason for involving students more closely in
school self-evaluation is that it enables students to develop their skills in
analysing, reflecting on, and evaluating their own learning, thus helping
them to take charge of and take responsibility for their own work and
progress, which is essential for effective learning. Asking pupils for feedback on their learning, and what they and the school might do to enhance
it, not only provides teachers with ideas for improving curricular provision
and teaching and learning approaches, but also, and equally importantly,
engages students in reflection and self-evaluation, enabling them progres-
sively to develop responsibility for managing their own learning. Such
skills are increasingly important in the 'information age' where rapid developments in ICT and changes in the nature of the workplace mean that
young people joining the workforce will need to become 'portfolio people'
(Handy, 1995), flexible and adaptable, with highly developed skills in managing their own ongoing learning and shaping the direction of their working lives.

A study of stakeholder views on what makes a good school (Macbeath,
1999; MacBeath *et al.*, 1997) identified ten sets or clusters of characteristics
reported as important by respondents. The study suggests five indicators
for each cluster, together with qualitative and quantitative evidence and
possible data collection instruments, which provide a helpful framework
for school self-evaluation drawing on the views of stakeholders. For example, the two clusters most frequently mentioned by pupils were school

climate or ethos and support for learning. The five indicators for school climate are shown below. Seeking pupil views on these indicators, by means of questionnaires or interviews, would provide useful evidence in evaluating this aspect of the school.

1) The school is a safe and happy place.
2) There are places for pupils to go and constructive things to do outside class time.
3) Pupils and staff behave in a relaxed and orderly way.
4) Pupils, staff and parents feel that their contribution to the school is valued.
5) The school is welcoming to visitors and newcomers (MacBeath *et al.*, 1997, p. 34).

# CONCLUSION

This chapter has explored various dimensions of curriculum evaluation, examining two broad approaches to evaluation, and external accountability requirements. It has been argued that schools need to set their own evaluation agendas, focusing on what is important rather than merely what is required or easily measured. Otherwise, they risk being 'colonised' not just by specific external demands, but more subtly by the currently dominant discourse of evaluation which emphasises immediate output measures and gives little attention to values, contexts, and the complexities and 'non-rational' issues involved in evaluation.

Studies of effective schools (for example, NCE, 1996) suggest that a key factor in their success is the ability to set and maintain their own agendas, despite external pressures. Rather than being overwhelmed by external imperatives, successful schools move in 'a self propelled virtuous circle' of development, in which they pursue their own priorities and year on year seek to improve their own 'previous best' performance; 'the energy released in these schools is generated primarily by what the school believes it can and must do' (NCE, 1996, p. 354).

In establishing the agenda for evaluation, it has been argued that three key issues need attention: the importance of values, building a community of enquiry where reflection and evaluation become a routine part of school life, and involving stakeholders, especially students. Student perspectives are necessary to give us a better understanding of the received curriculum and how it might be improved, and equally importantly to help pupils develop their own skills in self-evaluation and managing their own learning. Focusing evaluation on what is important is likely, of course, to raise some problematic and fundamental issues. One of these is how far are current curriculum structures, centred round traditional academic subjects and based on a transmission of knowledge approach to teaching and learning, appropriate for the needs of the information age, where all knowledge is provisional, and which requires thinking skills, creativity and the ability to locate, analyse and select from ever increasing quantities of new knowledge and information?

## NOTES

1 Ofsted – the Office for Standards in Education – inspects and reports on educational standards in state-maintained schools and 16–19 provision in colleges.
2. The DfEE has laid down four key stages in 5–16 education. Pupils are tested in the core subjects (English, maths and science) towards the end of Key Stages 1–3 at ages 7, 11 and 14 approximately, using nationally prescribed standard assessment tasks. Assessment at the end of Key Stage 4, at age 16, takes place by means of a public examination – the GCSE.

## REFERENCES

Adelman, C. and Alexander, R. (1982) *The Self Evaluating Institution*, London, Methuen.

Department of Education and Science (DES) (1989) *National Curriculum: From Policy to Practice*, London, DES.

Department for Education and Employment (DfEE) (1997a) *Excellence in Schools*, White Paper, London, HMSO.

Department for Education and Employment (DfEE) (1997b) *From Targets to Action: Guidance to Support Effective Target-setting in Schools*, London, DfEE.

Department for Education and Employment/Office for Standards in Education (DfEE/Ofsted) (1999) *Helping Schools to Carry Out Self-Evaluation*, London, DfEE.

Gardner, H. (1993) *Multiple Intelligences: The Theory in Practice*, New York, Basic Books.

Gipps, C. (1990) *Assessment: A Teachers' Guide to the Issues*, London, Hodder and Stoughton.

Gray, J. (1993) The quality of schooling: frameworks for judgement, in Preedy, M. (ed.) *Managing the Effective School*, London, Paul Chapman.

Handy, C. (1995) *Beyond Certainty*, London, Random House.

Jeffrey, B. and Woods, P. (1998) *Testing Teachers: The Effects of School Inspection on Primary Teachers*, London, Falmer Press.

Kelly, V. (1999) *The Curriculum: Theory and Practice*, 4th edn, London, Paul Chapman.

Keys, W. and Fernandez, C. (1993) *What Do Students Think about School?* Slough, NFER.

Kogan, M. (1986) *Education Accountability: An Analytical Overview*, London, Hutchinson.

MacBeath, J. (1999) *Schools Must Speak for Themselves*, London, Routledge.

MacBeath, J., Boyd, B., Rand, J. and Bell, S. (1997) *Schools Speak for Themselves: Towards a Framework for Self-evaluation*, London, NUT.

Maden, M. (2000) *Shifting Gear: Changing Patterns of Educational Governance in Europe*, Stoke-on-Trent, Trentham Books.

National Commission on Education (NCE) (1996) *Success Against the Odds*, London, Routledge.

Norris, N. (1998) Curriculum evaluation revisited, *Cambridge Journal of Education*, Vol. 28, no. 2, pp. 207–19.

Office for Standards in Education (Ofsted) (1999) *Handbook for Inspecting Secondary Schools*, London, HMSO.

Parlett, M. and Hamilton, D. (1975) Evaluation as illumination, in Tawney, D. (ed.) *Curriculum Evaluation Today*, London, Macmillan.

Peck, B. T. and Ramsay, H. A. (1998) *Managing Schools: The European Experience*, Commack, NY, Nova Science.

Rudduck, J., Chaplain, R. and Wallace, G. (1996) *School Improvement: What Can Pupils Tell Us?* London, David Fulton.

Skilbeck, M. (ed.) (1984) *Evaluating the Curriculum in the Eighties*, London, Hodder and Stoughton.

Stake, R. (1986) Evaluating educational programmes, in Hopkins, D. (ed.) *Inservice Training and Educational Development*, London, Croom Helm.

*Times Educational Supplement (TES)* (2000) Massaging the figures? 23 June, p. 4.

Williams, C. (1997) Managing motivation, *Managing Schools Today*, June–July, pp. 28–9.

## Section C: Roles and responsibilities in curriculum management

The focus of this section is to examine the management structures and roles that may exist within an educational institution for the smooth operation of the curriculum. David Middlewood, in Chapter 7, focuses on the responsibility of senior management to establish and communicate the curriculum vision within the role of leading the institution. Chapters 8, 9 and 10 each take a different view of curriculum management from the perspective of the 'middle manager' based upon different models of curriculum organisation which may coexist in many institutions. The role of the subject leader has been thoroughly researched by Hugh Busher and Christine Wise, who discuss their findings here. Les Bell examines the role of the curriculum managers who are responsible for co-ordinating the input of various teachers to ensure that students receive a coherent learning package. Daniela Sommefeldt explores issues surrounding the management of individual learning from the perspective of special educational needs.

# 7

# LEADERSHIP OF THE CURRICULUM: SETTING THE VISION

## *David Middlewood*

## INTRODUCTION

This chapter considers the curriculum management and leadership of the most senior professionals in a school or college. For the purposes of the chapter these are seen as principals/headteachers and vice-principals/ deputy headteachers although in some establishments they will include those with titles such as 'assistant principal'/'assistant headteacher'. Although such people have many specific responsibilities, the assumption is made that the 'core business' of a school or college being effective learning then the overriding responsibility of the senior staff *is* the curriculum. The chapter considers the importance of their roles and suggests there are four main aspects to the effective fulfilling of these roles:

- Having a view of the whole curriculum.
- Ensuring accountability for high standards in learning and teaching.
- Developing an appropriate culture and environment.
- Being a role model for both learners and teachers.

Each of these could merit a chapter of its own but it is hoped that they will serve as a framework for conceptualising the role of the people 'at the top' of the school or college in terms of their curriculum role, at a time when the business orientation of education may encourage them to focus on external relations, financial management etc.

## THE IMPORTANCE OF THE ROLE OF SENIOR CURRICULUM STAFF AT SCHOOL/COLLEGE LEVEL

In most countries, no matter how uniform, prescriptive or centrally dictated the formal curriculum is, it remains an inescapable fact that individual institutions differ. These differences may be because of factors such as:

- differences in location (for example, urban, rural, suburban)
- consequent differences in local community and nature of student intake (including different attitudes to learning, achievement and formal education itself)
- differences in physical resources, such as buildings
- differences in human resources, especially staff (including different attitudes to the school and job itself).

These factors need to be acknowledged in considering the role of those leading the curriculum at institutional level because, although a prescriptive curriculum (which may be perceived as being equivalent to a syllabus – Jansen and Middlewood (2001) – or timetable) appears to demand that teachers and students will do the same for example in each classroom in each school, in fact of course some schools do it very much better than others. Even if physical and financial resources were identical in each school, the competence and motivation of the individual teachers would still vary and this is one area where the influence of senior curriculum managers can be most evident.

The influence of teachers on curriculum effectiveness is considerable, even when a national curriculum appears to leave school and college teachers with a role limited to the implementation of national directives. In England and Wales, the introduction of a schools' national curriculum, described by Lawton (1996) as a 'top-down plan imposed on teachers by civil servants', meant that its implementation began with teachers 'treated as hirelings to be instructed rather than as professionals to be involved at all stages and at all levels' (Lawton, 1996, p. 41).

One of the risks in a tightly prescribed curriculum is that professionals may resort to covert adaptation of the intended curriculum, a process leading to what Becher (1989) describes as an 'implementation gap' between government plans and classroom practice. This could lead to wide discrepancies in practice, probably widening the gap between best and worst provision, exactly the opposite of a government's intentions. If, as writers such as Duffy (1990), and Fullan (1992) claim, teacher ownership of curriculum change is essential for it to succeed, then teacher participation in curriculum management at school level may be essential for any curriculum to be effective. 'There is a substantial body of evidence to indicate that the most effective schools – the schools that are high-achieving, highly regarded and adaptable – are those that have found ways of involving teachers in decisions and hence in the ownership of them' (Duffy, 1990, p. 95).

In all this, the role of the most senior staff in a school is critical and the remainder of this chapter suggests that, even in implementing a centrally prescribed curriculum, their actions will have the major influence on whether that curriculum is effective at institutional level. The success of these senior teams obviously depends partly upon their effectiveness *as a team*, but that aspect of management performance is dealt with elsewhere (for example, in Bush and Middlewood 1997). However, this chapter is concerned with the senior staff's roles in curriculum management and suggests that there are four main aspects of these roles to consider.

## 1) HAVING A VIEW OF THE WHOLE CURRICULUM

With the main task of classroom teachers being their effective work in learning and teaching, and with subject teachers focusing on their subject specialisms, it is essential 'for somebody to look at the curriculum as a whole' (Ribbins and Marland, 1994, pp. 57–8). The importance of this can be envisaged if the curriculum is seen as operating through four levels:

1) The *rhetorical* curriculum (what is stated in policies and statements of aims).
2) The *planned* curriculum (found in schemes of work, syllabuses).
3) The *delivered* curriculum (how it is taught in the classrooms or through other media).
4) The *received* curriculum (what is ultimately in the minds and some would say hearts of the students).

Since the fourth level, the curriculum as received by the individual learner, is one that he or she takes away (for example, takes home), and eventually leaves formal 'schooling' with as an individual person, it is critical that the curriculum experience is envisaged as a whole, not just as a number of separate unconnected strands. The individual learner's experience, post-formal education provision, will be as a whole, the whole being the identity of that individual.

Duffy (1988, pp. 116–17) describes this whole curriculum view as one that sees what the institution provides:

> in two distinct dimensions. It is a lateral view in the sense that it looks across the curriculum, to identify the totality of the learning that the curriculum offers a particular student at a particular stage. But it is also a longitudinal view in the sense that it adds continuity and progression in the student's learning experience, and searches out the gaps and repetition that the subject-centred approach inevitably produces.

The received curriculum of each individual student is the responsibility of the principal and other senior staff and in this sense it is their task to ensure that 'the whole *is* greater than the sum of the parts.' They may approach this through two ways, for example:

1) If the curriculum as envisaged by the institution's leaders is the sum of all learning experiences encountered there, and the sum of the parts of

this curriculum still leaves gaps in the overall received curriculum experience as envisaged by the leaders, they may wish to fill such gaps by the provision of voluntary or 'extracurricular' activities, outside of formal provision or statutory hours. Since this will be dependent upon the motivation and commitment of staff, it emphasises the earlier point that the involvement of teachers in school processes and decisions is crucial.

2) The two-dimensional view is also essential because it helps to ensure that senior staff view such processes as record-keeping and assessment as a whole, so that the grades for each student are not just a collection of separate pieces of information but give a total picture of each individual's progress and achievement.

While middle managers are increasingly involved in strategic thinking, their operational roles, especially as leaders of specialist teams, will understandably mean they are excited and challenged by new developments and opportunities in their own field. It is critical that those with a view of the whole curriculum experience offered at the school or college help to ensure that those specialist or sectional developments cohere with this whole.

In summary, leaders in schools and colleges will have a vision of the curriculum based probably upon some kind of postmodernist paradigm. Usher and Edwards (1994, p. 7) suggest this is 'a condition, a set of practices, a cultural discourse, an attitude and a mode of analysis' and not any kind of systematic theory or comprehensive philosophy. Primarily this is because they are preparing learners for a world which is characterised by complexity, multiplicity and ongoing change, where they will need to construct new knowledge and understandings throughout their lives. This therefore assumes that a curriculum of the future might well be very different than the one in operation at present. The *sharing* of this view with others is a key role for leaders so that the developments in specific areas of the offered curriculum led by others are in the context of this whole, which keeps the needs of learners at its centre.

## 2) ENSURING ACCOUNTABILITY FOR CONSISTENTLY HIGH STANDARDS IN LEARNING AND TEACHING

The principal/headteacher ultimately is accountable for the standards of education in the school or college, and a key aspect of the role therefore is ensuring that these standards are of consistently high quality. The word 'consistently' is critically important since the task is to ensure that each individual student's received curriculum experience is of similar quality. 'Consistency' therefore is less important over all periods of time (since 'ups' and 'downs' of human performance may be unavoidable), than across the different teachers and subjects experienced by the student. The key to how effectively this is carried out is likely to lie partly in the way in which monitoring, evaluation and feedback is managed in the school. This aspect of curriculum management is examined in detail in chapters in Section B of this book.

The effectiveness of procedures for accountability will depend to a large extent upon the *structures* which senior managers establish and develop. These structures, if effective, will facilitate:

- co-ordination
- monitoring
- flexibility to respond to future developments
- accountability (based on Mullins, 1989).

However, structures themselves are bureaucratic expressions of the above and the reality may be very different. Hargreaves (1997) argues that teachers' practices are grounded not only in expertise and altruism but in structures and routines in which considerable self-interest may be invested. Such structures may have evolved historically to meet certain political and moral purposes (for example, of 'control') and to achieve very different purposes now, changes in structures may be necessary.

Effective teacher development for collective school improvement may depend upon controlling vested interests. Developing a collaborative culture, for example, may require the modification of isolated, subject-specific departmental structures in the secondary school.

The school or college principal and senior colleagues may wish to consider what the specific purposes of structure should be, as far as the curriculum is concerned, before modifying existing ones. These purposes may include:

- ensuring that the needs of the 'whole' students are addressed
- supporting the implementation of whole school/college policies
- ensuring internal and external accountability for curriculum standards
- responding to externally imposed curriculum changes appropriately
- ensuring that the development of the whole curriculum is coherent.

There are a number of processes essential to effective management of the curriculum which can be hindered unless the structures facilitate the achievement of the above purposes. A few of these to be considered are:

1) A consideration of the emotional and behavioural needs of the learner as well as academic ones is crucial, since effective learning is affected by these. They need to be regularly identified and monitored. Clearly this is least effectively done if the academic and pastoral/welfare structures of a school are managed separately, instead of being integrated. Consideration of the progress of the learner as a 'whole person' needs therefore to be built into the way structures are developed. Martinez (2000) comments on how more schools and colleges are moving away from a pastoral-based tutoring system to an emphasis on monitoring, reviewing and supporting student progress.
2) A whole-institution policy on assessment is essential for consistency in maintaining learner progress. This will involve bringing together assessment data and the structures needed to facilitate this, not making the

process a cumbersome one through, for example, it having to be collected in different ways.
3) Certain structures which keep key areas of the curriculum separately
managed make it difficult to identify duplication in the curriculum.
More critically, they can hinder the adoption of a new curriculum initiative which a school or college is required to implement. In institutions
with rigid structures, such initiatives may well be 'bolted on' rather than
integrated, adding to administrative workload and to communications
problems.
4) The allocation of resources within a school or college can be a sensitive
issue. Since these resources are actually for the benefit of the learner,
there is a danger in allocating via certain separate structures, encouraging competition and territorialism between managers of separate curriculum sections. Whalley and Watkins (1991, p. 20) cite one of the worst
elements of a solely departmental structure as 'development of "subject-
barons" with an associated focus on competitive power struggles' such
as allocation disputes.

Senior managers need to address, in considering structures, the composi-
tion of staff teams and the quality and content of the meetings of these
teams. It is often through staff discovering *for themselves* the effectiveness
of these that the inadequacies of certain structures are exposed, making
changes easier to propose and manage. Paechter's (1993) work on introducing cross-curriculum work found that a balance was essential between a
stress on working through structures and working through interpersonal
links. She concluded that the management styles of the school leaders
tended to emphasise one approach or the other and suggested 'We need to
find ways to help senior managers to recognise the fluid and continuous
nature of the structures/personnel balance . . .' (Paechter, 1993 p. 178).
It is reasonable to conclude that in countries with a centralised curriculum, as in South Africa for example, the need for centralised accountability
for its delivery in the early days will reinforce the need for certain bureaucratic structures for routine functions at school level. The need for
flexibility in a fast-changing world, bringing unfamiliar activity, may suggest that the existence of a clearly articulated culture may be much more
significant.
In the context of today's ever-changing world, in which writers such as
Handy (1994) have suggested that the wealth of the Western world now lies
in intelligence, attention in the business world and to a lesser extent in
education has focused on the 'learning organisation'. As its name implies
such an organisation flourishes through the individuals in it who are committed to learning and, since this is the central purpose of colleges and
schools, it is difficult not to see it as applicable. Senge (1993) and other
influential writers, such as Covey (1989), argue that the key lies in the
integrity of the organisation's leaders and their commitment to 'generative
learning'. For senior curriculum managers, this implies that their respon-

sibility is to try to ensure that the whole curriculum experienced by the student is a process itself which is enriching and part of a 'journey' which will continue after formal education.

This learning culture has significant implications for the learning of teachers as well as of students, and therefore the role of senior managers in staff development may be seen in this context, that is not merely providing or enabling appropriate training for skills to deliver the curriculum, but to enable staff to learn, so as to enrich interdependency among staff. Rosenholtz (1989) identified the characteristics of 'learning enriched' schools as including:

> principals who supported teachers and removed barriers for them
> principals who fostered collaboration as opposed to competition.

In contrast, in 'learning impoverished' schools, norms of self-reliance flourished, leaving most teachers to develop in isolation (Rosenholtz, 1989). Thus, although one senior manager might have specific responsibility for staff development, the operation of this development needs to be seen in the context of the learning culture that the senior management team (SMT) as a whole is striving to develop, so that the changes that become necessary in any school or college ideally arrive through the 'inverted pyramid' approach usually known as 'bottom up' development rather than 'top down'.

In managing the conditions for such a culture to flourish, the senior managers are able to draw upon the research reflected in the 'effective school' literature. Summarised by Mortimore (1993), effectiveness can be promoted in schools in which:

- learning is highly valued
- expectations are pitched high and are sustained over time
- the environment is both safe and intellectually stimulating
- accurate but positive feedback is available
- there is a consistent approach to teacher–pupil relations
- rewards rather than punishments are stressed
- learners are involved and given responsibility.

The first in this list, the valuing of learning, is possibly the key to the culture to which senior staff aspire. This valuing of learning and the commitment to learning effectively that comes from it is vital, and if leadership is 'the art of mobilizing others who want to struggle for shared aspirations' (Kouzes and Posner, 1996, p. 9), then the role of the leaders may be to develop strategies which will encourage this.

## 3) DEVELOPING AN APPROPRIATE CULTURE

Headteachers/principals and senior colleagues will have a vision of the kind of place of 'learning for high achievement' that the school or college will become. The culture of such a place will be supportive and challenging to both learners and teachers through its establishing of norms and a consequent lesser reliance on rules and systems. Features of such a culture are likely to include:

- Conceptualising and communicating the institution's notion of an effective teacher/tutor.
- Conceptualising and communicating the institution's notion of an effective learner.
- Reducing bureaucracy – and stress – to enable motivation of learners and teachers to be kept at a high level.

## The institution's idea of an effective teacher and tutor

Theoretically, the notion of an effective learner should come first since schools and colleges exist for learning, but the reality for school and college leaders is that when they take up their posts the staff are there and have to be led and managed. For example, in a school where student behaviour is poor and inevitably affecting learning and achievement, it is almost certain that the new headteacher will need to focus upon the quality of teaching to address this. Other measures of course will need to be taken, but all the research upon behaviour in schools underlines that the quality of teaching is central to improvement in overall behaviour in the school (see Figure 7.1).

Is the teacher essentially

- a classroom manager?
- a manager of student learning?
- a researcher in the classroom, exploring change and development?
- a co-learner, exploring opportunities with the student?

If the ultimate ideal of the leaders is the last named in this list (and it may not be), there are almost certainly stages to be worked through for some teachers. The teachers on the staff of a school or college are inevitably at different stages of development, through age, experience, confidence or capability, and it is through the development of a culture such as we are discussing that most will be encouraged towards the ideal held. Moving staff from the notion of being an effective deliverer at classroom level of a 'given' curriculum (externally and organisationally influenced) to a manager of student learning is likely to involve understanding some of the following:

- Effective learning, including a range of theories of learning.
- The contribution of others to student learning, for example, parents.
- The importance of personally generated data, at classroom, sectional and whole-school/college level in developing personal practice.
- The relationship between the teacher and other learning support staff.
- Motivation, both of students and of teachers.
- The significance of ICT in learning and teaching.

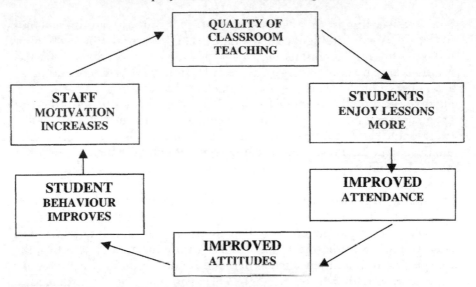

**Figure 7.1** The central importance of good teaching

To summarise then, the school/college leaders' vision of the institution may envisage a culture within which a 'typical' teacher would be one who is up to date with theories of learning, notions of multiple intelligence, recent understanding of how the human brain works, emotional intelligence, 'mind-mapping' and the range of learning styles which may exist in a group of learners. However, this teacher would not be a slavish adherent to any one set of theories for the very important reason that, since the last 20 years have massively increased our understanding of human learning, it is virtually certain that our knowledge and understanding will continue to increase and that theories will change. This aspect of curriculum strategic management is critical for leaders, since the external environment of the curriculum will be constantly changing and the teachers with the qualities described above may be best equipped to help their learners in this. The importance of this will be emphasised if we briefly consider the first three of the above.

- The teacher's essential need to have an understanding of and an intellectual curiosity in the meaning of 'learning' is essential if the teacher is not to be a mere transmitter of knowledge or skills. An awareness, for example, of different models of learning styles, whether it be consideration of predominantly visual, auditory or kinaesthetic learning or the activist, theorist or reflector modes of Honey and Mumford (1986), or others (for example, Butler, 1996) will enrich the teacher's thinking and encourage challenge to routine practice. Challenges to the outmoded notions of intelligence offered by the multiple intelligences of Gardner (1993) or Handy (1989) are essential to the teacher whom the leader wishes to facilitate learning in the twenty-first century. Similarly, an understanding of emotional intelligence (Goleman, 1996) is essential in a school or college where the emotions play a very significant role, simply because relationships lie at the heart of effective learning and teaching and these relationships are often expressed in emotional terms. In most areas of the curriculum, whether general such as thinking skills (Fisher, 1995) or specialist (cognitive acceleration in science – Adey and Shayer, 1994), traditional learning models are challenged and, while it is totally unrealistic to expect any teacher to be involved with all of them, an interest in or fascination by any of them is an essential element in the context envisaged.

• In arguing for parents to be more closely involved in learning partnerships with schools, Middlewood (1999a) points out that, while most schools talk of partnerships with parents, '(as) new technologies will involve more learning from home and learning together in families, the recognition of the importance of parental involvement may need to take on a sharper reality in practice' (p. 111). The point can be extended to those in further education since, although parents specifically may not be as influential, the relationship between the formal educators (in schools and colleges) and 'co-educators' (ibid., p. 112) outside needs to be reconceptualised. The teacher in the context of the school or college envisaged will have a clear view of the role of others such as parents in the learning process. The 1990s emphasis, for example, on the role of parents as consumers, is already giving way to a view of them as co-educators and even co-learners (Wolfendale, 1996). Real lifelong learning may mean a radical rethink as to who are the main educators and who is intervening in whose programme (Bull, 1989; Macbeth and Ravn, 1994). Middlewood (1999a, p. 127) suggests that those schools that have fostered an effective co-learning partnership with parents will be 'powerfully placed to manage the next stage', that is, joint learning ventures with a whole range of partners, such as further education colleges at present have.

• Teachers as researchers have the benefit of not only bringing an extra dimension to reflection on their own practice, but also to accumulate data which is regarded as a key element in organisational improvement. (Hopkins, Ainscow and West, 1994). Hargreaves (1998, p. 54) suggests there are powerful arguments for teachers as researchers: 'More research that is relevant and teachers to do more of that research. This involvement ensures its relevance and helps teachers make better decisions about what is effective.

   Teachers become "co-producers" of research, when teachers become creators of research knowledge, the research act in itself is a fundamental form of the professional development of teachers.'

The encouragement of the teacher as researcher will be a powerful tool for school or college improvement though different levels of change are likely to occur. Coleman (1999, p. 157) suggests these may be small-scale change (or 'instrumental'), potential long-term change, or whole-school or college change (with a 'conceptual' outcome).

Since the headteacher/principal seeks the development of the appropriate culture, the use of on-site and in-classroom research by teachers can have important, sometimes subtle, influences upon school or college culture. Studies by Middlewood (1999b) showed these changes and indicated that for school leaders their jobs had been made easier (ibid., p. 117).

## 4) BEING A ROLE MODEL FOR LEARNERS AND TEACHERS

If a key focus for senior staff is on the task of providing the right conditions in the school or college for learning and teaching to flourish, the role of the leaders as embodying those conditions through the way they *act* is critical. If, as Weindling (1999, p. 6) suggests, 'You have to believe passionately that all (children) can learn more than they currently do', then school or college leaders surely need to demonstrate that they are also capable of learning more. The use of ICT provides an example of this. It is by no means essential and is unlikely that the leader will be technically the most proficient user of ICT in the institution but 'if they demonstrate in their work that ICT is a genuinely useful tool, then their staff are more likely to accept the challenge of change and development which access to ICT brings' (Leask, Terrell and Falconer, 1999, p. 2).

Brighouse and Woods (1999) advocate the construction and displaying or publicising of a personal learning plan for the headteacher of a school, to demonstrate to all that the person in that role is committed in his or her life to continuous learning. Such a plan embraces those aspects of learning not directly relevant to the professional work of the school or college, but which are simply life-enhancing for the leader as an individual learner. For example, the commitment to learning a foreign language sufficient for use on holiday abroad simply demonstrates the leader's appetite for learning that is part of the person, not just the role. This demonstration of the values of the leaders being focused upon learning may be significant in helping to address any gap that may be seen to occur between leaders and other staff. Elliott and Crossley's (1997) research in further education found such a gap between the senior managers' focus upon quantitative performance indicators required of them from external agencies and lecturers' concern for student welfare. Staff believed that formal quality assurance systems were marginalising the emphasis on the quality of what actually occurs during student learning. This conflict between learner-centred approaches and a client-led approach (ibid., p. 8) needs to be mitigated by a visible emphasis by senior staff on 'learning as central'.

Being a role model as a teacher does not necessarily mean that headteachers/principals actually need to teach. This may be a vexed issue for some, although for many headteachers of smaller primary schools, teaching will be a normal part of the role, and at deputy head/vice-principal level there will be a range of practice. In secondary schools and colleges, where the leader has taken on more of the role of chief executive, a choice will often exist in larger schools and colleges. However, some headteachers hold the view that their leadership contribution to curriculum development is only meaningful if founded on current direct curriculum experience:

> I have often relished the space a non-teaching role would afford. However, the advantages of first-hand knowledge of the demands of class teaching at our school and the learning experiences of the pupils far outweigh the minimal gains that might accrue from a less superficial reading of the multitude of DES guidelines. This is not to mention the 'street-cred' rating a teaching head gets.
>
>                 (Cutler, quoted in Mortimore and Mortimore, 1991, p. 148)

The school or college leader can also emphasise the importance of personally generated data by being involved in 'practitioner research', as described earlier, particularly if this focuses upon aspects of staff or student learning, rather than quantitative data required for external agents, such as inspectors.

Finally, Bowring-Carr and West-Burnham (1997) sum up much of the element of the role model described above in their persuasive argument for the leader as intellectual:

> When leaders are intellectuals, they are then able to articulate the intellectual climate of the school (college), typify its virtues and be the model reflective practitioner. The leader has an awareness of social trends, is up to date in the relevant fields of research and cares passionately about learning. The leader as intellectual reifies the vision . . . as an interpretive community creating and extending its meanings and always challenging itself – it is essential to develop a critical and creative perspective for all and one exemplified most visibly in the leader.
>
>                                                     (ibid., p. 126).


## CONCLUSION

The headteachers/principals of schools and colleges and their senior colleagues need to see and remind themselves constantly that their organisational leadership rests primarily in leadership of the curriculum or of learning, since this is the core purpose of the organisation. Theirs is the strategic role which focuses on the achievement of the vision for the school or college as a place of learning. They will be responsible for putting in place strategies for raising achievement, such as:

- target-setting
- increasing learning time
- providing additional support
- changes in group organisation
- use of ICT
- greater involvement of parents and other external agents (adapted from Weindling, 1999).

However, it can be argued that, unless such strategies are accompanied by a relentless concern with learning and teaching, the kind of achievement that will be raised will remain one which is measurable only by quantitative, externally imposed results. Such achievement may satisfy short-term demands for 'raising standards', but will not fulfil the requirements of a society committed to genuine lifelong learning.

In research into the introduction of ICT into learning and teaching situations, Leask and Terrell (1997) suggested that there was a need to, among other things:

- establish experiments and exemplars
- support risk-taking
- create and manage new relationships
- raise fundamental questions.

These seem to be at the heart of approaches that leaders need to take, and the 'fundamental questions' above all relate to learning and teaching. As Tillotson (2000, p. 27) suggests, among the most difficult tasks 'is to develop a language of learning for students and teachers that permeates the school (college), gives meaning to lessons, builds self-esteem in students, provides job satisfaction to teachers, and enables everyone in the school (college) to celebrate success'. That 'success' will be the achievement in learning in one form or another.

## REFERENCES

Adey, P. and Shayer, M. (1994) *Really Raising Standards: Cognitive Intervention and Academic Achievement*, London, Routledge.

Becher, T. (1989) The national curriculum and the implementation gap, in Preedy, M. (ed.) *Approaches to Curriculum Management*, Milton Keynes, Open University Press.

Bowring-Carr, C. and West-Burnham, J. (1997) *Effective Learning in Schools*, London, Pitman.

Brighouse, T. and Woods, D. (1999) *How to Improve your School*, London, Routledge.

Bull, T. (1989) Home-school links: family oriented or business oriented, *Educational Review*, Vol. 41, no. 2, pp. 113–19.

Bush, T. and Middlewood, D. (1997) *Managing People in Education*, London, Paul Chapman.

Butler, K. (1996) *The Strategy Chart for Learning Styles, Levels of Thinking and Performance – Viewpoints*, Columbia, Learner's Dimension.

Coleman, M. (1999) Conclusions, in Middlewood, D., Coleman, M. and Lumby, J. *Practitioner Research in Education*, London, Paul Chapman.

Covey, S. (1989) *The Seven Habits of Highly Effective People*, London, Simon and Schuster.

Duffy, M. (1988) The school curriculum, in Frith, D. (ed.) *School Management in Action*, Harlow, Longman.

Duffy, M. (1990) A view from a secondary school, in Brighouse, T. and Moon, B. (eds.) *Managing the National Curriculum: Some Critical Perspectives*, Harlow, Longman.

Elliott, G. and Crossley, M. (1997) Contested values in further education, *Educational Management and Administration*, Vol. 25, no. 1, pp. 79–92.

Fisher, R. (1995) *Teaching Children to Think*, Cheltenham, Stanley Thornes.

Fullan, M. (1992) *The New Meaning of Educational Change*, Toronto, Cassell.

Gardner, H. (1993) *The Unschooled Mind*, London, Fontana.

Goleman, M. (1996) *Emotional Intelligence*, London, Bloomsbury.

Handy, C. (1989) *The Age of Unreason*, London, Business Books.

Handy, C. (1994) *The Empty Raincoat*, London, Hutchinson.

Hargreaves, A. (1997) Restructuring: postmodernity and the prospects for educational change, in Halsey, A., Lauder, H., Brown, P. and Wells, A. (eds.) *Education: Culture Economy, Society*, Oxford, Oxford University Press.

Hargreaves, D. (1998) Improving research to enhance teaching, *Professional Development Today*, Vol. 1. no. 2. pp. 47–55.

Honey, P. and Mumford, A. (1986) *The Manual of Learning Styles*, Maidenhead, Honey Publications.

Hopkins, D., Ainscow, M. and West, M. (1994) *School Improvement in an Era of Changes*, London, Cassell.

Jansen, J. and Middlewood, D. (2001) From policy to action: issues of curriculum management at school level, in Coleman, M., Graham-Jolley, M. and Middlewood, D. (eds.) *Managing the Curriculum in South African Schools*, Johannesburg, Amabhuku.

Kouzes, J. and Posner, B. (1996) *The Leadership Challenge*, San Francisco, Jossey-Bass.

Lawton, D. (1996) *Beneath the National Curriculum*, London, Hodder and Stoughton.

Leask, M. and Terrell, I. (1997) *Development Planning and School Improvement for Middle Managers*, London, Kogan Page.

Leask, M., Terrell, I. and Falconer, A. (1999) The Internet and school management, *Topic*, no. 22, Autumn, pp. 1–6.

Macbeth, A. and Ravn, B. (1994) Expectations about parents in education, in Macbeth, A. and Ravn, B. (eds.), *Expectations about Parents in Education: European Perspectives*, Glasgow: University of Glasgow.

Martinez, P. (2000) *Raising Achievement: A Guide to Successful Strategies*, London, FEDA.

Middlewood, D. (1999a) Managing relationships between schools and parents, in Lumby, J. and Foskett, N. (eds.) *Managing External Relations in Schools and Colleges*, London, Paul Chapman.

Middlewood, D. (1999b) Influencing school culture, in Middlewood, D., Coleman, M. and Lumby, J. *Practitioner Research in Education*, London, Paul Chapman.

Mortimore, P. (1993) School effectiveness and the management of effective learning and teaching, *School Effectiveness and School Improvement*, Vol. 4, no. 4, pp. 290–310.

Mortimore, P. and Mortimore, J. (1991) *The Secondary Head: Roles, Responsibilities and Reflections*, London, Paul Chapman.

Mullins, L. (1989) *Management and Organisational Behaviour*, 2nd edn, London, Pitman.

Paechter, C. (1993) Managing cross-curricular work: focusing on structures or persons?, in Busher, H. and Smith, M. (eds.) *Managing Educational Institutions: Reviewing Development and Learning*, Sheffield, BEMAS.

Ribbins, P. and Marland, M. (1994) *Headship Matters*, Harlow, Longman.

Rosenholtz, S. (1989) *Schools, Social Organisations and the Building of a Technical Culture*, New York, Longman.

Senge, P. (1993) *The Fifth Discipline*, London, Century Business.

Tillotson, V. (2000) The impact of research on a head's leadership: meeting the challenge, *Management in Education*, Vol. 13, no. 5, pp. 22–7.

Usher, R. and Edwards, R. (1994) *Post-modernism and Education*, London, Routledge.

Weindling, D. (1999) Kissing the frog: moving from school effectiveness to school improvement, *Topic*, no. 21, Spring, pp. 1–6.

Whalley, C. and Watkins, C. (1991) Managing the whole curriculum in a secondary school – a structure, *Management in Education*, Vol. 5, no. 3, pp. 11–19.

Wolfendale, S. (1996) The contribution of parents to children's achievements in school, in Bastiani, J. and Wolfendale, S. (eds.) *Home-School Work in Britain*, London, David Fulton.

# 8

# THE SUBJECT LEADER

## *Christine Wise and Hugh Busher*

## INTRODUCTION

Subject leaders hold multifaceted roles in schools that force them to play a variety of different parts. In hierarchical terms the subject leader is a middle manager. He or she is not part of the senior management team, responsible for the overall strategic development of a school, but someone responsible for the operational work of others, namely classroom teachers and the students with whom they work. Heads of year in secondary schools and Key Stage co-ordinators in primary schools might also be classed as middle managers as they, too, are operationally responsible for overseeing and developing the work of their colleagues and the students who work with them.

In schools these organisational hierarchical distinctions are not neatly delineated. As Glover *et al.* (1998) have argued recently, the distinction between middle and senior management remains blurred and leadership functions are still not adequately delineated, or defined. Expectations, parameters and authority of role must be clearly spelled out (Fielding, 1996) because 'an ill-defined role can be of great concern to many staff' (Howard, 1988, p. 87).

Many staff in secondary schools are involved in a complex switching of roles and lines of accountability between different aspects of their work. For example, most teachers will be responsible to both subject leaders and pastoral heads of year in secondary schools for different aspects of their work. Subject leaders will also be classroom teachers in their own or other subject areas, accountable to pastoral year heads, while pastoral year heads will work in subject areas and be accountable to the subject leaders of those areas. Indeed, senior staff will also work in classrooms and be accountable for this aspect of their work to middle managers.

Within this complex matrix of leadership and accountability, subject leaders are increasingly acknowledged to be key figures (Hopkins, Ainscow and West, 1994). In view of the overwhelming evidence of the influence of subject-area performance upon school performance (for example, Sammons, Thomas and Mortimore, 1997) clarity concerning leadership at middle management level would seem imperative.

Although the material on which this chapter is based is mainly drawn from research into schools and colleges, it has applicability to all sectors or phases of education, including further and higher education. Furthermore, because the chapter uses an international literature to create its conceptual framework, it is asserted that the constructs of the subject leader's role are applicable more widely than just in England and Wales to at least those countries – North America, UK, Australasia, Hong Kong for example – with similar cultures in their education systems.

## THE SUBJECT LEADER'S ROLE

The Teacher Training Agency (TTA, 1996, p. 4) suggested that: 'Evidence from OFSTED inspections and other sources has shown that pupil achievement is higher when the role of the subject leader is clearly identified and effectively implemented.' Several writers (Adams, 1987; Armstrong, Evans, and Page, 1993b) argue that it is important for role incumbents to fully understand their role. To do this subject leaders 'need to know role expectations and the theoretical ideal for performance so that degree of effectiveness can be monitored and strategies for growth in effectiveness planned' (Midwood and Hillier, 1987, p. 6).

Role is more than a list of tasks and responsibilities attached to a particular post within an organisational structure. It is not synonymous with a job description because tasks and responsibilities are only a part of a role. It has more to do with the relationships with relevant others and the associated behaviours expected of a post holder (Adey, 1988; Ribbins, 1988; Webb and Lyons, 1982).

Unfortunately many of the models of the subject-leader role focus on its structural aspects. Further, they offer little discrimination between that role in primary and secondary schools, although Bell and Ritchie (1999) suggest there is little substantive difference. The Teacher Training Agency (TTA, 1998, p. 6), in the National Standards for subject leaders, outlines a model for the role in primary and secondary schools:

- Strategic direction and development of the subject.
- Teaching and learning.
- Leading and managing staff.
- Efficient and effective deployment of staff and resources.

This complements a model developed for secondary school heads of department by Morris and Dennison (1982, p. 40) which also focuses on structural organisational aspects:

- A professional role as a teacher in the classroom.
- An organisational role as part of the responsibility for management of the department.
- A corporate role within whole school as a 'middle manager' in the administrative structure of the institution.
- A personal role.

However, as they point out, 'the boundaries between each of these roles is diffuse [and in any discrete situation] . . . a head of department could be playing a single role, [or] . . . elements of all four roles' (ibid.).

In an attempt to focus on the relationships involved in being a subject leader, Busher and Harris with Wise (2000) proposed a process model, which builds on that of Glover *et al.* (1998). Figure 8.1 shows the five aspects of this model.

The last model implies that subject leaders need to understand the implicit as well as the explicit relationships linked to their role (Armstrong, Evans and Page, 1993a), and 'how their roles fit into the overall organisation of an institution' (p. 1). As such, role must be thought of as dynamic because it is dependent on relationships for its definition. This is because a role is in 'a constant process of negotiation, which involves not only the expectations of others, but how the individual perceives these expectations [and] . . . which he perceives as legitimate [along with] . . . the manner in which he responds to them' (Howard, 1988, p. 87).

The definition of any individual's role in any situation is a combination of the role expectations of the role incumbent and the members of her or his role-set about the focal aspect of the role (Handy, 1993). For subject leaders, their role-set might include not only the teachers within their own subject area but also their fellow subject leaders, pastoral leaders, headteachers, governors, parents and the students. The extent to which each of these impinges on each individual subject leader's behaviour will depend on many factors. Bullock (1988, p. 63) notes that there is frequently a 'conflict of loyalty to headteacher and to departmental members'.

How a role is performed depends on an individual's personality, attributes and skills, as well as the tensions and pressures in the situation. Ribbins (1988, p. 61) believes that 'social actors do not merely "take" roles as they are presented to them, but actively "make" them what they are'. In

| Bridging or brokering | Involves transactional leadership with senior staff, colleagues and students |
| --- | --- |
| Creating social cohesion | Involves transformational leadership to create a shared vision and collegial culture within a subject area |
| Mentoring | Improving staff and student performance |
| Creating professional networks | Liaison with public examination and subject knowledge associations. Knowledge of changing government policy; Liaison with local authority support and parents |
| Using power | Expert; referent; reward; coercion; legitimate |

**Figure 8.1**  The pentagonal role of a subject leader
*Source:* Busher and Harris with Wise, 2000, p. 15.

reality role incumbents can and do influence their role sets and it is necessary to accept that 'the manager can be the source of or otherwise effect the expectations sent by the role set' (Fondas and Stewart, 1994, p. 88). However, Best and Ribbins (1983, p. 54) question the extent to which role incumbents can change expectations within the school situation because the role-set for a subject leader is very diverse and a number of its members are not necessarily education professionals, although they are still very powerful.

The demands and competing expectations on subject leaders that arise from their diverse role sets lead to role ambiguity and uncertainty about the limits of authority vested in their job. Coupled often with a lack of a clear job description about the extent of individual responsibilities it makes the role of subject leader difficult and stressful to fulfil (Health and Safety Commission, 1990, p. 9). However, according to Blandford (1997, p. 3) the recognition and reconciliation of multiple roles is 'central to effective middle management'.

## CULTURE

In many secondary schools departmental or subject cultures often differ from those of the whole school (Busher, 1992; Huberman, 1990). If the subject leader is actively to change the culture to better support improvements in teaching and learning, there needs to be a move towards the development of a shared culture both between members of the subject-area team, and between a subject-area team and the whole school. Schein (1992, p. 5) suggested that 'the only thing of real importance that leaders do is to create and manage culture', while Siskin (1994) argued that leaders have a central role to play in shaping departmental culture. Departmental culture is constructed from 'the enacted views, values and beliefs of teachers and support staff about what it means to teach students in particular subject areas within particular institutional contexts' (Busher and Harris, 1999, p. 311).

This is important because so much of a teacher's professional growth and development is achieved through formal and informal processes of sharing practice with colleagues. The formal aspects of this are likely to be managed by the subject leader, particularly under the new scheme of performance appraisal being put in place by central government in England and Wales (DfEE, 1998).

In single-subject areas the subject epistemology and its underpinning values is a unifying focus of identity. However, how teachers construct their understandings of what it means to be a teacher of a particular subject goes beyond being part of a particular curriculum structure or using certain books as texts. It also includes accepting the values, processes of study and underlying beliefs about how knowledge is constructed that shape a particular subject. This gives teachers of each subject a common base on which to develop a departmental culture (Siskin, 1994). Such shared understanding may not be as readily constructed in departments which consist of more than one subject or in primary schools where teachers teach more than one subject. In such institutions it may be that the primary focus of teacher professional identity is the age of the pupils whom they teach (Nias, 1999).

## IDEOLOGY AND THE EQUITABLE ALLOCATION OF RESOURCES

At the core of these shared understandings are a set of often unquestioned beliefs or ideologies about how the curriculum should be delivered or taught, and how students should be organised into teaching and learning groups. Each teacher has an educational ideology formed of their values, beliefs and assumptions about children, learning, teaching, knowledge and the curriculum (Morrison and Ridley, 1989, p. 41). Consciously or not these ideologies shape teacher behaviour in the classroom. Decisions about 'whether streaming, setting or mixed ability teaching best serve the interests of the pupils and make work feasible for the teachers' (Busher and Hodgkinson, 1997, p. 108) make visible the decision-maker's educational and social values.

Within the secondary school the various subject epistemologies are usually shared by teachers of the subject, they are part of the induction into the subject throughout its study, usually while a person is attending an institution of higher education, and become a part of the subject culture. As Siskin (1994 p.180) states:

teachers bring the distinct perspectives, procedures, values and discourses of their fields into the school . . . As subject specialists, they share a sense of who they are, what they do and what they need to do . . . Whether they are looking at pedagogical practice, at how courses should be arranged or students assigned to them, or what makes a useful professional development experience, these teachers bring the perspectives of their particular knowledge realms to bear on what they see.

If the ideology held by teachers is different to that which underpins the curriculum for the subject area or Key Stage area, or the values of the school or subject leader, then there is likely to be conflict or a lack of implementation of the curriculum. In these circumstances it is for the subject leader to begin to establish a common culture for the subject area by engaging his or her colleagues in a debate about the core ideologies of the subject area, making visible what may be taken for granted or not thought out. Morrison and Ridley (1989, p. 41) suggest that as a minimum such a curriculum debate should include the development of the following seven theories:

*[handwritten margin note: Ideologies you should know]*

- A theory of knowledge, its content and structure – what is considered worthwhile or important knowledge, how it is organised and who shall have access to it.
- A theory of learning and the learner's role – an active or a passive style, doing or listening, co-operative or competitive learning, producing or reproducing knowledge, problem-solving or receiving facts.
- A theory of teaching and the teacher's role – formal or informal, authoritarian or democratic, interests in outcomes or processes, narrow or wide.
- A theory of resources appropriate for learning – firsthand or secondhand.
- A theory of organisation of learning situations – criteria for grouping pupils.
- A theory of assessment that learning has taken place – diagnostic or attainment testing, written or observational assessment, defining what is to be assessed.
- A theory of aims, objectives and outcomes – a view of what is desirable for society, the child and knowledge.

An outcome of developing a coherent set of views about the values inherent in these theories is to allow staff in a subject area, under the guidance of their subject leader, to construct development plans to meet the needs of their pupils. To be most effective, subject-area development plans need to be internally consistent (have a common values framework) and to interlock with agreed school development plans. They are likely to focus on a range of aspects of a subject area's work:

- the curriculum (syllabus, teaching, learning, assessment, progression)
- human relations processes and values
- staff development
- decision-making and resource allocation
- links with the external contexts (both within a school and outside it).

They also need to include targets for what the subject area staff want to achieve within a given time frame to meet the identified needs of the students. The DfEE (1996) argues that target-setting is a powerful means of identifying what needs to be implemented to bring about change, and provides a framework against which progress can be monitored. Busher and Harris with Wise (2000, p. 148) suggest that effective planning is based on five interlocking processes:

- working with staff
- establishing baselines: measuring current performance
- having a clear vision of where to go
- creating sensible maps, timetables and ladders to achieve the preferred goals
- creating a means of monitoring progress on the road to achieving the goals (target-setting).

The successful construction of a subject area plan leads subject leaders into a series of difficult value choices. As Simkins (1997) points out, resource allocation involves subject leaders and their colleagues weighing and prioritising the competing claims of different groups of students for support. Busher and Harris with Wise (2000, p. 153) argue that these value conflicts can be summarised as:

- balancing efficiency and effectiveness
- balancing professional and managerial approaches to resource allocation
- balancing performance maintenance and performance development
- ensuring equitable resource allocation between student groups
- balancing resource creation and generation against student benefits and staff time.

# PROGRESSION

The subject curriculum is everything that is experienced, organised and delivered within the subject area. This means that not only what is taught but how it is taught and how it is assessed are crucial elements of the curriculum. Further, what is taught is not merely the subject content and skills but also the styles of teaching and learning and the social processes of how people as teachers and students interact with each other through the process of teaching and learning to facilitate that process. It is important, then, that subject leaders provide written guidance on not only *what* is intended to be achieved by each group of pupils but also *how* it is to be achieved (Mathematical Association, 1988, p. 19). This means that the curriculum might have particular pieces of work where particular resources are to be used: a computer package utilised, group work incorporated or team-teaching encompassed. It implies that it is not sufficient for subject leaders and their colleagues only to focus on delivering the National Curriculum content attainment targets.

None the less it is the description of subjects as set out in the National Curriculum that has become the main vehicle through which teachers in England and Wales have helped students to understand the subjects taught in schools. The National Curriculum was originally established in England and Wales in 1988, under the Education Reform Act, and heavily modified by the Dearing Review (Dearing, 1994). It is for children of compulsory school age, from 5 to 16 years in England and Wales. The National Curriculum establishes detailed programmes of study in three core subject areas (English, Mathematics and Science) and several foundation areas, such as Modern Foreign Languages, History and Geography. It also requires that Religious Education is taught and, since 2000, that Citizenship is taught, too.

The curriculum for each subject has a linear structure through which students have to progress during their years of compulsory schooling.

These structures are divided into Key Stages that are related to students' ages. Students' performances and progress through these stages are tested nationally, in addition to whatever tests teachers might administer. The tests are held at the end of Key Stage 2, when children are approximately 11 years old, and Key Stage 3, when children are approximately 14 years old. As almost all students who are 16 years old have to take the GCSE examinations, which act as national school-leaving examinations, there is no Key Stage 4 test. Each subject area is divided into a series of strands or attainment targets, and students are expected to perform at different levels on each of these attainment targets depending on their age.

It is for subject leaders and their colleagues to devise a coherent set of subject area and lesson plans to allow students to make sufficient progress in the subject to meet the benchmark levels of performance set by the DfEE for whatever age the students are at. To be effective, such planning needs to break down the subject syllabus into fragments that are achievable within a particular timeframe – the last are sometimes called targets – and identify what particular steps need to be taken, resources used and people to act in certain ways to achieve these. Even within lessons, teachers, under the guidance of subject leaders, need to carry out this process in order to ensure sufficient variety and continuity to sustain the interest and enthusiasm of the students.

Such planning and target-setting is not, however, straightforward. Fletcher-Campbell, Tabberer and Keys (1996) point out how difficult it is for small primary schools to match the curriculum structure required by the National Curriculum – which focuses on individual subject teaching, rather than integrated subject teaching – because of the few staff such schools have and the relatively few resources they possess. Becher (1989, p. 60–1) suggests that:

> Those responsible for shaping the curriculum need to remember that their best laid plans are vulnerable to the non-conformity of individual practice . . . teachers who strongly dissent from existing national or school or departmental policy will retain the professional's scope to do things in their own way. The classroom is a private place not easily invaded by opposing forces. As must always be the case in human affairs, even strongly coercive legislation has its limits.

It is important, then, that subject leaders carefully monitor not only the teaching but the learning experienced by pupils while in their areas. It is for the subject leader to ensure that the intended curriculum is actually delivered rather than remaining a collection of ideals on paper. This means that not only must teacher delivery be monitored, but so must how students receive and perceive the curriculum. The latter helps teachers to tailor the curriculum to meet individual student needs (Cooper and McIntyre, 1996; Riding and Raynor, 1998).

Monitoring the curriculum also involves more than using a variety of appropriate means for testing and measuring student performance and understanding, formatively and summatively. It also means exploring how students are perceiving and responding to the forms of assessment they are receiving and considering how they can be helped to view them in the most positive light possible. This can be achieved through what Stoll and Fink (1996, p. 124) call 'assessment literacy' by teachers:

- Are these the best assessment practices to assess this learning outcome?
- How well does this assessment sample students' achievement?
- Do the students understand the achievement targets and assessment methods?
- Does this assessment assess outcomes that matter?
- Are assessment strategies fair for all students?
- How are the resulting data to be presented?
- Who will have access to the data?
- How will they be reported and to whom?

## HELPING COLLEAGUES TO IMPROVE LEARNING

One of the main means available to subject leaders to improve the quality of learning in their subject areas is to help their colleagues improve the quality of teaching which they perform and the quality of learning which their students undertake. To do this the Teacher Training Agency (TTA), through the National Standards for Subject Leaders (TTA, 1998), explains that subject leaders need to understand:

- The relationship of the subject to the curriculum as a whole.
- Statutory curriculum requirements for the subject and the requirements for assessment, recording and reporting of students' attainment and progress.
- The characteristics of high quality teaching in the subject and the main strategies for improving and sustaining high standards of teaching, learning and achievement for all students.
- How evidence from relevant research and inspection evidence and local, national and international standards of achievement in the subject can be used to inform expectations, targets and teaching approaches.
- How to use comparative data, together with information about students' prior attainment, to establish benchmarks and set targets for improvement.
- How to develop students' literacy, numeracy and information technology skills through the subject.
- How teaching the subject can promote students' spiritual, moral, social, cultural, mental and physical development.

To be effective in this aspect of their role, however, subject leaders need to be, themselves, effective teachers, and to act as leading professionals (Adey, 1988; Harris, 1998; Harris, Jamieson and Russ, 1995). As part of this process subject leaders need to attempt to operate by consent, using processes of transformational leadership as well as those of transactional leadership, by gaining commitment to change and improvement rather than compelling it through coercion (Bennett, 1995). It implies having a respect for their colleagues' legitimately held and principled views where these differ from their own, in order to establish a culture of trust which seems to be closely associated with effective teamwork (e.g. Blase and Blase, 1994; Busher and Saran, 1995; Stoll and Fink, 1996). It is necessary for subject leaders to develop these qualities in order to better help their colleagues reflect critically on their performance (Wise, 1999) so that they can carry out their work more effectively (Leask and Terrell, 1997). It implies that processes of professional review and appraisal as well as those of professional development to meet identified teachers' needs are essential to the effective leadership and management of a subject area.

## CODA

In leading and managing effectively their subject areas, subject leaders need to develop an acute awareness of the multiplicity of aspects involved in their role and to learn to balance and juggle these aspects with each other. The subject leader who cannot develop successful relationships with his or her senior management team is unlikely to be able to represent the subject area effectively to them, or gain the support which their subject area colleagues will need from time to time. On the other hand, subject leaders who neglect to sustain the collegial culture of their subject area may soon find that students are not working in an environment as conducive to learning as it could be. Yet again, subject leaders who do not remain alert to developments in their subject areas' knowledge and pedagogy cannot give the leadership that can help staff colleagues and students to grow and develop by challenging their existing views and understandings of working in particular subject areas.

Siskin (1994) described subject areas as a realms of knowledge, but it is at least as appropriate to describe them as arenas of conflict. In these cauldrons subject leaders have to build coherence and co-operation despite the tensions which their complex role sets impose on them.

## REFERENCES

Adams, N. (1987) *Secondary School Management Today*, London, Hutchinson Educational.

Adey, K. R. (1988) Methods and criteria for the selection of teaching staff for appointment to posts in secondary schools, with special reference to head of department appointments: a study of practice in one local education authority, *Collected Original Resources in Education*, Vol. 12, no. 3, seventh of 11 microfiches.

Armstrong, L., Evans, B. and Page, C. (1993a) *Managing to Survive: Vol. 1 Organisation*, Lancaster, Framework Press.

Armstrong, L., Evans, B. and Page, C. (1993b) *Managing to Survive: Vol. 2 Relationships*, Lancaster, Framework Press.

Becher, T. (1989) The national curriculum and the implementation gap, in Preedy, M. (ed.) *Approaches to Curriculum Management*, Milton Keynes, Open University Press.

Bell, D. and Ritchie, R. (1999) *Towards Effective Subject Leadership in the Primary School*, Buckingham, Open University Press.

Bennett, N. (1995) *Managing Professional Teachers: Middle Management in Primary and Secondary Schools*, London, Paul Chapman.

Best, R. and Ribbins, P. (1983) Politics and the head: two cases and a model, *C.O.R.E.*, Vol. 7, no. 1, D11–E13 on first of 11 microfiches.

Blandford, S. (1997) *Middle Management in Schools*, London, Pitman.

Blase, J. and Blase, J. (1994) *Empowering Teachers: What Successful Principals Do*, Thousand Oaks, CA, Corwin.

Bullock, A. (1988) *Meeting Teachers' Management Needs*, Ely, Peter Francis.

Busher, H. (1992) The politics of working in secondary schools: some teachers' perspectives on their schools as organisations, unpublished PhD, School of Education, University of Leeds.

Busher, H. and Harris, A. (1999) Leadership of school subject areas: tensions and dimensions of managing in the middle, *School Leadership and Management*, Vol. 19, no. 3, pp. 305–17.

Busher, H. and Harris, A. with Wise, C. (2000) *Subject Leadership for School Improvement*, London, Paul Chapman.

Busher, H. and Hodgkinson, K. (1997) Managing the curriculum and assessment, in Fidler, B., Russell, S. and Simkins, T. (eds.), *Choices for Self-Managing Schools: Autonomy and Accountability*, London, BEMAS/Paul Chapman.

Busher, H. and Saran, R. (1995) Managing staff professionally, in Busher, H. and Saran, R. (eds.) *Managing Teachers as Professionals in Schools*, London, Kogan Page.

Cooper, P. and McIntyre, D. (1996) *Effective Teaching and Learning: Teachers' and Students' Perspectives*, Buckingham, Open University Press.

Dearing, R. (1994) *The National Curriculum and its Assessment: Final Report*, York, School Curriculum and Assessment Authority.

Department for Education and Employment (DfEE) (1996) *Setting Targets to Raise Standards*, London, HMSO.

Department for Education and Employment (DfEE) (1998) *Teachers: Meeting the Challenge of Change*, London, HMSO.

Fielding, M. (1996) The muddle in the middle, School Management Update, *Times Educational Supplement*, 19 January, p. 26.

Fletcher-Campbell, F., Tabberer, R. and Keys, W. (1996) *Comparative Costs: Perspectives on Primary-Secondary Differences*, Windsor, NFER.

Fondas, N. and Stewart, R. (1994) Enactment in managerial jobs: a role analysis, *Journal of Management Studies*, Vol. 3, no. 1, pp. 83–103.

Glover, D., Gleeson, D., Gough, G. and Johnson, M. (1998) The meaning of management: the development needs of middle managers in secondary schools, *Educational Management and Administration*, Vol. 26, no. 3, pp. 181–95.

Handy, C. B. (1993) *Understanding Organisations*, London, Penguin Books.

Harris, A., Jamieson, I. and Russ, J. (1995) A study of effective departments in secondary schools, *School Organisation*, Vol. 15, no. 3, pp. 283–99.

Harris, A (1998) Improving ineffective departments in secondary schools, *Educational Management and Administration*, Vol. 26, no.3, pp. 269–78.

Health and Safety Commission (Education Service Advisory Committee) (1990) *Managing Occupational Stress: A Guide for Managers and Teachers in the Schools Sector*, London, HMSO.

Hopkins, D., Ainscow, M. and West, M. (1994) *School Improvement in an Era of Change*. London, Cassell.

Howard, T. (1988) Theoretical and professional perspectives of management in secondary schools with special reference to teachers' perceptions of middle management, unpublished MA thesis, University of Durham.

Huberman, M. (1990) The model of the independent artisan in teachers' professional relations, paper presented at the Annual Conference of the American Educational Research Association, Boston.

Leask, M. and Terrell, I. (1997) *Development Planning and School Improvement for Middle Managers*, London, Kogan Page.

Mathematical Association (1988) *Managing Mathematics: A Handbook for Heads of Department*, Cheltenham, Mathematical Association and Stanley Thornes.

Midwood, D. and Hillier, D. (1987) *Headsup: New Directions for Department Heads*, Ontario, Secondary School Teachers' Federation.

Morris, T. and Dennison, W. F. (1982) The role of the comprehensive school head of department analysed, *Research in Education*, no. 28, pp. 37–48.

Morrison, K. and Ridley, K. (1989) Ideological contexts for curriculum planning, in Preedy, M. (ed.) *Approaches to Curriculum Management*, Buckingham, Open University Press.

Nias, J. (1999) Primary teaching as a culture of care, in Prosser, J. (ed.) *School Culture*, London, Paul Chapman.

Ribbins, P. (1988) The role of the middle manager in the secondary school, in Glatter, R., Preedy, M., Riches, C. and Masterton, M. (eds.) *Understanding School Management*, Milton Keynes, Open University Press.

Riding, R. and Rayner, S. (1998) *Cognitive Styles and Learning Strategies: Understanding Style Differences in Learning and Behaviour*, London, David Fulton.

Sammons, P., Thomas, S. and Mortimore, P. (1997) *Forging Links: Effective Schools and Effective Departments*, London, Paul Chapman.

Schein, E. (1992) *Organisational Culture and Leadership*, 2nd edn, San Francisco, Jossey-Bass.

Simkins, T. (1997) Managing Resources, in Tomlinson, H (ed.) *Managing Continuing Professional Development in Schools*, London, Paul Chapman.

Siskin, L. (1994) *Realms of Knowledge: Academic Departments in Secondary Schools*, London, Falmer Press.

Stoll, L. and Fink, D. (1996) *Changing our Schools: Linking School Effectiveness and School Improvement*, Buckingham, Open University Press.

Teacher Training Agency (1996) *Consultation Paper on Standards and a National Professional Qualification for Subject Leaders*, London, Teacher Training Agency.

Teacher Training Agency (1998) *National Professional Qualification for Subject Leaders*, London, HMSO.

Webb, P. C. and Lyons, G. (1982) The nature of managerial activities in education, in Gray, H. L. (ed.) *The Management of Education Institutions*, Lewes, Falmer Press.

Wise, C. S. (1999) The Role of Academic Middle Managers in Secondary Schools, unpublished PhD thesis, University of Leicester.

# 9

# CROSS-CURRICULUM CO-ORDINATION

## Les Bell

## THE ROLE

Cross-curriculum co-ordinators in any educational institution have the responsibility for balancing and co-ordinating the whole curriculum for either specified cohorts of pupils or students on particular courses, sometimes termed 'phase responsibility'. Co-ordinators also have to ensure that issues such as special educational needs, teacher professional development and personal, social and moral development are adequately addressed and that the core institutional values and aims inform both teaching and learning. These functions are normally middle management responsibilities in most schools and colleges. As Southworth and Conner (1999, p. 12) put it, cross-curriculum co-ordinators: 'have to develop the skills of working with colleagues, create the work groups, teams and manage their meetings so that they accomplish their agreed tasks, establish systems of communication and plan and monitor them, create and sustain dialogues about teaching and the improvement of practice'.

Cross-curriculum, as distinct from subject-based, roles have become much more common in schools and colleges in Britain in recent years. Significant new roles have been established such as the special educational needs co-ordinators (SENCO), professional development co-ordinators and Key Stage co-ordinators. To these can be added teachers with responsibility for the cross-curricular themes and issues that permeate the National Curriculum including Personal, Social and Health Education (PSHE), Spiritual, Moral, Social and Cultural (SMSC) development, information and communication technology, welfare, health, economic and industrial understanding, careers guidance, environmental education and citizenship. The key skills identified in the revised National Curriculum will also require cross-curriculum management (QCA, 1999). Each of these skills transcends subject and, in many cases, age-group boundaries. Each will require cross-curriculum co-ordinators to develop roles that are defined by sets of responsibilities and expectations that make challenging demands and which are derived from a statutory national curriculum that contains both a subject emphasis and a cross-curricular element. Cross-curriculum co-ordinators, therefore, find themselves working with other middle managers such as subject leaders, heads of department and other colleagues with cross-curriculum responsibility. They may be responsible for particular aspects of learning such as literacy, numeracy, information technology, or for core skills that are taught across subjects. Inevitably these responsibilities will require cross-curriculum co-ordinators to work closely with colleagues from different departments and with a variety of interests and may cause them to be detached from a subject or departmental base. The extent to which this is the case and the impact that it has on the functions of the co-ordinators and the skills required to carry out those functions depends, to a large extent, on the nature of the curriculum itself.

## The curriculum

In previous chapters different models of the curriculum have been explored. Lumby, in Chapter 1, notes that the essential defining element of any curriculum is the content of what is taught, the subject area within which teaching and learning are located. Where subject boundaries are discrete and impermeable, the essential decision-making at this level is likely to rest with subject specialists rather than those with cross-curriculum responsibility. Where boundaries are permeable and subjects loosely defined, cross-curriculum co-ordinators will have a significant role to play as middle managers. In Chapter 2, Burton and Middlewood introduce Wragg's (1997) cubic curriculum, the three dimensions of which are the subject taught, cross-curricular themes and the forms of teaching and learning deployed. Here, the role of the cross-curriculum co-ordinator is to mediate between the three aspects of the curriculum, to seek to ensure that the learned experience of pupils is coherent and to ensure that themes that transcend subject boundaries or exist independently of subjects are adequately resourced and delivered. Wragg's cubic curriculum appears to be based on the assumption that, while subjects may be important, they will not be so tightly defined or dominant as to preclude cross-curricular elements. Burton and Middlewood go on to reformulate this cubic curriculum to emphasise three curriculum levels: that which is acquired, that which is taught and that which is resourced. They identify a hierarchy of perspectives that begins with a vision about the purpose of education and leads on to strategies for achieving that vision and an organisational structure to operationalise those strategies. It is possible, however, for a curriculum designed within this framework to incorporate a range of different beliefs about the essential nature and purpose of education. This, in turn, will help to shape the ways in which cross-curriculum co-ordinators carry out their responsibilities.

It has been argued (Egan, 1999) that most education systems and the curricula which they deliver, have, in the Western world at least, been shaped by three main sets of ideas. The first is that education is and should be a process of induction to the norms and values of society. The curriculum will reflect such notions of social utility and will select and differentiate as well as socialise children into adult roles. Here cross-curriculum co-ordinators will have a central role to play in articulating the significant norms and values, in contributing to the processes of selection and differentiation and communicating with a variety of audiences. The second is that education is a process of seeking the truth through the accumulation of high-level disciplined knowledge based on critical analysis of conventional wisdom. The curriculum will be shaped by a pursuit of such knowledge and will differentiate students according to their ability to cope with a critical, analytical search for truth. Here anyone with a non-subject specific role to play may be marginalised in the face of a strong subject knowledge-based emphasis to the curriculum but may contribute to the development of analytical skills and critical thinking. The third is that the educative process is one of spontaneous natural development. Here the curriculum will support and facilitate this natural process and ensure that children reach their maximum potential. The cross-curriculum co-ordinator, like other teachers, becomes a facilitator and a monitor of progress whose main function is to support pupils in finding their own path through the educative process.

Egan (1999) claims that nearly all modern conceptualisations of education from the most radical to the most conservative are constructed from these three ideas. It is assumed that schools should socialise children adequately, that they should achieve academically commensurate with their abilities and that the individual potential of each student should be developed. Yet these ideas are fundamentally incompatible. If education is a naturally occurring developmental process, then children should be isolated from the norms and values of any society for as long as possible to allow that process to take place untainted by the belief systems of a particular society or social group. If students are to attain skills of critical analysis, this will lead them to challenge existing values and conventional wisdom, yet if schools are to socialise children these beliefs must be accepted by those same children. These tensions may impact on the work of teachers in a variety of roles, but for cross-curriculum co-ordinators who have the responsibility of making a coherent whole of the entire curriculum, they cause particular problems. Egan goes on to argue that the way forward is for a subject-free, thematic curriculum. Such a curriculum would pose considerable challenges for cross-curriculum co-ordinators but, as yet, no education system has moved very far in this direction. What this brief consideration of Egan's attempt to reformulate the curriculum demonstrates, however, is that cross-curriculum management cannot be understood independently of the educational context within which they are located.

## SKILLS, COMPETENCES AND CROSS-CURRICULUM CO-ORDINATION

Although thematic curricula advocated by Egan (1999) have not yet been developed, significant attempts have been made to explore the possibility of curricula based on or incorporating core skills or generic competences. Marsh (1997) notes that examples of such curricula can be found in Australia, Britain, the Netherlands, New Zealand, Norway and Switzerland, although both the definition of and the incorporation of these skills into the curriculum has taken different forms. For example, in New Zealand the National Curriculum incorporates seven essential skills: communication, problem solving, numeracy, self-management, social and co-operative skills, work and study skills, physical skills. All pupils are to acquire these skills as part of their compulsory education. In Australia the delivery of key skills was targeted at students in further education and covered language and communication, mathematics, cultural understanding, problem-solving and personal and interpersonal skills (Finn, 1991). These were extended to incorporate collecting, analysing and organising data, planning and organising activities, working with others and in teams (Mayer, 1992). In both countries concern was expressed about the extent to which transferability of skills was taking place and about how this might be managed. It soon became apparent that the learning process needed to be managed by teachers working across the skill areas who could take an overview of the development of all students. In South Australia, for example, this was done through competence portfolios, the development of which was supported and monitored by cross-curriculum co-ordinators.

In Britain these developments followed a number of different patterns. Harwood (1992, p. 17) points out that cross curriculum management was then a relatively new concept in British education: 'The concept has been applied increasingly since the mid-1980s to describe leadership roles in the context of cross-curricular initiatives such as . . . Supported Self Study, Records of Achievement and associated In-service Education and Training'.

One of the earliest attempts to incorporate key skills into the work of both schools and colleges in a planned and coherent way was the Technical and Vocational Educational Initiative (TVEI). This was a Manpower Services Commission sponsored project designed to enable pupils and students to acquire a range of key skills and understandings linked to work experience and the world of work more generally. As Tomlinson (1986) reported, involvement in TVEI meant that teachers had to develop new skills, learning had to become more active and experiential and new forms of assessment based on profiles and criteria had to be designed. Above all, as Tomlinson (1986) argued, new forms of school organisation had to evolve as schools became more responsive to the needs of pupils, less constrained by traditional subject boundaries and timetables and where they needed to co-operate more effectively with each other and the wider community. Within schools and colleges these new approaches to the curriculum and the related new forms of organisation were managed by a new type of teacher, a TVEI co-ordinator. This was the first time that such a role had been established in British schools that was entirely separate from either the academic or pastoral structures but was still central to both the academic and pastoral development of pupils. It was a new role and one which still exemplifies many of the difficulties that face those who have cross curriculum functions within secondary schools and colleges today.

These co-ordinators were responsible for the academic and pastoral work of the students following the programme, for the day-to-day organising of courses, for work experience, careers guidance, the provision of profiles for students and for co-ordinating cross-institution co-operation. In spite of these onerous responsibilities, this group had no real job description or role definition. There was no common pattern to the ways in which school co-ordinators worked, nor was there agreement about the mechanisms for enabling them to fulfil their roles and report to the appropriate people within the school (Bell, 1988). The nature of the TVEI project itself, with its emphasis on cross-curriculum collaboration within schools and school co-operation and on organised and supported work experience and assessment through portfolios, was a significant element in shaping the nature of these posts. The post-holders needed to have, or rapidly to acquire, competence in negotiating, monitoring, evaluating and assessing the work of students and the contributions of colleagues. Their location within the school management structure also had a direct influence on the capacity of these co-ordinators to carry out their duties. Those who had come to the role from senior positions in the institutions, or who could establish for themselves direct access to the principal, head or senior management team, tended to be more successful than those from middle or junior positions. Those who had subject or pastoral expertise that were perceived by their colleagues as directly relevant to the project had more credibility than those who appeared to lack such expertise. Those who could create for themselves a definition of their role and identify a set of responsibilities that were coherent and manageable within the time available tended to function more effectively than those who were unable to do so. This was therefore, in a very real sense, a negotiated role (Bell, 1986). It was the forerunner of many of the posts that are termed 'co-ordinators'. These co-ordinator posts, like that of the TVEI co-ordinator, are partly shaped by the curriculum context and school management structure within which they are located and are partly a product of negotiation based on expectations and an understanding of what is possible and what has to be achieved.

## Cross-curriculum management in primary schools

In primary schools the demands of a highly prescriptive national curriculum have already generated a fundamental change in primary school organisation through an increased emphasis on subject expertise and pupil performance, especially in literacy and numeracy, that has led to an increasing reliance on subject co-ordinators (Alexander, Rose and Woodhead, 1992). Although Campbell (1985) has argued that it is possible to identify a broader rationale for this role that is based on collegiality and good practice based on teacher collaboration and expertise, it is now evident that the National Curriculum has been instrumental in firmly establishing the need for co-ordinators. This is largely because the National Curriculum in Britain is an archetype of a centre-periphery model of curriculum development that assumes that the exemplary curriculum product will be faithfully replicated in all schools (Hacker and Rowe, 1998). Even though, as Richards (1998) points out, it was capable of being tailored to suit particular purposes in individual schools, the National Curriculum is subject focused yet with some increasingly powerful cross-curriculum themes. In order to be managed effectively such a curriculum requires subject, cross-curriculum and phase management, each of which will require generic leadership and management skills in order to: 'provide professional leadership and management for a subject (or area of work) to secure high quality teaching, effective use of resources and improved standards of learning and achievement for all pupils' (TTA, 1998, p. 4).

There are, however, a number of ways that these roles may be interpreted or implemented in primary schools. Osborn and Black (1994) identify four possible models:

- Resource gatekeepers who manage resources and offer help if requested so to do.
- Planning and resource facilitators who play an active role in planning the implementation and development of their area of responsibility and disseminate ideas and materials.
- Consultants who meet regularly with colleagues to shape good practice and implement school policy.
- Critical friends who may spend some time working alongside colleagues in their classrooms, acting as catalysts, encouraging and supporting new ideas and approaches.

It is clear that the growing emphasis on skills and competences and on monitoring both pupil and teacher performance will shift the nature of the cross-curriculum role away from the reactive aspects of resource management towards the proactive consultant and critical friend functions. Lawn (1991, p. 72) claims that: 'Teaching has been redefined as a supervisory task, operating within a team of teachers . . . work is related to the overall development plan or whole school management policy.'

The Office for Standards in Education (Ofsted) emphasised this trend when it recommended that teachers' work should be managed more effectively and that cross-curriculum and subject leaders should become more involved in the reviewing, monitoring, evaluating and appraising of the work of their colleagues. The National Literacy Strategy in primary schools requires all schools to have literacy advisers appointed to manage the strategy across phases and subjects. The interim evaluation of the implementation of that strategy notes that, in order for them to be effective, two things are necessary for literacy advisers. The first is the provision of non-contact time to enable the co-ordinator to support the planning of lessons by colleagues and to monitor and evaluate those lessons. The second is to give co-ordinators a leading role in audit and action planning in order to facilitate the improvement of children's learning (Ofsted, 1999).

Thus, the success of these middle management roles in primary schools depends on two crucial factors. The first is the extent to which non-contact time is allocated to incumbents to allow them to develop their role and status. The second is the degree to which cross-curriculum co-ordinators are located or incorporated within the senior management structure of their schools. As Campbell (1989) pointed out even before the full implementation of the National Curriculum and the raft of policies that followed it in the UK, policy changes have undoubtedly increased the workload of primary teachers. It has proved extremely difficult for most primary teachers to be allocated the appropriate time to carry out their normal duties let alone shoulder the additional management burdens that cross-curriculum and subject leadership brought with them. Moore (1992) has shown that four years after the publication of the National Curriculum, only 12 per cent of primary schools were able to provide a regular amount of non-contact time for teachers with co-ordination responsibility. In many schools the issue of time allocations remains a prime determining factor in the construction of their middle management roles.

Harwood (1992) identified the extent to which management styles and practices can create or exacerbate difficulties for cross-curriculum co-ordinators while O'Neill (1996, p. 31) argues that: 'Individual schools need to redefine a role for the co-ordinator that builds on the values of the school, an awareness of what is desirable and attainable . . . and a clearer understanding of the cost of co-ordination. Co-ordinators can only change and develop classroom practice with the active consent of colleagues.' O'Neill uses Fullan and Hargreaves's (1992) models of management cultures to make this point. Where a management style based on individualism exists, O'Neill (1996) claims that the professional isolation and experiences of working alone make it difficult, if not impossible, for cross-curriculum co-ordinators to operate effectively. In the style termed 'Balkanisation', O'Neill (1996) suggests that while there may be disputes over territory, expertise and resources, cross-curriculum co-ordinators may be able to work with specific groups. Where 'comfortable collaboration' exists, limited advice and help may be offered but in 'contrived collegiality' there may be considerable cross-curriculum activity but little tangible outcome.

Thus, preconditions for effective cross-curriculum management in primary schools will include openness, trust, a clearly articulated set of aims, a willingness to give and receive advice and an organisational structure that allows, supports and encourages the necessary professional interchanges that are required for such middle management to be of value.

## Cross-curriculum management in secondary schools

In secondary schools factors similar to those in primary schools appear to be operating but the management structure is more complex. The size of most secondary schools means that more formal structures, usually based on subject departments, are used as a basis for allocating resources and for organising staff, resources and pupils. Hannay and Ross (1999, p. 356) suggest, with particular reference to secondary schools in Australia: 'The power of the taken-for-granted middle management departmental structure cannot be underestimated as it has defined teachers' roles, interactions patterns, knowledge considered of worth and learning opportunities offered to students.'

There is also a clearer division of responsibility between middle and senior managers. As Busher and Harris (1999) have identified in their study of middle managers in secondary schools, the distinction between middle and senior management is that while the latter are responsible for overall school policy, the former are operationally responsible for overseeing and developing the work of their colleagues. Much of this involves a brokering role based on the translation of school policies into classroom practice. This complexity of management structure is not simply a function of size. The increasingly complex curriculum, the emphasis on subject-specific teaching, learning and related patterns of assessment have forced secondary schools to face similarly complex management issues. Coleman, Middlewood and Bush (1995) argue that the changes in curriculum content have raised critical organisational issues for schools such as managing the arrangements for post-16 provision, which, in turn, will have implications for other areas of school management. Consequently it is important for secondary schools to have a management structure that recognises the importance of the coherence of the educative experience for all pupils. Such a whole-school approach, within which cross-curriculum co-ordinators have an important role to play, will have two distinct dimensions (as discussed by Middlewood in Chapter 7):

> a lateral view in the sense that it looks across the whole curriculum, to identify the totality of the learning that the curriculum offers [and] . . .
> a longitudinal view in the sense that it adds continuity and progression in the student's learning experience, and searches out the gaps and the repetition that the subject-centred approach inevitably produces.
>
> (Duffy, 1988, p. 116–17)

If anything, it has been exacerbated (Ribbins and Marland, 1994). As a result, the role of the cross-curriculum co-ordinator, while becoming more difficult, is even more essential because each subject in the National Curriculum was developed separately so, as one head points out: 'The crucial issue . . . is the necessity for somebody to look at the curriculum as a whole' (Ribbins and Marland, 1994, p. 57–8).

Similarly, if cross-curriculum themes and responsibilities are to be fully developed and implemented, the importance of this work must be recognised and cross-curriculum managers need to be able to gain access to necessary resources. Nevertheless, there are key factors that inhibit the performance of cross-curriculum co-ordinators. These are the time available to do the work and the matter of the status and position within the management structure: 'Co-ordinators share certain difficulties with heads of faculty, including limited contact time, but their relatively low status in many schools makes their role even more difficult. The impact of cross-curriculum activity in schools is likely to be limited by such weaknesses' (Coleman, Middlewood and Bush, 1995, p. 31).

At the same time, role definition is weak with no formal recognition of function or responsibility. It proved difficult for co-ordinators to recruit colleagues to provide support, and their low status produced extremely limited outcomes (Coleman, Middlewood and Bush, 1995). This situation was made worse in many schools because cross-curriculum managers did not have access to the support structure provided for many of their colleagues through their membership of a subject department. In a study of information technology co-ordinators, Owen (1992) found that co-ordinators in his study had limited time to fulfil their role, had weak formal status within their schools and were perceived as having a lower status than subject based leaders. Owen concluded that: 'Where the role incumbent has low status and restricted curriculum experience then delegating the production of policy . . . becomes fraught with danger. The degree of danger is increased by organisational factors, such as little designated time for strategic planning, lack of . . . support and resource' (Owen, 1992, p. 39).

In pastoral care, the traditional location of much cross-phase work in secondary schools, the situation is remarkably similar. Harrison (1998) reports that there exist ranges of conflicts that impact on the contemporary pastoral domain. These include:

- A lack of shared understanding as to the nature and purpose of pastoral provision.
- A lack of confidence in the pastoral domain on the part of many teachers.
- Inappropriate management structures for effective pastoral care.
- Inadequate support for pastoral care.

The subject-focused nature of the National Curriculum in Britain has tended to devalue this form of cross-curricular provision in many secondary schools and has created a situation in which many pastoral managers are reactive rather than proactive in providing support for pupils and colleagues. This is largely because they have been marginalised both by recent developments in curriculum content and organisation and by an increasingly subject focused management structure in many schools, driven by the emphasis on the publication of examination results. A similar situation exists in Singapore where: 'the preoccupation with providing a good academic education and securing excellent results in the national examinations has tended to eclipse the guidance and caring aspect of education' (Salim and Chua, 1994, p. 76). Once established, however, it was noted how the pastoral care systems enhanced the teaching and learning processes even in the most academically focused schools. Nevertheless, as in British schools, pressures of time and inappropriate management structures inhibited the extent to which pastoral leaders could fulfil their roles (Ong and Chia, 1994).

This situation appears to be continuing in Britain in many schools even for new roles. By September 2000 all secondary schools were required to have appointed a literacy adviser to manage the implementation of the National Literacy Strategy at Key Stage 3. It is evident from a pilot study that teachers appointed to those posts are being drawn from relatively junior members of staff or from staff with very limited relevant expertise. They are not being located centrally within the management structure of the school nor are they recognised by colleagues in subject departments, including English departments, as having a significant role in cross-curriculum matters (Weston, 2000). Thus the situation in which the literacy advisers in the schools in this pilot study find themselves is very similar, especially in regard to their status within the schools' management structure, to that of the co-ordinators in the earlier research project. Nevertheless, Megahy (1998, p. 46) can still argue that the way forward in secondary education is for staff to be appointed: 'To be responsible for the whole curriculum experience on offer to a particular group of pupils, information on their individual progress, and proposals for action to bring about improvement.'

## Cross-curriculum management in further education

In post-compulsory education settings in Britain both the curriculum and college organisation have been subject to even more radical change than has been the case in the primary and secondary sectors. The further education sector is complex with an emphasis on vocational training (DTI, 1994). It comprises over 400 tertiary, sixth form, agricultural, arts and performing arts colleges, and other specialist institutions (Lumby, 1995). The introduction of new patterns of funding, an earlier adoption of modular courses than either the higher education or the compulsory sectors, new vocational and skills-based courses and qualifications and the increasing recognition of the importance of lifelong learning have all served to reshape further education. Specific curriculum developments have also been important. The specification of modules as units of teaching and learning, the use of learning outcomes to define learning and the development of units of credit have all had a singular impact on the work of further education colleges. The increased flexibility and choice that these developments have brought emphasise the importance of effective cross-curriculum management generally and phase management in particular (Robertson, 1995).

A learner-centred curriculum leads to a situation in which students make more of their own choices. This, in turn, must lead to new relationships between students and tutors and, in turn, to new approaches to curriculum management. All teachers with cross-curriculum responsibility, therefore, are now required to recognise the importance of core skills, guidance and counselling, and not the delivery of subjects, as central to their work (Lumby, 1995). As with cross-curriculum co-ordinators in other sectors, having the time to carry out their duties is important since the tasks to be achieved are extremely time consuming. These new management challenges might be summarised as developing the skills necessary to manage student–tutor partnerships, to manage student use of resources and to manage the new student learning pathways (Nash, 1995). This implies changes in both the organisational structure of colleges and a shift in the power relationships that underpin those structures.

Cross-curriculum managers who work in colleges that have moved away from the traditional hierarchical and bureaucratic structures are better placed to function effectively than those who do not. They are more able to co-ordinate curriculum development and student support across layers of hierarchy but may, as Lumby (1995) has noted, face the problem of having responsibility without authority. In order to fulfil this complex and demanding role, cross-curriculum co-ordinators in further education will need to undertake the following tasks:

- Curriculum planning including
  - identifying and organising the delivery of key skills
  - developing flexible learning pathways
  - evaluation and quality assurance.
- Administrative support including
  - co-ordinating admissions, guidance and support systems
  - liaising with industrial and other partners in the learning process
  - managing physical and staff resources.
- Implementation including
  - ensuring that flexible learning pathways are available
  - developing and sustaining a team approach to teaching and learning
  - monitoring student and staff progress (after Lumby, 1995).

In further education, then, as with the other sectors, these roles are shaped both by the nature of the curriculum and the organisational structure of the individual college. They are complex roles that demand specific skills to meet the challenges that are presented.

## Supporting cross-curriculum management

Effective curriculum management depends on a number of interrelated factors. For the individual middle manager, training has widely been acknowledged as important. As long ago as 1975 the Bullock Report recommended that all teachers with responsibility for language and literacy should receive regular training. By 1999 Ofsted noted that in-school training should be high profile and properly resourced and was still commenting on the need for training for the same group of teachers, the National Literacy Project literacy advisers, noting that: 'Many co-ordinators reported that they also need help to develop their training skills and the skills to manage change' (Ofsted, 1999, p. 9).

Tan noted the importance of training for pastoral leaders in Singapore. An innovative role required an innovative approach to training:

> In order to meet the demands of training a great number of pastoral care-givers [we] experimented with two non-traditional approaches . . . Since pastoral care and career guidance in the Singapore context adopts a whole school approach, we were convinced that the most effective way to prepare front-line care givers would be to conduct school-based in-services course for the staff of pilot schools . . . In addition . . . we also conducted . . . campus-based, school-focused in-service courses.
>
> (Tan, 1994, p. 200–1)

Training is undoubtedly important but it needs to recognise the extent to which the challenges of cross-curriculum management are now different from those which faced these middle managers hitherto: 'The job has changed from modelling desired behaviours and attitudes into leadership, strategy, deployment and negotiation . . . This is a much more daunting role' (Waters, 1996, p. 5).

In order to meet the demands of cross-curriculum responsibility, the incumbents of those posts need a clear understanding of what is expected of them. This may be transmitted partly through training and partly through experience. They will be expected

> to apply professional knowledge, understanding, skills, attributes and the most appropriate leadership style . . . However, leadership is not about the application of separate or specific knowledge, skills or attributes to a specific task, but rather about the integration of the most appropriate knowledge, skills and attributes to a task or set of tasks in a given context or situation.
>
> (Field, Holden and Lawlor, 2000, p. 9)

The main focus of any cross-curriculum responsibility now is to support and improve pupil learning, although this also involves supporting staff in relation to students. This will be achieved by contributing to policy-making, working with colleagues, deploying resources effectively, monitoring and evaluating performance and progress, and managing change. There are five different but related activities that cross-curriculum co-ordinators must undertake if they are to be effective. These are:

- Orientation – reviewing the current strengths and weaknesses in their area of responsibility.
- Elicitation – considering views of colleagues about how co-ordination should operate, what needs to be done and identifying what skills are required.
- Intervention – acquiring new skills, refining strategies, tactics and approaches.
- Review – reflecting on progress, monitoring what has been achieved and what needs further attention.
- Application – tackling new aspects of the post using acquired skills and learning (after Bell and Ritchie, 1999, p. 22).

These activities cannot take place in a vacuum. It is clear that certain approaches to management are more likely to produce effective cross-curriculum management than others. Cheng (2000) notes the importance of organisational structures that allow for teacher involvement in implementing curriculum change and developing cross-curricular approaches in Hong Kong. Lee and Dimmock (1999) confirm, in the Hong Kong context, that teacher collaboration must be meaningful, principals and senior administrators need to engage fully in planning across the curriculum and whole-school policies must be formulated if effective cross-curriculum management is to be secured. Thus, some types of management structures are more likely than others to facilitate and support good practice for cross-curriculum managers. Such structures tend to have common elements. They will be: 'organisations in which face-to-face relationships dominate . . . in which people routinely interact around common problems of practice and . . . that focus on the results of their work for students rather than on the working conditions of professionals' (Elmore, 1996, p. 20).

In Norway it has been concluded that in order to support cross-curriculum initiatives, the most important thing a headteacher can do is to foster a climate in which such activity is considered to be important (Midthassel, Bru and Indsoe, 2000). Thus, cross-curriculum co-ordinators, if they are to be effective, need to be located within a management structure that allows them to be empowered and to empower others, and that creates a collegial and collaborative culture. As Yui Chun Lo (1999) has shown, on the basis of an analysis of a curriculum innovation in Hong Kong, key elements similar to those found in British and European schools foster the work of cross-curriculum co-ordination. These include participation in decision-making and in school committees in an open and highly supportive climate in which the relationships were based on low directiveness on the part of the principal and high collegiality.

Cross-curriculum management is further enhanced where teachers as a group are motivated and the head is concerned with teacher professional development (Yoi Chun Lo, 1999).

It should not be assumed, however, that these elements are relevant in all cultures. In Thailand, for example, where there is considerable emphasis on the need to change the nature of the school curriculum to develop problem-solving and other analytical skills (Charoenwongsak, 1998), fundamental cultural norms influence how such changes might be managed. The apparent lack of sincerity in the governmental rhetoric that exhorts Thai educators to change, the lack of a clarity and sincerity of purpose for educational reform and the lack of certainty over what is to be achieved all mitigate against such changes (Hallinger *et al.*, 2000). Curriculum change here is driven by exhortation which relies on compliance from Thai teachers who, when instructed to change by educational administrators in this highly centralised system:

> will politely accept their orders and try to 'do it' – *within the scope of their capabilities*. Such polite acquiescence does not, however, begin to suggest that change has been implemented . . . the monitoring of reform seldom goes beyond the use of checklists. Supervisors perform what principals refer to as 'hit and run' missions to check on implementation at site level . . . the system is satisfied that change has taken place . . . What we describe here is a shared mythology of change. Participants at each level . . . are doing *what is expected of them* and all agree that everyone has done what was asked. Yet, change fails to occur.
>
> (Hallinger *et al.*, 2000, p. 218–19)

For this situation to be avoided in British schools cross-curriculum management in all schools and colleges must be inextricably linked to a whole-school perspective through a coherent management structure that enables school improvement plans to inform and be articulated through the work of middle managers and classroom teachers. At its most strategic, management involves formulating a vision for the school based on strongly held values about the aims and purposes of education and their application to specific institutions and translating this into action. Cross-curriculum management involves the articulation of this vision and its communication to others. Management at the strategic level involves translating the vision into broad aims and long-term plans. It is at the organisational level, however, that the strategic view is converted into medium-term objectives supported by the allocation of appropriate resources and the delegation of responsibility for decision-making, implementation, review and evaluation. Here the cross-curriculum manager has a crucial role to play in planning, implementing, monitoring and evaluating the work of colleagues across the curriculum. In turn, the implementation of these medium-term plans requires them to be further subdivided into the totality of the delegated tasks that have to be carried out. At the operational level, therefore, resources are utilised, tasks completed, activities co-ordinated and monitored. Cross-curriculum co-ordinators need to be involved in this co-operationalisation of policy on a day-to-day basis. The three levels of management must work in harmony towards a common purpose, especially if cross-curriculum co-ordination is to work effectively. This will not happen if all members of the school community do not share the vision and if values are not largely communal. Each level of management depends on the other two. To emphasise one and ignore the others is fundamentally to misunderstand the nature of educational management.

# CONCLUSION

In Britain, many of the recent government initiatives in education, such as the literacy and numeracy strategies, Inclusive Education and the development of information technology, are predicated on the assumption that cross-curriculum co-ordination in schools and colleges can work successfully. It has been argued in this chapter that this assumption is not well founded. In fact, there is a fundamental paradox in the assumptions about school management that are implicit in much current educational policy. Considerable emphasis is placed on the centrality of headteachers at the pinnacle of their organisational hierarchy. As the latest DfEE document indicates, heads are responsible for, among other things:

- the internal organisation, management and control of the school
- the formulating of overall aims ad objectives . . . and policies for their implementation
- deploying and managing all . . . staff
- determining, organising and implementing an appropriate curriculum
- keeping under review the work and organisation of the school
- evaluating the standards of teaching and learning
- ensuring that the progress of pupils of the school is monitored and recorded (adapted from DfEE, 2000, p. 78–84).

The critical issue here is the relationship between policy and its implementation. It may be true that headteachers and principals cannot manage schools and colleges alone and that it is extremely difficult for them to carry the burden of motivating others to achieve objectives and complete tasks without significant support from colleagues. This set of functions gives scant indication that this may be the case. At the same time, however, an increasing number of policies that headteachers are required to implement in their schools are to be delivered by middle managers working across the curriculum (DfEE, 1997; Ofsted, 1999). Cross-curriculum co-ordinators can have a crucial role to play here, but for them to succeed, schools and colleges must move towards inclusive forms of management and leadership that challenge the current hierarchical orthodoxy. This will lead to a considerable shift in the power relationships as these key middle managers further develop their expertise. What is needed if policy initiatives are to be implemented successfully and if cross-curriculum co-ordinators are to be enabled to play their full part in supporting these developments is a more fluid approach to school and college management as well as more fluid definitions of management (Ainscow, 1991; Blandford and Gibson, 2000). Contemporary models of management in educational institutions are based on Newtonian (Bell, 1999; Zohar, 1997) or modernist (Blandford and Gibson, 2000) assumptions about the nature of hierarchical organisational structure. These reinforce the subject divisions in secondary schools and further education colleges and, in primary schools, emphasise the age-specific and, increasingly, subject-related nature of the school origination. Working across these boundaries is difficult, as this analysis of the work of cross-curriculum co-ordinators has shown. If cross-curriculum management is to be successful these boundaries have to be permeated.

The first step towards this is the acknowledgement of the nature of these boundaries and the power relations that underpin them. As Haw (1996, p. 324) has shown: 'Our everyday lives, socially, culturally and institutionally are made up of a web of discourses which are fluid and shifting, which compete or co-exist and which are always related through these webs . . . that . . . illuminate and reveal how power is exercised.'

Effective cross-curriculum co-ordination must be based on an understanding of these webs of power and on the capacity, taken or given, to work through and across existing networks. To achieve this a step beyond understanding the nature of the relations is necessary. Cross-curriculum co-ordinators need to recognise that: 'There are no answers "out there" . . . the basis for changed action is reflection and analysis on current ways of working, we need to avoid quick fix solutions' (Cunningham, 1990, p. 212). The outcomes of such reflection on the practice of cross-curriculum management might be similar to that reported by Hannay and Ross in Australia where it is has been argued that: 'middle management leadership is gradually shifting from a hierarchical model . . . to a perspective based on collaboration and teacher leadership . . . The middle management model based on whole-school functions and processes is contributing to cultural change and is impacting the learning opportunities offered to students' (Hannay and Ross, 1999, p. 346).

As Busher and Harris (1999) point out, this implies a transactional leadership role by which working agreements are secured with departmental colleagues about how to achieve school goals. A transformational approach to leadership will also be required to enable cross-curriculum co-ordinators successfully to manage the many changes that will be necessary.

Here cross-curriculum co-ordinators will be involved in setting directions, developing people, fostering shared decision-making and building relationships within the school based on an analysis both of their own practices and of the organisational exigencies of their institutions.

## REFERENCES

Ainscow, M. (ed.) (1991) *Effective Schools for All*, London, Fulton.

Alexander, R., Rose, J. and Woodhead, C. (1992) *Curriculum Organisation and Classroom Practice in Primary Schools: A Discussion Paper*, London, Department of Education and Science.

Bell, D. and Ritchie, R. (1999) *Towards Effective Subject Leadership in the Primary School*, Buckingham, Open University Press.

Bell, L. (1986) An investigation of a new role in schools: the case of the TVEI co-ordinator, in Simkins, T. (ed.) *Research in the Management of Secondary Education*, Sheffield City Polytechnic, Sheffield Papers in Educational Management, no. 56.

Bell, L. (1988) Technical and Vocational Educational Initiative: criticism, innovation and response, in Bondi, L. and Matthew, M. H. (eds.) *Education and Society: Studies in the Politics, Sociology and Geography of Education*, London, Routledge.

Bell, L. (1999) Back to the future: the development of educational policy in England, *Journal of Educational Administration*, Vol. 37, nos 3 and 4, pp. 200–28.

Blandford, S. and Gibson, S. (2000) Middle management in schools: a special educational needs perspective, paper presented at the British Educational Research Association Annual Conference, University of Cardiff, 7–9 September.

Busher, H. and Harris, A. (1999) Leadership of school subject areas: tensions and dimensions of managing the middle, *School Leadership and Managing*, Vol. 19, no. 3, pp. 305–17.

Campbell, R. (1985) *Developing the Primary School Curriculum*, London, Holt, Rinehart and Winston.

Campbell, R. (1989) The Education Reform Act 1988: some implications for curriculum decision-making in primary schools, in Preedy, M. (ed.) *Approaches to Curriculum Management*, Buckingham, Open University Press.

Charoenwongsak, K. (1998) Higher-value products and better education seen as vital, *Bangkok Post*, 25 November, p. 2.

Cheng, Y. C. (2000) Educational change and development in Hong Kong: effectiveness, quality and relevance, in Townsend, T. and Cheng, Y. C. (eds.) *Educational Change and Development in the Asia Pacific Region: Challenges for the Future*, Lisse, Swets and Zeitlinger.

Coleman, M., Middlewood, D. and Bush, T. (1995) *Managing the Curriculum in Secondary Schools*, Leicester, University of Leicester, Educational Management Development Unit.

Cunningham, I. (1990) Beyond modernity: is post-modernism relevant to management development?, *Management Education and Development*, Vol. 21, no. 3, pp. 207–18.

Department for Education and Employment (DfEE) (1997) *The SENCO Guide*, London, The Stationery Office.

Department for Education and Employment (DfEE) (2000) *School Teachers' Pay and Conditions Document 2000*, London, The Stationery Office.

Department for Trade and Industry (DTI) (1994) *Competitiveness Helping Business to Win*, London, HMSO.

Duffy, M. (1988) The school curriculum, in Firth, D. (ed.) *School Management in Practice*, Harlow, Longman.

Egan, K. (1999) Education's three old ideas and a better idea, *Journal of Curriculum Studies*, Vol. 31, no. 3, pp. 257–67.

Elmore, R. F. (1996) Getting to scale with good educational practice, *Harvard Educational Review*, Vol. 66, no. 1, pp. 1–26.

Field, K., Holden, P. and Lawlor, H. (2000) *Effective Subject Leadership*, London, Routledge.

Finn, B. (1991) *Report of the Australian Education Council Review Committee, Young People's Participation in Post-compulsory Education and Training*, Melbourne, Australian Education Council.

Fullan, M. and Hargreaves, A. (1992) *What's Worth Fighting for in your School*, Buckingham, Open University Press.

Hacker, R. and Rowe, M. J. (1998) A longitudinal study of the effects of implementing a National Curriculum project upon classroom practices, *Journal of Curriculum Studies*, Vol. 9, no. 1, pp. 95–103.

Hallinger, P., Chantarapanya, P., Sribooma, U. and Kantamara, P. (2000) The challenge of educational reform in Thailand *Jing Jai, Jing Jung and Nae Nron*, in Townsend, T. and Cheng, Y. C. (eds.) *Educational Change and Development in the Asia Pacific Region: Challenges for the Future*, Lisse, Swets and Zeitlinger.

Hannay, L. M. and Ross, J. A. (1999) Deputy heads as middle managers? Questioning the black box, *School Leadership and Management*, Vol. 19, no. 3, pp. 345–58.

Harrison, B. T. (1998) Managing pastoral care in schools: taking responsibility for people, in Calvert, M. and Henderson, J. (eds.) *Managing Pastoral Care*, London, Cassell.

Harwood, D. (1992) In at the deep end: a case study of the co-ordinator role in a 'low key' innovation, *School Organisation*, Vol. 12, no. 1, pp. 17–28.

Haw, K. (1996) Exploring the educational experiences of Muslim girls: tales told to tourists – should white researchers stay at home?, *British Educational Research Journal*, Vol. 22, no. 3, pp. 319–30.

Lawn, M. (1991) Social construction of quality in teaching, in Grace, G. and Lawn, M. (eds.) *Teacher Supply and Teacher Quality: issues for the 1990s*, Claverdon, Multilingual Matters.

Lee, J. C. and Dimmock, C. (1999) Curriculum leadership and management in secondary schools: a Hong Kong case study, *School Leadership and Management*, Vol. 19, no. 4, pp. 455–81.

Lumby, J. (1995) *Managing the Curriculum in Further Education*, Leicester, University of Leicester, Education Management Development Unit.

Marsh, C. J. (1997) *Perspectives: Key Concepts for Understanding the Curriculum*, London, Falmer Press.

Mayer, E. (1992) *Employment-Related Key Competencies for Post-Compulsory Education and Training*, Canberra, Australian Government Printing Office.

Megahy, T. (1998) Managing the curriculum: pastoral care – a vehicle for raising student achievement, in Calvert, M. and Henderson, J. (eds.) *Managing Pastoral Care*, London, Cassell.

Midthassel, U. V., Bru, E. and Indsoe, T. (2000) The principal's role in promoting school development activity in Norway, *School Leadership and Management*, Vol. 20, no. 2, pp. 247–60.

Moore, J. L. (1992) The role of the science co-ordinator in primary schools: a survey of headteachers' views, *School Organisation*, Vol. 12, no. 1, pp. 7–15.

Nash, C. (1995) Flexible learning and outcomes, in Burke, J. (ed.) *Outcomes, Learning and the Curriculum: Implications for NVQs, GNVQs and other Qualifications*, London, Falmer Press.

O'Neill, J. (1996) The role of the co-ordinator, in O'Neill, J. and Kitson, N. (eds.) *Effective Curriculum Management*, London, Routledge.

Office for Standards in Education (Ofsted) (1999) *The National Literacy Strategy: An Interim Evaluation*, Bedford, Nenworth Print.

Ong, T. C. and Chia, E. (1994) The pastoral care and guidance programme in an independent school in Singapore, in Lang, P., Best, R. and Lichtenberg, A. (eds.) *Caring for Children: International Perspectives on Pastoral Care and PSE*, London, Cassell.

Osborn, M. and Black, E. (1994) *Developing the National Curriculum at Key Stage 2: The Changing Nature of Teachers' Work*, Bristol, NAS/UWT.

Owen, G. (1992) Whole school management of information technology, *School Organisation*, Vol. 12, no. 1, pp. 29–40.

Qualifications and Curriculum Authority (QCA) (1999) *The Revised National Curriculum for 2000. What Has Changed?* London, QCA.

Ribbins, P. and Marland, M. M. (1994) *Headship Matters*, Harlow, Longman.

Richards, C. (1998) Curriculum and pedagogy in Key Stage 2: a survey of policy and practice in small rural primary schools, *Curriculum Journal*, Vol. 19, no. 3, pp. 319–32.

Robertson, D. (1995) Aspirations, achievement and progression in post-secondary and higher education, in Burke, J. (ed.) *Outcomes, Learning and the Curriculum: Implications for NVQs, GNVQs and Other Qualifications*, London, Falmer Press.

Salim, J. and Chua, E. (1994) The development of pastoral care and career guidance in Singapore schools, in Lang, P., Best, R. and Lichtenberg, A. (eds.) *Caring for Children: International Perspectives on Pastoral Care and PSE*, London, Cassell.

Southworth, G. and Connor, C. (1999) *Managing Improving Primary Schools: Using Evidence-Based Management and Leadership*, London, Falmer Press.

Tan, E. (1994) Teacher training in pastoral care: the Singapore perspective, in Lang, P., Best, R. and Lichtenberg, A. (eds.) *Caring for Children: International Perspectives on Pastoral Care and PSE*, London, Cassell.

Teacher Training Agency (TTA) (1998) *National Standards for School Leaders*, London, TTA.

Tomlinson, J. (1986) *Crossing the Bridge*, Sheffield City Polytechnic, Sheffield Papers in Educational Management.

Waters, M. (1996) *Curriculum Co-ordinators in Primary Schools*, London, Collins Educational.

Weston, J. (2000) The National Literacy Strategy and its effect upon literacy teaching and the management structures in the primary and secondary school. A pilot study, unpublished Doctorate of Education Assignment, University of Leicester School of Education.

Wragg, E. (1997) *The Cubic Curriculum*, London, Routledge.

Yui Chun Lo (1999) School-based curriculum development: the Hong Kong experience, *Journal of Curriculum Studies*, Vol. 10, no. 3, pp. 95–103.

Zohar, D. (1997) *Rewiring the Corporate Brain: Using the New Science to Rethink How We Structure and Lead Organisations*, San Francisco, Berrett-Koehler.

# 10

# MANAGING INDIVIDUAL NEEDS WITHIN AN INCLUSIVE CURRICULUM

## Daniela Sommefeldt

## INTRODUCTION

In the present climate, when central government initiatives in a number of countries are concentrated on promoting the notion of school improvement, it is easy for curriculum managers in schools to lose sight of individual student needs within this wider context of league tables, prescriptive teaching practices and ever more closely defined student outcomes. A substantial proportion of students can be seen to be underachieving and schools are, therefore, urged to 'raise standards'. At the same time, increasing numbers of students, in the UK and the USA, for example, are losing contact with the education system, some through their own choice (truancy) and some through the action of schools (exclusion).

In recent years, the concept of 'inclusion' has been applied to social issues in general and to education in particular. In *Meeting Special Educational Needs: A Programme of Action* (DfEE, 1998, p. 23), inclusion is described as a term which

> can be used to mean many things including the placement of pupils with SEN in mainstream schools; the participation of all pupils in the curriculum and the social life of mainstream schools; the participation of all pupils in learning which leads to the highest possible level of achievement; and the participation of young people in the full range of social experiences and opportunities once they have left school.

The idea that children have an entitlement to a worthwhile educational experience is not new but, in most parts of the world, the inclusion of *all* children is. Even the development of the 'comprehensive' ideal in Britain during the 1960s did not take account of those with certain disabilities. There is a strong logical, as well as moral, imperative to the promotion of inclusion: whilst society may be judged by how it provides for its most vulnerable members, it is also the case that good provision for children with disabilities has been associated with benefits for all children in the institution. The converse is also true; thus, in the mid-1960s, at a time when children with an IQ of below 50 were deemed ineducable in England and Wales, admissions to universities were around 3 per cent of eligible 18-year-olds (3.3 per cent in 1965–6). Whilst I would not wish to postulate a straightforward correlation between these two examples, it serves as a reminder of how recently some learners have been excluded from opportunities which are now taken for granted.

In this chapter, I wish to look at what *inclusion* means in educational terms, taking as my starting point the inclusion of students of statutory school age (5–16 years) with special educational needs (hereafter, SEN). This is the context within which individual student progress will, increasingly, be judged. At the beginning of the twenty-first century, schools in the UK are at different points on the inclusion continuum, which ranges from little formal provision for SEN within the school to fully inclusive classes catering for all abilities. Policies and practices will, therefore, reflect a diversity of belief and provision. The common thread, which unites all schools, is a requirement and a desire to meet the needs of its students across all aspects of the curriculum. Developments have also occurred beyond statutory schooling. The Tomlinson Report, *Inclusive Learning*, published in 1996, was the first national inquiry into FE provision for students with disabilities/learning difficulties undertaken in England. The findings and recommendations of the inquiry mirror the situation to be found in many parts of the developed world within the further and higher education sectors at that time and form the basis for fundamental changes within the system. The most significant aspect of the report is the view that difficulty or deficit should not be seen to reside in the individual, but within the institution, leading to the expectation that colleges will increase their capacity to respond to the needs of individual learners. This is described as an 'individual learning environment'. Where the report differs from school-focused developments is in its assertion that inclusive learning is not synonymous with integration; sometimes the best placement for an individual student will be partially or totally discrete specialist provision.

The first annual report (1998–9) of the Further Education Funding Council (FEFC), on progress towards inclusion, highlighted projects such as the inclusive learning quality initiative. The observations made by the FEFC's chief inspector about the quality of provision also included a number of shortfalls which need to be addressed, particularly in the area of curriculum development for students with learning difficulties. The FE sector in England and Wales has not been as proactive as the statutory sector in seeking to develop opportunities for inclusive practices within its institutions. There are many reasons for this, not least the absence of a legal obligation such as Statements of SEN placed on schools. However, recent legislative changes, influenced by the European Union, are starting to have an impact. The implementation of the Disability Discrimination Act 1995 has required FE colleges, as service providers, to make 'reasonable adjustments' from October 1999, to any of their policies, practices and procedures which have effectively excluded disabled people. Full implementation of the Act is scheduled for 2004.

In this chapter, the focus is specifically on school provision and, by concentrating on how schools deal with the SEN dimension of their work, I hope to identify those elements which contribute towards that aim and which suggest whole-school strategies for managing the individual progress of every student.

## THE RATIONALE FOR INCLUSION

Inclusion is a process, not a fixed state. As Booth *et al.* (2000, p. 13) explain, inclusion 'involves a different approach to identifying and attempting to resolve the difficulties that arise in schools'. It is not just another name for SEN, which is a label that can become a barrier to learning and promote lowered expectations. Labels have always been problematic in the area of SEN and reflect current attitudes towards disability. Thus, someone with limited intellectual capacity has been known, variously, over the years as 'idiot', 'subnormal', 'retarded', 'intellectually impaired', 'having learning difficulties' and 'having special educational needs'. I have not included those terms in common usage which are deliberately offensive. Some of these labels, particularly the earlier ones, are now perceived as unacceptable, but all were originally coined to be descriptive, rather than derogatory. It is the prevailing attitude towards disability that ultimately gives meaning to such descriptors. The holistic approach inherent in the inclusive process postulates the 'identification and minimising of barriers to learning and participation and the maximising of resources to support learning participation' (Booth *et al.*, 2000). The key point here is that inclusion will benefit everyone, not only those with SEN. This represents a significant move forward from the earlier thinking about 'integration' of students with SEN into the mainstream of educational provision, which has always been an 'add-on' system, smacking of patronage and resulting in few fundamental changes to existing practice. The concept of integration is similar to that of 'normalisation', in that the problem is seen to reside in the individual, who has to change in order to fit the dominant mould, whether that be 'normal' (implying acceptable) behaviour or 'normal' (mainstream) schools. While it is true to say that all children are expected to adapt to some extent to the school experience, children with SEN have been expected to prove their suitability for normal schooling, rather than schools having to adapt to meet their needs.

The Warnock Report (DES, 1978) gave impetus to the move towards inclusion by acknowledging that up to 18 per cent of children experiencing learning difficulties in mainstream schools do so because of SEN and that most students, at some point in their school life, will experience temporary difficulties in learning. If so many students with learning difficulties were already being catered for in mainstream schools, then it must be possible to include more of those currently being educated in separate special schools. The 1981 Education Act took up many of the recommendations of the Warnock Report, and the removal of 'medical' labels, to be replaced by 'educational' descriptors, was a further attempt to de-stigmatise children with SEN and bring them, if not into the educational mainstream, at least on to the continuum.

One of the results of this reclassification, with its accompanying emphasis on assessment of needs, was to start to separate the idea of impairment from the notion of disability, leading to a radical rethink about how we use these terms. If we accept that inclusion is a human rights issue, we will understand that while someone may be born with a physical, sensory or intellectual impairment, that, in itself, is not disabling. The argument is that society produces the disability, by not making adequate provision for the impairment to be overcome and thus restricting access to what society has to offer. An obvious example of how society can help overcome the disabling effect of impairment would be the provision of ramps at the entrance to every building for wheelchair users. A more complex example would be the introduction of fully inclusive schools. *The Salamanca Statement* (UNESCO, 1994), suggested that most of the required changes are part of a wider reform of education, and that the principle of inclusion raises 'fundamental questions about the nature and purpose of our education system'. The ideal is set out as schools for all – institutions which, 'include everybody, celebrate differences, support learning and respond to individual needs'. The *Index for Inclusion*, sent to all schools in England and Wales in May 2000, is built on this premise of how disability is created, and includes a statement, part of which is reproduced below, from 'Disability in Education', a complementary training organisation:

> Disabled people are oppressed by a deeply rooted 'disablist' ideology. This is associated with a 'medical' model in which problems are seen as arising from an individual's impairment, rather than the barriers to participation created by society. In a 'social' model, barriers in the school environment, organisation and attitudes are seen as the major obstacles to inclusion.
>
> (Booth *et al.*, 2000, p. 108)

The current distribution of pupils with SEN in England clearly shows that not only has there been a growth in the numbers of pupils classified as having special educational needs, but that the majority of these are to be found in mainstream schools. In January 2000, the DfEE published

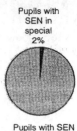

Pupils with
SEN in
special
2%

Pupils with SEN
in mainstream
98%

**Figure 10.1**   Placement of pupils with
SEN, January 2000.
*Source:* DfEE

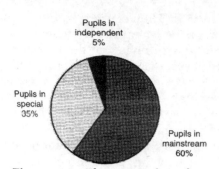

Pupils in
independent
5%

Pupils in
special
35%

Pupils in
mainstream
60%

**Figure 10.2**   Placement of pupils
with Statements, January 2000.
*Source:* DfEE

statistics derived from the annual schools' census, about the provision for pupils with SEN in England. The placement of pupils in English schools is illustrated in Figure 10.1, which shows the percentage of pupils with SEN in mainstream schools, compared with the significantly smaller percentage attending special schools. Figure 10.2 shows where pupils with Statements of SEN are placed. As these clearly illustrate, the great majority of pupils with special educational needs are already being educated in mainstream schools.

In addition to growing numbers of pupils classified as having SEN now within mainstream schools, there has also been a recognised increase in the numbers of pupils diagnosed as having more complex difficulties, as well as a worrying increase in the numbers of disaffected and violent pupils in schools. This is seen as a problem in other parts of the world, as studies from countries such as the USA and South Africa will testify.

## ARGUMENTS AGAINST INCLUSION

While the humanistic and political arguments in favour of inclusion have gathered pace, there has, at the same time, been a growing disquiet amongst educationalists and schools. Few would disagree with the human rights aspect of inclusion, although some, such as Wilson (1999), would question the difference between the social and learning functions of a school, or, like Parsons (1999), fear that the inclusion of all children within our schools conflicts with school improvement as measured by test results, a point also made by Feiler and Gibson (1999, p. 149) who believe that 'the inclusive movement needs to take a realistic look at the way in which schools have been placed in the unenviable position of needing to consider the effect upon published standards of welcoming low-achieving children'.

Vaughn and Schumm (1995) found that decreased funding and the pressure of market-led services work against inclusion and went on to say that 'the pressures on ordinary schools are having the effect of making them both less able and less willing to provide for children with SEN'

(p. 156). They claim a lack of research evidence for the effectiveness of inclusive practices, a stance supported by Farrell (1997) whose comprehensive review of the literature relating to the integration of children with severe learning difficulties highlights the fact that much of the literature takes a socio-political perspective and frequently does not draw on research evidence in support of integration. Sebba and Sachdev (1997), while enumerating the positive aspects of inclusion, also admit to a lack of research evidence. Blamires (1999) identifies the lack of a theoretical framework which can hinder the evaluation of inclusive practice and asks for clarity on what might be seen as the 'indices of inclusion'. The National Association for Special Educational Needs (NASEN) in its *Policy Document on Inclusion* (1999) recognises that attendance at mainstream school does not guarantee that needs are met and further acknowledges that 'there are those who see inclusion . . . as either impractical or too demanding of resources', an idea echoed by Feiler and Gibson (1999) who highlight the problems of catering for the few at the expense of the many.

Manset and Semmel (1997) assert that, 'the evidence clearly indicates that a model of wholesale inclusive programming that is *superior* to more traditional special education service delivery models does not exist at present' (pp. 177–8, my emphasis). This view is one shared by most teachers and a significant number of other educationalists. However, there are examples of good practice from a number of schools and colleges across the world and the publication and distribution of the *Index for Inclusion* (Booth *et al.*, 2000) gives a strong message from the DfEE that a 'good enough' framework has been found to bring all schools in England and Wales on board. As with so many government initiatives affecting the education service over the last 20 years, no doubt models will emerge, be modified and/or abandoned until something takes root. By insisting that inclusion is a process and not a state, it will be easy to defend the inevitable impetus for change.

The implications for school managers have yet to be fully realised. The London Borough of Newham, one of the UK's 'flagship authorities' for inclusion, recognises that a root and branch reform of the education service was required to bring about total inclusion in all its schools. This could not have been achieved without the full support of the local council and staff in schools. Over time, staff who were unable to subscribe to the new climate for inclusion have left the authority, to be replaced by people who are committed to this new way of working. The schools in Newham are now claimed to be fully inclusive, with some schools being resourced for particular categories of SEN. All the special schools, except one, have been closed. The LEA has been at pains to ensure that schools are adequately resourced and that support teams are in place. A shared understanding and willingness to move forward in a new way has been crucial to the success of this venture; what is essential to a whole local authority is no less important to individual schools.

# INCLUSION IN PRACTICE

In this section, I wish to look at the common strands running through studies of inclusion projects, in order to try and come to an understanding of what works for individual institutions.

In 1995, the Organisation for Economic Co-operation and Development (OECD) published its findings, from research carried out in 19 member countries, into integration practices. Part of the work included agreement on a definition of *integration* as 'that process which maximises the interaction between disabled and non-disabled pupils'. Among their conclusions was the belief that effective integration requires the development of a number of key features:

- Access to the curriculum via buildings/equipment and pedagogy.
- School organisation which is flexible and supportive.
- Staff training at all levels to develop the necessary skills and attitudes.
- Working with parents to enable involvement in their children's education.

A follow-up OECD study, published in 1999, added to this by identifying several additional influences which promoted inclusion:

- equal opportunities
- civil rights
- parental attitudes
- information technology.

In Chapter 4 of the original report the importance of whole-school approaches is discussed in the case studies, and examples from Australia, the UK and USA are used to define those features which relate to successful integration. These are listed as being (OECD, 1995, p. 193):

- Catering for individuals, rather than just offering standard programmes.
- Involving members of the broader school community in decision-making.
- Recognising social and life skills, as well as academic achievement, as contributing to the success of the school.
- Providing leadership through role models and clearly stated goals.
- Organising activities designed to achieve the stated goals and periodically to assess progress made towards these goals.
- Offering a responsive programme of staff training.

Case studies from other countries showed marked differences in practice, depending on where along the continuum from specialist class to full integration any one institution was placed. However, flexibility emerged as a key aspect of all examples.

Where problems were encountered in the implementation of integration practices, the cause could usually be ascribed to one or more underlying causes from the following:

- lack of expertise
- lack of time
- poor motivation
- insufficient material resources.

This list may sound depressingly familiar to headteachers/principals, who have been involved in the implementation of a long series of educational reforms, so what are the benefits for the school? These were identified as:

- Increased insight into strengths (and weaknesses) of students with SEN.
- Changed perceptions of disability.
- Better differentiation of teaching for *all* children.
- Increased co-operation amongst teaching staff.
- Greater sharing of teaching skills through the practice of shared class-room observations and lesson evaluation.

A cautionary note is sounded in chapter 10 of the report (OECD, 1995), where it is noted that the 'observed virtues' do not equal good practice across the board. Schools do what they can within their own circumstances and no school gets it all right, all of the time. The researchers also found that inclusive schools lean towards a comprehensive intake and seek to achieve a balance between conflicting imperatives such as:

- Individual entitlement vs. collective need.
- Targeted funding vs. finite budgets.
- Adequate support for children vs. learned dependency.

In the second OECD report (1999) *Inclusive Education at Work*, eight countries from the original 19 were included in the study (Australia, Canada, Denmark, Germany, Iceland, Italy, UK, USA). The major finding was that none had yet constructed a fully inclusive public education system, although Italy was cited as the country which had gone a long way towards the ideal, possibly as far as is achievable. Germany was regarded as less advanced but more experimental, and the UK was seen as in the middle of the continuum from segregation towards full inclusion. The researchers concluded that the process of inclusion remains fragile, with some countries, such as Denmark, showing a 'significant move away' from integration (between 1981 and 1988). Parental choice is cited as a strong factor in the resistance to mainstream education, but government attitudes are also influential, particularly with regard to funding and an understanding of the support required by schools. Within schools, even in those countries where central government actively promotes inclusion, resistance can be found in the classroom. In Italy, despite its excellent record, examples were found in small, rural schools of teachers ignoring pupils with disabilities in their classes or expecting the special education support teacher to withdraw pupils from mainstream lessons for the majority of the time. It is also useful to note that statutory schooling in Italy is between 6 and 14 years and the number of 'certificated' students with SEN attending school drops dramatically post-14, from 2.23 per cent at lower secondary level to 0.22 per cent at upper secondary level (1993 figures). The report concludes that, 'The main factors blocking reform to inclusion would seem to be a mixture of lack of political will and human beings' interminable resistance to change' (OECD, 1999, p. 22).

A review of the available research evidence from studies undertaken in the UK shows the same pattern of findings as the OECD case studies. All the lists which have been compiled to show the characteristics of effective practice will have at least a couple of the features identified above and there is generally a high degree of similarity among them. This is not surprising, in some respects, since many of the features seen as good *inclusive* practice are the same as those identified as good practice for *any* school. One of the most consistent features of most lists was the emphasis on leadership. Thus, we find in the DfEE Research Report No. 90 (Daniels *et al.*, 1999), on provision in mainstream schools for pupils with emotional and behavioural difficulties (EBD), that one of the necessary conditions for working effectively was seen as school leadership which ensured the existence of appropriate values, ethos and aspirations for the school. Richards (1999), in another study of EBD inclusion, cites senior management beliefs in the rights of access as a crucial aspect of success. Lipsky and Gartner (1998) place visionary leadership at the top of their list of key factors for successful inclusion, while Ainscow *et al.* (1999) reported that many LEA officers, in a study of 12 local authorities, admitted a need for 'guidance and leadership' in relation to how inclusion relates to raising standards. Smith (1996) stresses the importance of SEN co-ordinators (SENCOs) being assured of the support of the headteacher and senior management if they are to succeed in their role. O'Neill (1996) goes further and defines the SENCO as having a major leadership role with the potential to help restructure learning and teaching approaches across the curriculum. Booth *et al.* (2000) stipulate that headteachers and senior staff must be involved in planning for inclusion at a very early stage of the process, because they have a clear responsibility for school development.

This emphasis on leadership is not inconsistent with the idea of shared responsibility within the inclusive school. Of course, ideally, all members of the school community should become involved in promoting an inclusive ethos throughout the institution. However, without a clear sense of direction and purpose, this is unlikely to achieve much more than a warm, 'touchy-feely' overlay to the existing systems and structures, even supposing that it were possible to create such a collegial response without direct intervention. Status is also an issue when talking about leadership. In terms of current practice, it seems clear that SENCOs are often expected to carry the burden of responsibility for SEN throughout the school, without the authority required to ensure that expectations are met. At a training session (May 2000) for SENCOs and other SEN support teachers in Leicestershire, I was able to ascertain that over three-quarters of the 33 teachers present had no direct access to senior management decision-making processes. Many, almost exclusively in primary schools, had the responsibility for SEN as an 'add-on' to their other class teaching and subject co-ordination work. Little wonder that they felt unable to sufficiently influence practice within their schools. In many smaller primary schools, it is common for the headteacher to also be the SENCO, in the absence of an available alternative. This does not necessarily mean that SEN thus enjoys a higher status; often a hard-pressed headteacher will only have time to ensure that the minimum legal requirements are met.

A National Foundation for Educational Research (NFER) report (Lee and Henkhusens, 1996) on research into SEN provision clearly made the point that the new strategies being developed by mainstream teachers to enable pupils with SEN to learn effectively were also appropriate for teaching *all* pupils. They found that subject teachers tended to adopt one or both of the following approaches (ibid., p. 3):

- Differentiation, by materials, teaching style, expected outcomes.
- Individual attention to give further explanations or help.

The availability of learning support staff was seen to greatly enhance the opportunities available to pupils. Resources, in terms of time, staffing and funding, were highlighted as important for successful inclusion practices to take root, a finding with which all schools would heartily concur. Other areas identified as contributing to good provision were ongoing training for staff and the monitoring and evaluation of school practices, in order to learn what was effective and what could be improved.

So far, it has been possible to identify a number of common strands running through studies of successful integration or inclusion projects. I would summarise the most significant as being (in no particular order):

- Positive attitudes towards inclusion.
- Flexibility in approach and practices.
- Committed and supportive leadership.
- Adequate resourcing, creatively applied.

Implicit in all the research is that *all* pupils are capable of learning and that it is the job of schools to promote and support them in this, whatever their individual needs may be.

## INDIVIDUAL SCHOOL RESPONSES

In considering how schools manage the individual progress of pupils with SEN, the practices of four schools in the English Midlands were examined. For the purposes of this study, I visited three schools and interviewed either the headteacher or deputy head about how SEN was managed in their school. For the fourth example, I drew on my own headship experience of an integration link between a special school and a mainstream school. The types of school represented are: secondary special for pupils with moderate learning difficulties (MLD); mainstream primary with nursery provision; mainstream middle school (10–14 years) with designated special provision and a link between an all-age special school for pupils with severe learning difficulties (SLD) and a secondary mainstream school (11–16 years). The schools were chosen to provide a typical range of provision across the statutory age group. In addition to gaining an understanding of the culture and ethos of each school, I gathered information about the roles and responsibilities of key staff, curriculum delivery and resourcing. All the schools, including the special schools, claimed a wide range of ability amongst their pupils.

## Roles and responsibilities

Responsibility for SEN provision varied across the four schools. The SENCO was the key member of staff in three of the schools, while responsibility within the integration link was shared between the team leader (special school) and the curriculum deputy (mainstream school). In all the schools, the headteacher was said to have a key role, offering a clear line management function to the responsible member(s) of staff. In one special school and two out of the three mainstream schools, this member of staff was also part of the senior management team. All schools expected every member of staff to take responsibility for the pupils with SEN in their classes, supported by the SENCO and/or team leader. In the link group, day-to-day management of the group was shared between the relevant team leader in the special school and the curriculum deputy in the secondary school, while the two headteachers retained responsibility for strategic direction of the project. In all the mainstream schools, SEN issues had a high profile and priority, as evidenced by the policies and practices of the institution.

## Curriculum delivery

The use of individual education plans varied across all the schools in design, content, the use made of them and the involvement of different staff in their creation. The linkage between IEPs and the whole-school curriculum was not always clear; although all the schools understood the need to incorporate individual learning targets within lesson plans, how this was achieved differed. Differentiation of curriculum delivery was approached in a variety of ways, often with schools using a number of strategies to achieve a satisfactory outcome. This diversity of approach is illustrated in Figure 10.3. All the schools expected their teaching staff to differentiate lesson content and delivery to take account of the wide range of ability levels in their classes. Specific strategies were adopted to respond to individual student needs as identified within IEPs. An example of this would be the physical placement of students with, say, a hearing impairment so

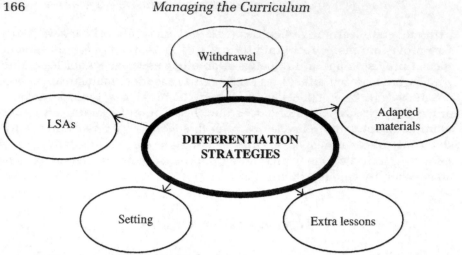

**Figure 10.3**   Approaches to differentiation

that the teacher was in clear view, to assist in lip-reading. Adapted materials were often produced in collaboration with learning support assistants (LSAs) and could include something as simple as worksheets geared to different abilities or the assisted use of sophisticated computer equipment for a student with limited functional movement.

Setting is becoming an increasingly popular response to the need to cater for individual rates of learning within a wide ability range. All the schools used some form of setting for a number of activities or subjects. Thus, the primary school used setting within the literacy and numeracy sessions, while the middle school grouped children within lessons as necessary. The secondary MLD school was considering the introduction of formal setting arrangements in some subjects, while the SLD link group practised setting across the whole of the special-school age group (5–19 years) and included students in streamed classes in the host secondary school. The rationale for setting was seen as enabling a more focused response to be made to all student needs, as well as allowing a more efficient and effective use of scarce resources.

Where LSAs were used, their role and function was defined by individual need. Thus, students with a high physical support need tended to be allocated an LSA for most of the time, while others with lower support needs received help from the class-based LSA, who worked with all students. All the schools were aware of the need to avoid setting up a 'learned dependency' culture for their students with SEN and actively encouraged independent practices. Withdrawal from timetabled activities usually occurred to accommodate the visits of therapists, although the primary school did withdraw pupils for a time-limited series of 'booster classes' in basic skills, numeracy and literacy. For students with behaviour disorders, withdrawal was often used as a 'time-out' technique to allow for a calming-down period.

It was in the area of extra lessons that most creativity could be seen. All the schools were concerned at the lack of time available to fit in everything they saw as necessary for students with SEN. The extra input seen as being required included follow-up or reinforcement of work arising out of lessons, coaching in basic skills, work on specific IEP targets, social skills work and language work. Opportunities to work on these identified areas were created at the beginning and end of the school day or at lunchtimes. The middle school, for example, had its SEN cohort bussed into school at 8.10 a.m. in order to fit in 35 minutes of extra tuition before registration. A similar amount of time was built in at the end of the school day for the same purpose. The work focused on the individual targets contained in the IEPs. This additional time was seen as invaluable in ensuring that all students were enabled to gain a fuller access to the core curriculum than would otherwise have been the case. In order to minimise the stigma associated with 'special' provision, the facilities and activities were open to any student in the school who wished to join in. Since this meant access to computers, the option was a popular one with many 'ordinary' students in the school.

The primary school had a large number of initiatives, designed to provide extra support and educational opportunities for its lower-achieving pupils. Activities were on offer to pupils before and after school and at lunchtimes every day. These included lunchtime 'Betterme' clubs providing individual coaching sessions, a homework club for Year 5/Year 6 which included support for SEN, games club at lunchtime to promote language development and social skills, a lunchtime story club for reception age children, and breakfast and lunchtime literacy clubs aimed at Year 2/Year 5 pupils. None of these activities were aimed exclusively at pupils with SEN, but at all children attending the school. The school has a strong commitment to equal opportunities and community education in an area where pupils score well below average on baseline assessment. Many of the techniques and approaches developed for pupils with SEN have been found equally useful for working with children across the ability range and therefore distinctions are often unnecessary. As the headteacher explained, 'When we say every child in this school is included, we mean *every* child. The ethos and underpinning philosophy of this school are to do with enabling children to achieve. Our watchwords are flexibility and adaptability.'

The two special schools are designed and equipped to offer optimum learning opportunities for their students, and the smaller classes and modified curriculum allow differentiated, individual support to be more easily provided within the normal school day. There were built-in opportunities for students to experience work in mainstream classes as far as possible. As in the mainstream schools, there is a growing recognition that everything cannot be fitted into the formal part of the day, resulting in the introduction of a range of out-of-school clubs or activities to meet perceived needs. Activities may focus on developing or supporting basic study skills or may be geared towards promoting social skills. Work with parents is seen as an important part of promoting student progress and achievement, although opportunities for generating casual contacts is difficult in special schools, which serve a wider catchment area than neighbourhood mainstream schools.

Inclusion practice was encouraged by the special schools, who provided staffing support and expertise to the mainstream schools with whom they worked. A difficulty experienced by both special schools was that of gaining access to mainstream provision when there is no duty placed on ordinary schools to respond to requests for inclusion links. Where pupils with SEN are on the roll of the school, provision has to be made, whereas there is no comparable duty to provide for pupils on the roll of other schools. Both schools felt that dual rolls could be the answer to this problem by firmly linking the pupil to both mainstream and special provision, thus allowing more flexibility in the system and, through this, opening up more possibilities of appropriate placement. At the moment, link arrangements between schools are agreed on an *ad hoc* basis and can be withdrawn, as the SLD school has found. The integration link group has been running for over 11 years, but inclusion opportunities have decreased as pupil numbers in the mainstream school have grown. There is now, literally, no space in many classes for the pupils from the special school link group to be included, despite the commitment of the mainstream staff to the link.

An added complication of setting up inclusion links has been the steady increase in the placement of pupils with more complex needs in LEA maintained special schools. Thus, in the SLD school, there has been a growing proportion of children admitted with profound and multiple learning difficulties (PMLD), none of whom can be physically accommodated in most neighbouring mainstream schools. The MLD school has been expected to cater for a widening range of abilities and conditions to the extent that the headteacher now considers the school to be a *generic* special school, having youngsters on roll with emotional and behavioural difficulties, autism, physical and sensory impairments, psychiatric disorders, all in addition to their moderate learning difficulties. As the headteacher pointed out, the MLD school is inclusive in its own right!

There was a high level of agreement across all the schools about effective teaching practices, which benefit students with SEN. The common strands which were identified fall into four main categories, as illustrated in Figure 10.4. An understanding of how children differ in the way they learn was seen as the key to effective teaching. The information on individual students, provided by the SENCO, identified in Statements or through detailed assessments, all assisted the teachers to tailor their delivery to encompass the areas of access, style, content and pace.

Teaching can be seen as a personal response by the teacher to that student or group of students; as such, no two lessons can ever be exactly the same and no one approach will serve to meet every situation. This understanding forms part of the pedagogy of teaching, but is brought into sharp relief when the student has a learning difficulty and the usual norms do not apply. In finding a way of helping a child with a specific difficulty to learn

| Buildings<br>Aids<br>Staff Support | ACCESS | STYLE | Teaching<br>Learning<br>Presentation |
|---|---|---|---|
| Relevance<br>Meaning<br>Complexity | CONTENT | PACE | Matched to understanding<br>Challenging<br>Revisiting |

**Figure 10.4**   Effective teaching practices

successfully, the teacher is often being stretched to the limits of his or her ingenuity and ability. However, once a technique or approach has been found to be helpful for a particular learning challenge, the teacher is able to adapt this technique to use in other situations and with other pupils who do not have specific learning difficulties. The teacher's expertise can thus be seen to be enhanced by the experience of working with pupils who have special educational needs.

## Resourcing

The largest differences across the schools occurred within the area of re-sourcing for SEN. Funding for supporting the teaching of students with SEN comes from a number of different sources:

- school budgets
- targeted funding from the DfEE, for example, for improving disabled access
- LEA centrally held funding, through Statements
- fund-raising.

The way that resources are allocated differed from school to school. For example, the middle school in my study spent less than the average on staffing in order to increase the physical resources within the school, whilst the majority of the SLD school's budget went on staffing to support the work seen as necessary for students with high levels of need. West *et al.* (2000), in a study of 13 schools, found that headteachers directed most of their additional SEN resources to staffing, as did four out of the five schools in this sample. Both special schools spent far in excess of the mainstream schools on staffing – over 90 per cent of the total budget.

Specific aids, such as computer equipment or specialised tools such as a Brailler, were provided by the LEA, through the Statementing system. Training was seen as a valuable resource for staff, as a way of increasing knowledge and improving expertise. All the schools felt underfunded for SEN, and the primary and middle schools claimed to spend far more than their designated SEN funding on the work they chose to do. The special schools do not receive additional funding to support the inclusion links they operate, despite having responsibility for providing the staffing and back-up required. Transport costs for operating inclusion links are all found by the special schools and can curtail learning opportunities if the school budget can only support a small, finite amount. All the schools highlighted the lack of time available to undertake all the work they would wish to do.

# SUMMARY

Since the early 1970s, there has been a gathering momentum for change across the developed world in the way that children with disabilities are educated. Inclusion is seen as a human rights issue and schools are being encouraged to extend and improve upon their policies and practices in this area: 'Although there is still substantial debate over the desirability and feasibility of inclusion, including students with special needs in regular schools is an internationally supported policy initiative that operates alongside others, such as concerns for equity, human rights and the development of strategies for lifelong learning and decentralisation' (OECD, 1999, p. 46). Worldwide studies of successful inclusion projects suggest that a number of key factors contribute towards the development of inclusive schools. These include positive attitudes, flexibility, committed leadership and adequate resourcing. Most of the research into successful inclusion projects has found that improved provision and practices that include children with SEN also improve the educational experience of all students. The emphasis on meeting individual needs within an inclusive environment places the focus clearly on the learner and, therefore, the institution has to adapt to a wider range of abilities and learning styles than has previously been the case.

Individual schools approach inclusion in a variety of ways and from a number of different perspectives, and examples of good practice can be seen around the world. In England and Wales, the government is currently backing a drive to promote inclusion in all schools, within the context of raising educational standards for all. This will have implications for how schools manage their SEN provision in the future, particularly in the areas of curriculum delivery and resource allocation. The increasing interest in individual learning styles is already starting to have an effect, particularly in primary schools, and ideas such as differentiation and positive behaviour management, which have been familiar to special schools for decades, have now begun to infiltrate the mainstream. The concept of managing individual progress across the curriculum is steadily gaining ground as the way forward, not only for the minority of children with special educational needs but, ultimately, for every student within the system.

# REFERENCES

Ainscow, M., Farrell, P., Tweddle, D. and Malki, G. (1999) *Effective Practice in Inclusion, and in Special and Mainstream Schools Working Together*, London, DfEE Research Brief No. 91.

Blamires, M. (1999) Universal design for living: re-establishing differentiation as part of the inclusion agenda?, in *Support for Learning*, Vol. 14, no. 4, pp. 158–63.

Booth, T., Ainscow, M., Black-Hawkins, K., Vaughan, M. and Shaw, L. (2000) *Index for inclusion*, Bristol, CSIE.

Daniels, H., Visser, J., Cole, T. and de Reybelall, N. (1999) *Emotional and Behavioural Difficulties in Mainstream Schools*, London, DfEE Research Report No. 90.

Department for Education and Employment (DfEE) (1998) *Meeting Special Educational Needs: A Programme of Action*, London, DfEE.

Department for Education and Employment (DfEE) (2000) *Statistical First Release: Special Educational Needs in Schools in England*, London, DfEE.

Department of Education and Science (DES) (1978) *Special Educational Needs*, Warnock Report, London, HMSO.

Farrell, P. (1997) The integration of children with severe learning difficulties: a review of the recent literature, *Journal of Applied Research in Intellectual Disabilities*, Vol. 10, no. 1, pp. 1–14.

Feiler, A. and Gibson, H. (1999) Threats to the inclusive movement, *British Journal of Special Education*, Vol. 26, pp. 147–52.

Further Education Funding Council (FEFC) (1996) *Inclusive Learning*, Tomlinson Report, Coventry, FEFC.

Further Education Funding Council (FEFC) (1998–9) *Annual Report*, Coventry, FEFC.

Lee, B. and Henkhusens, Z. (1996) *Integration in Progress: Pupils with Special Educational Needs in Mainstream Schools*, Windsor, NFER.

Lipsky, D. K. and Gartner, A. (1998) Taking inclusion into the future, *Educational Leadership*, Vol. 58, pp. 78–81.

Manset, G. and Semmel, M. I. (1997) Are inclusive programmes for students with mild disabilities effective? A comparative review of model programs, *Journal of Special Education*, Vol. 31, pp. 155–80.

National Association for Special Educational Needs (NASEN) (1999) *Policy Document on Inclusion*, Tamworth, NASEN.

O'Neill, J. (1996) *Managing Special Educational Needs in Schools*, MBA coursebook, University of Leicester.

Organisation for Economic Co-operation and Development (OECD) (1995) *Integrating Students with Special Needs into Mainstream Schools*, Paris, OECD.

Organisation for Economic Co-operation and Development (OECD) (1999) *Inclusive Education at Work*, Paris, OECD.

Parsons, C. (1999) Social inclusion and school improvement, in *Support for Learning*, Vol. 14, pp. 179–83.

Richards, I. C. (1999) Inclusive schools for pupils with emotional and behavioural difficulties, *Support for Learning*, Vol. 14, pp. 99–102.

Sebba, J. and Sachdev, D. (1997) *What Works in Inclusive Education?* London, Barnado's.

Smith, H. (1996) *Procedures, Practice and Guidance for SENCOs*, London, NASEN Enterprises.

United Nations Educational, Scientific, and Cultural Organisation (UNESCO) (1994) *The Salamanca Statement and Framework for Action on Special Needs Education*, UNESCO, Paris.

Vaughn, S. and Schumm, J. S. (1995) Responsible inclusion for students with learning disabilities, *Journal of Learning Disabilities*, Vol. 28, pp. 264–70.

West, A., Pennell, H., West, R. and Travers, T. (2000) Financing school-based education in England: principles and problems, in Coleman, M. and Anderson, L. (eds.) *Managing Finance and Resources in Education*, London, Paul Chapman.

Wilson, J. (1999) Some conceptual difficulties about 'inclusion', *Support for Learning*, Vol. 14, pp. 110–12.

# Section D: Resourcing the curriculum

This final section examines how learning resources need to be appropriately identified and managed to ensure effective curriculum provision. In Chapter 11, Ann Briggs, taking examples from different phases, begins by exploring how the nature of the learning environment, the classroom and beyond, can be enhanced through the recognition of educational potential. David Middlewood and Richard Parker present models based on research as to how support staff can be developed to enhance the delivery and overall operation of the curriculum. In the final chapter Neil Burton and Ann Briggs discuss the importance of effective resource management and examine the ways in which the financial support for the curriculum can be addressed at different levels within the organisation.

# 11

# MANAGING THE LEARNING ENVIRONMENT

## Ann Briggs

## INTRODUCTION

The physical surroundings of our schools, colleges and universities provide a learning environment for many during the formative years of life. This is also the working environment for countless teachers and lecturers world-wide. It is therefore a crucial factor in the way people assess and respond to education, and is inextricably tied up with school and college culture.

This chapter looks at the learning environments of schools and colleges, considering ways in which they can produce a climate conducive to learning. The physical environment is linked to the conceptual design of the institution, and where its educational focus lies. Classroom walls are permeable: learning may take place within the remit of the curriculum partly or wholly beyond the classroom, or elements of the 'world outside the class-room' may be brought in to enhance the learning experience. Virtual worlds may be set up within which learners can access knowledge and develop skills through the medium of information and learning technologies.

Included in the chapter are case studies carried out at a UK primary and secondary school and a further education college, where particular attention is being paid to the way that the learning environment can enhance the learning experience of children and students. They have not been chosen as representative in any way, but are examples of how good practice in managing the environment can impact upon the way people learn.

## A CLIMATE CONDUCIVE TO LEARNING

Learners bring with them to their school or college the encouragement and encumbrances of their daily lives. One role of the educator is to create a culture which harnesses the positive elements and removes or lessens the effect of those which inhibit. If we examine Stoll and Fink's (1996) characteristics of effective schools (Figure 11.1) we can see that the *physical environment* – the building and the resources within it – contributes directly to a climate conducive to learning.

> In twenty years of reading research on the characteristics of effective schools I have only once come across a case where the physical environment left something to be desired; interestingly, in that particular case, working on the environment had been one of the new principal's first priorities, as indeed it appears to be with most headteachers.
>
> (Gray, 1993, p. 30)

This supports the notion that the physical environment is a visible sign of the school's culture: tangible evidence of its values, norms and behaviours: the stage upon which the rituals and ceremonies which go to make up school culture (Deal, 1988) are played out. This does not mean that effective learning can only take place in technologically advanced classroom environments, rather that the environment needs to be in harmony with the preferred learning and teaching styles. The Hay McBer (2000) report on

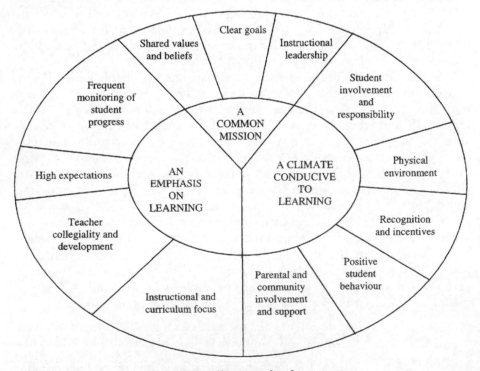

**Figure 11.1** Characteristics of the effective school
*Source:* Stoll and Fink, 1996, p. 15.

teaching effectiveness in England noted that classroom climate is a much greater determinant of teacher effectiveness than classroom environment.

The physical environment will also encourage or inhibit other characteristics of effectiveness. The *instructional and curriculum focus*, as we shall see later in the case studies, can be greatly enhanced by creating a learning environment which matches and supports the aims of the curriculum. *Positive student behaviour* can be fostered by the decorative state of the building and its surroundings, classroom design and the display of student work and achievements of all kinds: reinforcement of the concept that learning is a prestige activity. *Support and involvement from parents and community* will be encouraged where the physical environment is welcoming and pleasant. Hargreaves and Fullan (1998, p. 67) note in this context that structure and culture often go hand in hand: '[Schools] have created all kinds of structural and cultural habits of keeping people out. In Kantner's words (1996 p. 91) "leaders of the past often erected walls. Now they must destroy these walls and replace them with bridges".'

*Teacher collegiality and development* can be encouraged through appropriate clustering of classrooms and the provision of staffroom areas which are conducive to sharing ideas and working effectively. For example, in two examples of the work of departmental heads researched by Brown and Rutherford (1998, p. 82), devolved money had been spent on accommodation for staff:

> The department had its own staffroom for which the head of department had purchased a large oval table and matching chairs . . . we observed the collegium in action when members of the department gathered around the table in the staffroom during their free periods and at lunch.

> Another example was observed where the head of department had spent a significant amount of the departmental monies on the establishment of a departmental staffroom, furnished with individual desks and workspaces for staff. She had purchased good quality pictures to hang on the walls, to enhance and improve the appearance of what otherwise would have been a rather barren environment.

It is through addressing this 'barren environment' for both staff and students – the staff and pupil facilities in one UK case study school investigated by Levačić (1998) were described as 'appalling' and 'squalid' – that the growth of a learning culture can be fostered.

To such basic requirements as adequate light, heat and fresh air, a table and chair suitable for the age and build of the student, can be added classroom surroundings which encourage. The configuration of tables, chairs and storage facilities can enable student interaction and student movement, or promote quiet individual study.

# THE PLACE OF LEARNING IN SCHOOL AND CLASSROOM DESIGN

Hargreaves (1994, pp. 43–4) observed that 'schools are still modelled on a curious mix of the factory, the asylum and the prison'. Nixon (1996) comments that this implies a focus on 'repetition, segregation and surveillance.' In recent years, the growth of educational philosophies which are learner centred, and which place an emphasis upon students' learning styles and learning needs has produced a strong counter-culture.

These developments may have come about through an increasing concern for student welfare, through seeing the pupil or student as customer, or through the pressures of increased openness and accountability, but underlying them are emergent frameworks of understanding both how people learn and the nature of learning itself (see Chapter 1). Learning theories should, and do, have a major impact on classroom design and the range of resources available to students as well as the teaching styles adopted.

Published classroom studies show examples of such rethinking. Research by Fraser, Rennie and Tobin (1990) into science teaching in an Australian secondary school focused upon the classroom environment of two teachers, Peter and Sandra. When asked to conceptualise his role in the classroom, Peter saw himself as 'entertainer' and 'captain of the ship', whereas Sandra saw herself a 'resource'. The learning environment in each classroom was shaped by the teacher's knowledge and beliefs: Sandra's classroom was configured for learning through small-group activities and Peter's through whole-class teaching. Peter was better able to keep order than Sandra, as all desks faced the front and he could easily see all the students, whereas Sandra in moving around her small groups frequently had her back to students, resulting in lower levels of perceived order. On the other hand, learning was more personalised in Sandra's classroom as she was in constant interaction with her students. One important observation of this study was that because of each teacher's adherence to a particular stance in classroom organisation, different learning environments existed for different students within the same classroom, according to how well they related to the teacher's style.

The often very physically stimulating environment of the 'early years' (nursery or kindergarten) classroom is designed to enable children to learn through an exploratory approach based upon adapting and interacting with their environment, similar to their pre-school learning. This is enshrined in the tenets of the High Scope philosophy (plan, do, review) (see Hohmann, Banet and Weikart, 1979) which builds upon pre-school experiences.

These examples show that while experimentation with different approaches to learning is not a panacea, changes in the classroom layout, curriculum design and access to resources can help students achieve their learning goals. The concept of 'adaptive education' is useful here, as it refers to: 'the modification of the school learning environments to respond effectively to student differences and to enhance the student's ability to succeed in learning in such environments' (Wang, 1992, pp. 3–4).

For the teacher to meet the learning needs of every student is an unattainable ideal; access to learning will remain inequitable to some extent. However, as Wragg (1997, p. 12) comments when considering the teaching and learning strategies available to the individual teacher: 'Matching what is desirable to what is feasible is part of the art of teaching effectively.'

In the past the distinctiveness of a learning environment may have been the visibility of specialist subject-based equipment – maps, gas taps, plants, musical instruments, paints and clay – the uniformity of desks and chairs in a 'generalist' classroom or the focused expanse of the lecture theatre. The unique 'feel' of a future learning environment may equally be the configuration of the students' chairs relative to each other and the teacher, the accessibility of subject-based equipment and materials by the students or the accessibility of learning technologies. The environment tells us not just *what* is to be learned, but *how* it is to be learned.

## LEARNING BEYOND THE CLASSROOM

If education for the young is an induction into adult life and the culture of the surrounding society, some of the necessary learning will take place in the broader environment outside the school or college. Learning begins, pre-school, in the home and, if it is to remain relevant, the curriculum must maintain these links throughout formal schooling. Home visits are often used by nursery teachers to prepare children (and their parents) for the start of formal education. The school or college then needs to offer an appropriate curriculum which will support students as they return to learning entirely within the wider environment. Transitions between learning environments need to be managed to make them as smooth as possible.

Schools and colleges generally work hard to create 'an appropriate, self-contained, institutional culture, and a strong belief in a set of educational values' (Bentley, 1998, p. 88). This set of values and institutional culture may be very different to the values and culture that the students are experiencing in the wider community. Thus, when educators and learners work together outside the school or college walls they may be operating within the learners' 'cultural territory'. Bentley offers many examples of community-based projects for older students, run by a wide range of agencies, where the aims are: 'to engage young people in dialogue and positive activities, to reduce behaviours which increase risks of unemployment, problem drug use and crime, and to assist young people in moving towards greater independence and integration into the common life of their communities' (ibid., p. 83). Here the learning is not circumscribed by the formal curriculum, but it is addressing issues vital to the young people's wider educational development, through engagement in positive activities within the local community, and through visits to places of interest and outdoor pursuits in locations beyond the locality. In this way, motivation, self-esteem and potential for educational attainment are increased.

Learning within a wider educational setting can make the walls of the classroom permeable, and give new relevance to what is taught in school. In one of a range of case studies presented by Hustler, Milroy and Cockett (1991), disaffected school students were involved in setting up a community farm during their final year at school. The new learning context enabled them to make gains in personal skills, and drew the school closer to the community: 'Apart from the more obvious learning experiences gained from this project, what I think has been really significant has been the rise in self-esteem of the students involved, and the involvement of the parents and the community in a school-based activity' (ibid., p. 70). The students also began to make more sense of what they had learned at school, and to see its applicability to life outside the classroom:

> The other vital element is that the students are beginning to see the relevance of much of what they have learned in the classroom; they now know that they need mathematics if they are to carry out measuring and planning exercises; that they need to be able to write letters, and communicate easily with people if they are to be involved in a community scheme, and so on.
>
> (ibid., p. 71)

Where teachers and learners venture from the school or college base into the wider environment together, for example on an investigative field trip or on outdoor pursuits activities, the change of environment can also effect a change in the formal learning process. As Baddely (1991, p. 103) comments, summing up the effects of a range of activities beyond the conventional classroom: 'Release from the confines of the classroom, into the wider community, changed the attitude of the pupils and teachers, both to each other and to that which is to be learned' and 'The divide between the teacher and the taught has blurred into a middle ground which can unselfconsciously be inhabited by all'.

Rather than constructing the environment to enhance the learning, the curriculum may need to be shaped by the environment. This is particularly relevant to educators working with learners who are engaged in learning activities within the workplace. These could be trainers employed by the workplace, or college lecturers who validate the learning achieved within the workplace, sometimes supplementing it with classroom learning. Here the primary learning environment is the working community, and the educator assesses within a formal framework the skills and understanding acquired within it. These include the technical or managerial skills specific to the job, and also generic skills valuable to the working environment, such as communication, working with others and competence in using information technology.

The Trident Trust in the UK links work experience to two other elements: personal challenge and community involvement. Students who undertake all three elements of the programme – the three 'prongs' of the trident – are encouraged to identify the skills they have developed and the goals they have achieved in the programme as a whole. A study of extended work placements in Australia by Cumming and Carbine (1997) identified school programmes where workplace learning became one of the options on the school curriculum, and was seen as part of the students' long-term development. The schemes were successful because learning achieved in the workplace was evaluated and acknowledged; students' motivation was increased, as they could identify skills which they had developed, and see how they contributed to their learning goals.

A further example of the permeability of classroom walls is where people from the local community bring their subject expertise or simply a commitment to other people's learning into the school or college environment. For the institution, this involves a process of 'developing and sorting out beneficial alliances with people and groups outside the school, even when you do not always initially know how it will turn out' (Hargreaves and Fullan, 1998, p. 67). To succeed, the alliances need to be mutually beneficial; the playwright or artist who contributes to a creative workshop in a school or college may be motivated by a desire to develop the creative passion in others; a class discussion with a 'grandparent' may help to bring local history to life. As Bentley (1998, p. 113) comments: 'There is a wide range of benefits for institutions when such partnerships work well: improved reputation, staff development, improved attainment, extra resources, wider understanding and approval for schools'.

Creating working relationships in which the multitude of cultures on either side of the classroom walls can be reconciled and work effectively to mutual benefit but, with a firm focus on positive outcomes for the learner, is a difficult task. Where such partnerships are effective, the learning environment of the school or college will be enhanced.

## A VIRTUAL ENVIRONMENT FOR LEARNING

A further way of enabling students to understand the 'real world' is – paradoxically – through creating 'virtual' learning environments. This can involve setting up virtual classrooms – managed learning environments – where students can access course materials and interact with other students and their tutor from their home, workplace, international location or from an area within the college itself. Equally, it could involve providing for learners a computer-controlled simulation of a work environment or a physical process with which it would be dangerous, difficult or time-consuming for the student to interact in real life. Finally, it can involve student exploration, for example, of the contents of an art gallery, or of academic, business or promotional material, through access to the Internet, as part of an investigation initiated by their tutor.

From these examples, it is apparent that the degree of control by the tutor of the learning environment will vary. In all of them, the teacher has been instrumental in either creating or setting up access to the learning environment, and framing the learning experience within it. However, in the first example, the student could be studying at times or in locations remote from the tutor; in the last example, the students could spend varying amounts of time exploring the internet sites, and could access a range of material beyond that known to the tutor. The tutor and fellow students will also have varying degrees of 'visibility' for the learner. Technology allows teacher–learner and learner–learner interactions to take place from remote locations.

A study by Gibbs (1999) reports on the setting up of a virtual learning environment for a topic with which students had previously failed to engage: a methodology and philosophy course for social science undergraduates. Students were given learning tasks to complete, and computer access to three virtual areas in which to work: an individual work area – for their own work, but accessible to selected others – a group work area, where tutor- and student-initiated discussion took place, and a resources area, with links to key external internet sites and to internal documents such as examination papers (and answers), lecture summaries and notes to support group work. Gibbs reports that the levels of debate and the handling of philosophical concepts of the 'virtual learning' group were superior to those of 'conventional' students in previous years, and that there was evidence of deep and strategic learning. Ninety-four per cent of the participants recommended that the system should be continued for the following year's students.

While it may be feared that using virtual learning environments may isolate the learner, the success of this project depended upon effective student interaction. Through clarifying their thoughts to each other in the protected environment of the computer, they engaged more deeply with the topic, and improved their learning capability. As with the other forms of resource-based learning considered earlier in the chapter, the needs of the learner and support for the learning process are key factors to bear in mind when setting up computer-based learning environments.

## CASE STUDIES

In order to investigate examples of supportive learning environments, three case studies in England were undertaken for this chapter. The first, at Booth Lower School, Northampton, shows how the environment inside and outside the school building was redesigned to promote particular learning activities, and to add to the children's sense of security and well-being. The second, at Leasowes School and Community College in Halesowen, illustrates how focus upon a particular educational philosophy led the school to reshape, not only parts of its learning environment, but its time-table and its whole approach to learning activities. The third, at a Midlands further education college, demonstrates the use of learning technologies to enhance the learning of students within and beyond the college walls. In carrying out the case studies, interviews with key personnel were supplemented with site observations and discussions with some of the staff and students involved.

## Booth Lower School, Northampton

Quotations are from the headteacher, Philip Buckle.

This lower school and nursery provision for around 550 children is housed in buildings which are around 30 years old. 'In parts it's looking quite sad: it needed its facelift.' On joining the school three years ago, the headteacher found a committed staff group working in a learning environment which was not wholly satisfactory: children with special needs were being taught in cloakrooms and corridors; computers and library stock were dispersed around the building, potentially underused; classrooms were open to each other, which discouraged noisy activities such as music and drama, and there was an external environment which was not friendly to all children. The head and staff were 'determined to move the school along in terms of improving the environment'.

The catalyst for change came in the form of a portable building – a gift from British Telecom – for which the school governors provided funding to transport to the school and refurbish. This building was adapted for multiple use: a staffroom, a teaching area for literacy teaching in the morning, an area for music and drama in the afternoons and an after-school club – a source of income for the school. Importantly, it also released the former staffroom area within the main building to be a library/learning resource room, large enough to seat 30 children. 'We felt that computers should be a group activity: a third of the children can work on computers, a third of the children work on dreamwriters – they're little laptops, not very expensive – and a third of the children work in a group being teacher led.'

An area adjoining the former staffroom was adapted to be a special needs room: 'It's in a very quiet place, and the children have really appreciated it. It's bright, it's well resourced and the resources are at hand for the learning resource assistant and the SENCO.' Transforming the environment had become possible, and other developments followed: in the nursery – 'The staff who are working in there have gone crazy with paint; they've made it a very bright and colourful environment, even down to the bathrooms, the cloakrooms. So each of the cloakrooms has a theme, like a weather room, a circus and under the sea.' Areas of school that might make very small children nervous – cloakrooms and toilets – had been made attractive and stimulating: 'they're learning just by looking'.

Little used areas of the school came to light: 'And then we had a real glory hole which was our kiln room, people used to close the door on it, it was an absolute waste of space, really.' The staff wanted to create an extra classroom area to enable setting for numeracy and literacy work. 'So, by getting rid of the sliding partitions and building partitions of nice wood, with pine doors and carpeting half the room, and putting up shelving, and making sure there was the right storage, we've now created a teaching space for about 20 children.'

The outside areas came under scrutiny: 'adjoining the nursery we've got a wonderful play area, because there's a big emphasis on that part of the children's learning'. The outdoor facilities for the schoolchildren are being improved 'by building play houses and an outside adventure trail. We want to create play and rest facilities for the children: we'd like to have raised flower beds and seats, opportunities for children to play away from where those who want to play football are having a really good time. I think we ought to cater for both.'

It can be seen from these examples of the many new learning environments created at Booth Lower School, that educational and child-centred philosophy was the starting point in each case:

- Learning on computers should be a group activity.
- Children receiving support for their special needs should have a quiet, well-resourced environment.
- Children can learn wherever they are in school – even in the cloakrooms.
- A safe, varied and stimulating outside environment is essential to child growth.

The larger developments created a culture where smaller, simpler improvements were readily undertaken. Learning can take place more effectively, and both children and staff can take pleasure in their achievements. 'The notion that the state of the building, the quantity and state of the books and the numbers in the classroom are all merely peripheral to learning shows a fine disregard for what learning really is' (Bowring-Carr and West-Burnham, 1997, p. 27).

## Leasowes Community College, Halesowen

Quotations are from the vice-principal, Sue Hill.

Leasowes is an 11–16 secondary school of around 1,200 pupils, which is 'absolutely centred upon learning . . . learning that's contextualised, where students have a problem to solve, or something to finish, something to achieve . . . instead of seeing learning as little disparate bits'. In order to achieve this focus, it has substantially changed the learning environment within the school.

In the mid-1990s, the school restructured its timetable – and later its building – in order to devote one day per week to 'contextualised learning events for every student in the school, every year group, every Friday'. From 8.30 in the morning to 1.30 in the afternoon, each year group focuses on one curriculum subject or one cross-curricular theme, explored through approaches and activities which may involve other curriculum subjects, in order to achieve an outcome, a product or a performance which can be shared with other members of their year group.

To support this curriculum approach 'we've been trying to improve the environment in which the children work, because we believe that learning should be seen to be important, valid – a prestige activity'. 'We try to create learning environments which we call curriculum learning centres in each major curriculum area, which are light, airy, spacious, well furnished, well equipped, with good artefacts or manipulatives, for whatever subject it is, within sight and easy to get at.' 'We're actually modifying classrooms, where we've robbed space from other parts of our geography like cupboards and bits of corridor. We've enlarged spaces.'

These curriculum learning centres, like other aspects of the learning at the school, are designed in response to Howard Gardner's (1983) work on multiple intelligences. They can hold around 75 children, and form the hub of the activity for the contextualised learning event. On a typical Friday, the year group of 230 students might have one or more whole-year plenary sessions, work as a single or pair of class groups, split into small working groups and carry out individual study. The learning centres act as the resource base and stimulus centre for the activity which is to be completed that day. 'About half past twelve it's a bit frenetic, because between half past twelve and one, we're getting to the point where it's finished, and at one o'clock we're actually looking at what we've achieved. We could have visitors in having a look at what we've been doing, or we could be presenting what we've been doing to other classes, to other teachers, or to an invited audience, or even just to each other.'

The learning is purposeful and memorable for the children, and the joint planning and performance of the events provides excellent staff development. 'Staff have used Gardner's multiple intelligence theories, which gives one possible framework of understanding the way that children are different in their learning and in their need for the things that we create for them, creating learning experiences so that all of them feel that "I can achieve" at their own different levels, and that all have value.'

The approach helps teachers to create ways of teaching the national curriculum 'not just looking at it as content . . . but with the emphasis on how to learn. And if you've five hours and a team of colleagues and you're all pulling the same way, and you're excited about what you're doing, it actually works very well, and the attitude spills over into the rest of the week.' An audit of National Curriculum targets achieved during the Friday events shows that a wide range of contextualised learning is achieved. This was confirmed during a recent school inspection: 'The flexible learning day makes a very good contribution to extending the range and depth of the students' learning' (Ofsted, 2000, p. 6).

Other outcomes for the children are that they 'have very good social skills; they have a certain "stickability" which is well liked and well admired'. The children learn from each other, and from members of the 'outside' community, such as artists, writers, business people and public service workers who may come to facilitate a learning event. A supportive school ethos means that students are helped to feel secure and 'learning ready' within the school environment.

Similarities with Booth Lower School can be seen in the emphasis on child security, on the light, airy, varied stimulating environments, on enabling pupil and teacher access to a range of resources. In both schools, the physical environment has been adapted to the needs of the child; at Leasowes School, the structure of the curriculum – the learning day and the learning experience for staff and pupils – has also been substantially adapted in order to support the learning process.

## Midlands Further Education College

Quotations are from the project co-ordinator, Sharon Dodds.

This case study focuses on development in learning technologies which have transformed the learning environment for further education students. 'We have a situation in which students can learn entirely on line, any time, any place, anywhere – the Martini route, as we call it.' This has been achieved by setting up a computer-based environment for learning, 'Our mainstream college tutors can build courses on to this managed learning environment which enables them to alter the way in which they deliver, moving towards the concept of totally individual learning programmes.'

Students working at the college can access course materials, debate with other students electronically, and access Internet sites such as the electronic library of Stanford University in California for further material. 'What the lecturer can then do is use the class time to develop seminar skills, presentation skills . . . really talk around subjects.' At other times, 'you can send away the students who are coping . . . to develop their standard further through individual self-study, and work with other students on a tutorial basis, so you are actually developing individuals: that's the whole concept behind it'.

For the lecturers, 'whilst it is time-consuming in the development stages, it actually releases the time to do what they really want to do'. They have control over what the students are doing: 'you can monitor exactly who is doing what in teamwork, which is more than you can do if you're setting up group work in a classroom'. They can also enhance the college learning environment for their students: 'You can set discussions within the chat rooms, not only within college but with other colleges wherever in the world, so you get your students to engage in conversation with them.'

Beyond the college, business students are also accessing on-line learning from their workplace or from home, through Internet links. They not only learn individually, but also 'you have workshops, you have fortnightly contact with your tutor. This can be through net tutoring, which is face-to-face provision through a camera on your PC, or net conferencing'. This electronic contact is used for the tutor to support the learning process, and for students to communicate with each other. The social aspects of learning are not lost by moving to on-line provision: for distance learners they may be enhanced.

Learning technologies are also the key to some of the college's community work, which 'is very much based on engaging learners. It's the issue of basic skills development, learning support development, family learning, engaging people in the use of e-mail and surfing the net, giving them demonstrable benefits from having internet access'. 'One of the schemes I'm hoping to launch is that businesses recycle their old PCs through our computer technician training course, which are then sold on to the community. The computer technicians themselves become a co-op: social entrepreneurs, the government calls them. And people get access to a computer for a very nominal sum.'

All of these developments at the college are based on providing innovative routes to learning for the individual learner. As with the learning environments at the two schools, a range of stimuli is provided, and in the college, the learners are not constrained by time or place in their access to learning, although they may be constrained by their access to technology. Counter to the popular perception of computer-based learning projects, the social aspects of learning are highlighted, and the tutor is not 'sidelined', but is essential in providing, monitoring and adapting the learning experience for the students, and in giving them personal support in their learning.

## CONCLUSIONS

Through the case studies, and through the examples quoted by other researchers, we can see the importance of the learning environment in enabling the student to access or 'tune in to' learning. Within the school or college, an environment which gives security and encouragement to learners, which is configured for their learning needs and contains a range of types of stimuli provides a consistent thread across the examples of good practice. In these environments, the learner feels respected, and feels that their needs have been assessed and acknowledged. But if the learning is also to be relevant within the wider culture and workplace, the classroom walls need to be permeable, so that learning can be accessed from outside, 'outsiders' can come in and 'insiders' go out. In a multitude of ways the 'bridges' described by Kantner (1996) are being built and crossed.

## REFERENCES

Baddely, G. (1991) Teachers and learners, in Hustler, D., Milroy, E. and Cockett, M. (eds.) *Learning Environments for the Whole Curriculum: 'It's not like normal lessons'*, London, Unwin Hyman.

Bentley, T. (1998) *Learning beyond the Classroom: Education for a Changing World*, London, Routledge.

Bowring-Carr, C. and West-Burnham, J. (1997) *Effective Learning in Schools*, London, Pitman.

Brown, M. and Rutherford, D. (1998) Changing roles and raising standards; new challenges for heads of department, *School Leadership and Management*, Vol. 18, no. 1, pp. 75–88.

Cumming, J. and Carbine, B. (1997) *Reforming Schools through Workplace Learning*, New South Wales, National Schools Network.

Deal, T. (1988) The symbolism of effective schools, in Westoby, A. (ed.) *Culture and Power in Educational Organisations*, Milton Keynes, Open University Press.

Fraser, B. J., Rennie, L. J. and Tobin, K. (1990) The learning environment as a focus in a study of higher-level cognitive learning, *International Journal of Science Education*, Vol. 12, no. 5, pp. 531–48.

Gardner, H. (1983) *Frames of Mind*, London, Fontana.

Gibbs, G. R. (1999) Learning how to learn using a virtual learning environment for philosophy, *Journal of Computer Assisted Learning*, Vol. 15, no. 3, pp. 221–31.

Gray, J. (1993) The quality of schooling: frameworks for judgment, in Preedy, M. (ed.) *Managing the Effective School*, London, Paul Chapman.

Hargreaves, A. and Fullan, M. (1998) *What's Worth Fighting for in Education?* Buckingham, Open University Press.

Hargreaves, D. (1994) *The Mosaic of Learning: Schools and Teachers for the Next Century*, London, Demos.

Hay McBer (2000) *Raising Achievement in Our Schools: Model of Effective Teaching*, http://www.dfee.gov.uk/teachingreforms/threshold/interim.html (accessed 11 July 2000).

Hohmann, M., Banet, B. and Weikart, D. (1979) *Young Children in Action*, Ypsilanti, MI, High Scope Press.

Hustler, F., Milroy, E. and Cockett, M. (eds.) (1991) *Learning Environments for the Whole Curriculum*, London, Unwin Hyman.

Kantner, R. M. (1996) World-class leaders: the power of partnering, in Hesselbein, F., Goldsmith, M. and Beckland, R. (eds.) *The Leader of the Future*, New York, Drucker Foundation.

Levačić, R. (1998) Coupling financial and curriculum decision-making in schools, in Preedy, M. (ed.) *Managing the Effective School*, London, Paul Chapman.

Nixon, J. (1996) Professional identity and the re-structuring of higher education, in Scot, D. (ed.) *Accountability and Control in Educational Settings*, London, Cassell.

Office for Standards in Education (Ofsted) (2000) *Inspection Report of Leasowes Community College, Halesowen*, Report No. 103861, London, Ofsted.

Stoll, L. and Fink, D. (1996) *Changing our Schools*, Buckingham, Open University Press.

Wang, M. (1992) *Adaptive Education Strategies: Building on Diversity*, Baltimore, MD, Paul Brookes.

Wragg, E. C. (1997) *The Cubic Curriculum*, London, Routledge.

# MANAGING CURRICULUM SUPPORT STAFF FOR EFFECTIVE LEARNING

## David Middlewood and Richard Parker

### BACKGROUND AND INTRODUCTION

Since the late 1980s, there has been a substantial increase in interest in the roles and management of all those staff employed in schools and colleges who are not teachers or lecturers. There appear to be two main reasons for this.

First, there is the recognition that schools and colleges, as people-centred organisations with young people at the heart of their business, depend for their success upon the work and support of *all* the people who work in them. Technicians, librarians, caretakers and cleaning staff all play important parts, and all these add to the diversity of individuals with different personalities, backgrounds and personal and professional needs. Staff such as midday assistants have professional development training needs (Naylor, 1999) and the poor performance of a receptionist (Fidler and Atton, 1999) cannot be accepted any more than that of a teacher. The principles of effective management of all staff as people has become crucial: '*all* people are entitled to effective and sensitive management' (Bush and Middlewood, 1997, p. ix). This awareness has been supported by the processes involved in such schemes as Investors in People (IIP) which highlight the importance of formal training opportunities for all staff in organisations. The number of schools in the UK gaining IIP status grew to 6,719 in 1999/2000.

The second impetus for a focus upon the importance of staff other than teachers was the movement towards self-governance of schools and colleges. In the UK, local management of schools (LMS) and the incorporation of further education colleges at the beginning of the 1990s placed responsibility for budget and resources management with the individual institutions, accentuated in the schools sector by grant-maintained schools and city technology colleges which received their funding directly from central government. Using the term 'associate staff', Mortimore and Mortimore's study (1994) examined the wide range of practices in primary and secondary schools post-LMS and found that schools had focused much of their practice upon cost-effectiveness. The growth in the number of associate staff was not surprising. In England, for example, the number of primary classroom assistants went up from 6,342 in 1991 to 9,304 in 1993.

However, this second context for the growth of associate staff, especially in classroom support, inevitably has brought into focus the question of whether the whole issue is one of cost-cutting through using cheaper resources. Given the current acute shortage of teachers in the UK, the question concerning an increase in support staff can be whether a vision for this growth 'is really a disguise for a growing recruitment crisis?' (Duffy, 2000, p. 30).

Whatever these arguments, the Green Paper, *Teachers Meeting the Challenge of Change* (DFEE, 1998,) envisaged a further 20,000 classroom assistants in schools in England and Wales by 2002, on top of 24,000 learning support assistants recorded in 1997 and 2,000 literacy assistants referred to as being needed to be recruited and trained.

Furthermore, as our understanding of the nature of learning increases, and with it the issue of the most effective forms of teaching and support for that learning, the role and the management of those staff who support student learning is likely to become increasingly important. This chapter examines the need for the role of the effective curriculum support staff (the generic term we have chosen to use), current practice in the UK in the management of that role, and suggests that this management may need a particular emphasis in the future if supporting effective student *learning* is to remain central.

We recognise that all those employed in a school or college contribute in one sense to the curriculum, however indirectly. Nevertheless, in the context of this book, this chapter focuses on the work of those who work directly with student learners in collaboration with a teacher.

## Why have curriculum support staff?

The historical origins of help in the classroom lay in the simple recognition that the multiple aspects of the teacher's work would gain from low-skill assistance from others. Many parents, mainly mothers, still operate as voluntary helpers in their own children's primary classrooms, relieving teachers of many basic chores, especially in preparing resources. The Hadow (1931) report noted its approval of school helpers! The fact that this has a community dimension to learning is not the concern of this chapter but it is also true that many current assistants commenced their involvement with schools in this way. A comment from an infants school headteacher (quoted in Haigh, 1996, p. 21) stressed that what her school's assistants did recognised those origins: 'They're not here to wash paint-pots and they're not round the back cutting up paper when they should be involved with the children.'

The key argument for using support staff still begins with the need *to give the teacher more time*, so that the teacher can concentrate more on using his or her expertise fully – as a teacher. Because of the pressures upon teachers' classroom time and the risk of individual children, especially those with any learning difficulties, being neglected, it was logical that the largest number of support staff, eventually known as learning support assistants, in the 1980s and early to mid-1990s, were those assigned to support individual children with special educational needs, especially those Statemented.

A second argument is in the *effective preparation and deployment of resources*. In the 1990s these have been increasingly focused upon assessment requirements, especially for measuring progress and in preparation or as part of national testing arrangements. As ICT developments have had increasing influence upon students' learning, so the resources involved have changed accordingly.

Third, *organisation* of the learners can be more effective and efficient. The working of students in groups, the withdrawal of individual learners, the prioritising of key tasks can all be improved. The Secretary of State for Education and Employment (Blunkett, 1999) made it clear that his view of the teachers of the future in the UK as 'learning managers' was dependent upon support from a well-educated, well-trained support staff of para-professionals.

There are areas of marked difference between the range and nature of work carried out by curriculum support staff in primary and secondary schools. There are, however, certain common features in what they do, for example, working alongside students with Statements of Special Need, giving extra help to individuals or small groups withdrawn from mainstream lessons, supporting the teachers in the delivery of the lesson (but not in the planning of it) and providing teachers with verbal reports of students' progress.

Our work in this chapter is focused primarily upon schools in the UK but it is interesting to note that a parallel development is occurring in tertiary education, especially in colleges of further education. The use of part-time staff, always a feature of the large-scale provision in further education, has in itself worked against such people feeling part of an integrated staff. The readjustments in the role of support staff of various kinds have made this even more so. Nevertheless, Kedney and Brownlow (1994, p. 12) noted that, owing to greater funding flexibility, support staff roles in further education were:

- more flexible
- more involved directly in support of students

- more likely to offer guidance and support
- more likely to be directly concerned with instruction, supervision and design.

In primary schools in particular, there is evidence to suggest that the line distinguishing the work of the LSA from that of the teacher can become increasingly blurred – particularly when the LSA's confidence and expertise develops. Farell, Balshaw and Polat (1999, p. 17) quote an LEA service manager articulating a not unfamiliar view of the distinction between a teacher's work and that of an LSA: 'She felt that the difficult and, by implication, more intellectually challenging part of helping pupils with special needs was in assessment and proforma planning. This required the expertise of an experienced teacher who could then advise and support the LSA in the implementation of the programme.' However, as studies in 1994 (Mortimore and Mortimore) and 1999 (Farell, Balshaw and Polat) showed, there were a number of factors affecting the effective development of classroom support staff.

- *Pay* – 'levels of pay are seen as being far too low when set against the work that LSAs undertake and the responsibilities they are given' (Farell, Balshaw and Polat, 1999, p. 28). In some schools, assistants were on different pay scales, although doing the same jobs.
- *Contracts* – the majority of contracts were temporary, many of them in schools tied to an individual student with a statement. This inevitably fostered considerable feelings of insecurity.
- *Undervaluing* – with no real career structure, formal induction and appraisal dependent upon the management of individual schools or colleges, and training opportunities spasmodic, many curriculum support staff felt undervalued.
- *Frustration* – given the abilities of many staff, the above, and treatment in some individual organisations, a sense of under fulfilment was widespread. Ironically, those receiving training could be the most frustrated, if not given development opportunities in their own institution.

## Current trends, practice and identified issues

In addition to using the literature and the research of others, the authors interviewed a number of curriculum support staff in various roles in primary and secondary schools, teachers and heads who work with these staff, participants on training courses, and managers (and trainers) from these courses.

### Aspirations and frustrations

All LSAs did not necessarily subscribe to the above view. Elizabeth Passarello (2000, p. 17) stated unequivocally: 'I am a qualified teacher and, unusually, have worked both as a secondary learning support teacher and an LSA. The duties and responsibilities of both jobs are the same and even the staff are not aware of the differences.' She adds that the only recognised distinction is the level of pay: almost twice as much per hour for the teacher.

Meriel Godfrey has been an LSA in her local primary school for nine years and is currently working towards achieving the Council for Awards in Children's Care and Education (CACHE) qualification. 'The role,' she says, 'has changed out of all recognition from the one I took on nine years ago.' Learning support assistants now spend the vast majority of their time in the classroom actively engaged in assisting in the children's learning:

> We are involved in the literacy hour and additional literacy support. We do group reading and writing; we work with teachers to target specific needs arising from national curriculum requirements. We are closely involved in assessment and recording. The work we are now demanding from relatively young children is much more challenging and sophisticated. A teacher needs a fellow professional in the classroom just to stay afloat!

The only thing that has not changed, according to Meriel Godfrey, is the status and the pay. Although there is no question that in the place of work she is clearly seen by teachers as a valued fellow professional, there is equally little desire or compunction demonstrated to address the issue of pay differentials:

> It is doubly frustrating. Inside the school we are accepted as part of the staff; our ideas are taken on board and we are acknowledged as professional educators. Outside in the playground, on the other hand, we are seen by parents as people doing a job that anyone can do, a job which in their view doesn't rate higher recognition or pay than a shelf-filler at their local supermarket.

Noreen Crook, an LSA at Lodge Park Technology College, articulated a common view when she recalled how nervous and apprehensive she was when she first began. Schools in themselves can be daunting places for new teachers at the best of times but going into a classroom full of 11-year-olds with little or no training can require considerable courage! However, experience and developing expertise have now made Mrs Crook much stronger: 'I now know what is expected. I know how the school operates. I'm much more confident in myself. I am, for example, no longer alarmed at expressing my complete ignorance in some subject areas. I don't need guidance any more. I work *with* the teacher, not *for* the teacher.'

The concept of working with rather than for the teacher is perhaps at the heart of the widening debate about the current and potential contribution LSAs have to make to students' teaching and learning. Where LSAs already believe they work with the teacher, there is the sense of frustration about their lack of status and absence of career progression. Learning support assistants do not necessarily feel undervalued by the schools in which they work – quite the opposite in fact – but they do feel underpaid and under-developed. Teachers feel guilty about the fact that LSAs attend out-of-school activities such as staff and planning meetings when their contracts preclude any possibility of additional payment but the reality is that governing bodies do not put pressure on their political masters to do anything about it!

The battle taken on by the teaching unions over the last 15 years to raise the profile, morale and professional status often brought with it a suspicion of other adults helping in schools. Even in July 2000 unions are warning that LSAs must not be given tasks best carried out by teachers. The General Secretary of the National Union of Teachers stated, 'the DfEE is using examples that denigrate and confuse the role of the teacher' and Nigel de Gruchy, (NASUWT General Secretary) made a similar point by emphasising that 'classroom assistants are rapidly becoming teachers in practice' (TES, 2000, p. 4). They were clear to avoid any public set of opinions which enhanced the view that anyone can teach: all that is needed, after all, according to some of these views, is a bit of common sense and a firm hand!

## Emerging career development opportunities

However, the introduction of LMS has given schools much more autonomy and flexibility with their budgets which has, in turn, encouraged greater flexibility and innovation with regards to staffing the curriculum effectively. This, together with the growing popularity of Investors in People and the increasing number of training courses and qualifications available, has created an opportunity for LSAs to take over a role in school with real career potential and progression. To date, that opportunity has not been widely grasped, so there is a real and significant sense of frustration and, in some cases, anger that the professional expertise of LSAs is not being recognised and promoted in the way it should.

Although currently Farell, Balshaw and Polat's (1999) evidence would suggest that only 20 per cent of LSAs would wish to become teachers, the reality is that such a percentage still represents a significant recruitment source for schools. Sandra Miles, an LSA at Fulston Manor School, makes the point clearly:

> I'd like to see structures in place to allow classroom assistants to train as teachers whilst on the job. I think that this could be an excellent teacher-training route. Because we see a variety of teaching and learning styles every single day, we really get to find out what works and what doesn't.
>
> (Elkin, 2000, p. 35)

The logic is difficult to counter. At present, there are a plethora of courses for LSAs and an equally varied range of options for graduates wishing to become teachers. What does not currently exist is a mechanism for LSAs to obtain qualifications which cater for and recognise their developing expertise.

Monica Farthing, the TTA's professional officer for teacher supply and recruitment, says that local authorities have a key role to play in developing routes into teaching. 'Lancashire County Council really talent-spots among classroom assistants and has got about 20 people through,' she says. However, a 1998 survey carried out by Southampton University, 'Career Ladders for Classroom Assistants', found a 'very patchy picture' of such provision, while other research suggests classroom assistants' enthusiasm and dedication are not being tapped. Surveys carried out in Essex, Kent and Yorkshire have found about 15 per cent were interested in becoming teachers (Mercer, 2000).

## Associate teachers: a way ahead?

It is primarily for this reason that University College Northampton is looking to introduce a qualification based on the foundation degree which will lead to a new role which they have termed 'associate teacher'. This qualification will not only enable LSAs to increase their subject expertise and classroom management skills; it will also create a career structure which in turn could allow an 'associate teacher' to progress to (fully) qualified teacher status. Ken Bland, head of Continuing Professional Development (CPD) at the college, is convinced that such a course and qualification will quickly become oversubscribed: 'It fills a gap; it answers a need; it presents a large number of talented people with the opportunity to develop their expertise and enhance their personal professional status. It cannot fail, in my view.'

His optimism was justified by the initial response when, at a recent meeting in Corby, 52 LSAs responded to an invitation to find out more about this new qualification. Although the notice had been short and the advertising low key, the reaction was significantly wide-ranging and upbeat. Many of those attending mentioned several others who would have come had they been able to. All those who could not attend requested the information be sent to them. What came from the meeting was a unanimously positive response to the possibility of progressing to associate teacher status and, in many cases, a real sense of excitement and anticipation about the potential route from associate teacher to qualified teacher status.

From interviews with LSAs carried out after the meeting came some clear messages:

• A sense of increasing frustration about the fact that even now additional qualifications do not equal greater status and increased pay.

- A real tension currently existing in some schools between teachers and LSAs where a good deal of suspicion, mistrust and even antagonism at middle and senior management, pervades the staffroom. This lack of partnership would appear to centre on a lack of understanding on the part of the teaching staff as to the aspirations, talents and potential contributions LSAs have to make to the teaching and learning dynamic in school.
- A high level of self-belief and confidence among the LSAs that they possess the ability, qualifications and experience to develop their teaching expertise. They know they could make a greater contribution!
- The introduction of a clearly defined career structure will give LSAs a greater sense of self-worth. It will enable them to confirm their own view that they have much more to offer schools.

The notion of the associate teacher is not, however, a prospect which Paul Rangecroft, headteacher of a large primary school, greets with the same undiluted enthusiasm. He employs 15 LSAs at his school and freely admits that he gets tremendously good value for money for them. 'They are,' he says, 'empowered, committed, loyal and resourceful.' They work with special needs students, they support the literacy hour, they prepare specific teaching materials and work with groups of children as and where appropriate. He acknowledges that without them his school would not be able to function effectively. However, he believes that the concept of associate teacher is flawed. He considers such a role would place the post-holder between a rock and a hard place and represent that worst of both worlds:

> It's a bridge too far: a primary school teacher has to deliver the whole range of the curriculum and possess a sophisticated knowledge of pedagogy. Equally, parents expect teachers to teach their children. They won't accept anything less; replacing them with anyone they consider less qualified just will not wash – it's too much of a quantum leap.

Whether or not this view would be widely supported is, of course, open to debate; what is uncertain at the present time is how popular such a qualification will turn out to be. One thing is certain, however: the consequence of introducing the role of 'associate teacher', a possible example of para-professionals (Hargreaves, 1996), could be wide-ranging. In terms of recruitment, they could, like LSAs, provide an answer to the current shortage in the UK of qualified teachers.

## PRINCIPLES OF THE EFFECTIVE MANAGEMENT OF CURRICULUM SUPPORT STAFF

### Clarification of the role

It is easy to say what support staff are *not*, but the starting point for managers must surely be that of student learning, that is, how best do students learn and who does what best to enable this to occur? A clear delineation of the role of teacher and support staff in the learning process is essential: 'there is a need for teachers and classroom assistants to define their own *unique* role in classroom processes and differentiate their tasks according to established expertise' (Moyles with Suschitzky, 1997 p. 13). As Moyles points out, it is not a question of being 'equal' in the classroom. It is much more, for managers, an issue of how all those involved in the learning process of students can best contribute using the particular skills they bring (parents are an obvious example of another group with a quite different contribution to make). It is vital therefore in the classroom that roles to support and extend student learning are *complementary*.

Our thinking upon the effective management of curriculum support staff draws upon certain assumptions about learning:

- that it will become more individualised and targeted
- that the focus in education will be more on learning than on teaching
- that the deployment of any resources supporting learning should be geared to their appropriateness first and foremost, and not merely to the sum total of resources available.

We suggest therefore that managers need to consider the roles of curriculum support staff in terms of three levels of support provision for learning (see Figure 12.1):

1) The compensatory level – where support is needed to relieve pressure on teachers, to enable teachers to concentrate on their key tasks. This will inevitably involve some 'technical' work and operate directly under teacher direction.
2) The interpretative level – where support is focused on the learners being helped to understand the task required of them. This may involve, for example, re-emphasising, rephrasing the original task for the learner.
3) The extension level – where the students' learning is extended from the original task to understanding what comes next. This will involve interpreting the *learning* taking place to enable the students to make their own decisions.

If a principle such as this is accepted by leaders and managers of schools and colleges, then they will need to think strategically about the support for learning provided by staff other than teachers in terms of such a model or a similar one. This will have implications for management in at least three key areas.

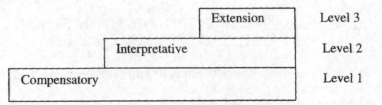

**Figure 12.1** The levels of curriculum support staff provision

## Implications for personnel requirements

Those staff employed to operate solely or mainly at level 1 will have skills such as resources management, time management, ability to follow instructions, demonstration skills and qualities such as unobtrusiveness. Their relationship to the teachers is essentially that of 'helper', and this is perceived as such by the student.

Level 2 staff will have the ability to understand the nature of the task the learner is to undertake and what is involved in the task for it to be successfully achieved. A key quality will be that of persuasiveness. The relationship is essentially a mediator between teacher and learner, reinterpreting if necessary the task on the learner's own terms. The student perceives this person as his or her personal 'aide' in learning, acting as a link between teacher and learner.

Staff employed at level 3 will have the ability to understand the learning process itself and the significance of the task in the context of the individual student's progress. Skills will include encouraging reflection and giving feedback, and students will view the support person as a resource, additional to the teacher, who helps them to decide for themselves as to their next step. It is at level 3 that the role is essentially a *proactive* one, which makes it differ from the other two.

If we take homework – or any learning task to be undertaken away from formal hours and setting – we see the different roles as possibly being:

- at level 1, to ensure that the task is carefully noted in diaries or planners (a task to which at present too much teacher time is often devoted)
- at level 2, to ensure that the task is fully understood in terms of what is required, and how it relates to other work done
- at level 3, to encourage the learner to develop an appropriate task for himself/herself in the light of previous and future learning, and even to set the specific task.

## Implications for deployment of personnel

Having looked at a model for the various levels of learning support intervention, managers will clearly need to be aware of ways in which personnel can be most effectively deployed. There are fascinating logistical and budgetary implications.

If, for example, a principal or headteacher has £100,000 to spend on educating 100 students, does he or she take the conventional route of employing £100,000 of qualified teachers or go for a more imaginative mix of teachers, associate teachers and LSAs? If the latter option is preferred, how best are the personnel to be utilised to ensure maximum educational benefit for the children? Whether or not such decisions are easier to make in larger organisations such as secondary schools where there is more flexibility, is equally open to question.

The successful utilising of LSAs, whether to sustain and develop their role as supporters of learning or allow them to move on eventually to become teachers, is, in the final analysis, in the hands of the government first and schools second. Clearly, there are budgetary implications in creating a new grade of professionally qualified teacher, but equally clear in the UK is the need to do something fundamental to address the current and growing teacher shortage. In addition, the introduction of alternative uses of curriculum support staff will encourage schools and colleges to challenge the stereotypical notion of one teacher per class, and begin to experiment with more flexible and innovative models of human resource deployment.

The proper targeted professional development of LSAs must be a part answer, albeit radical, to this problem. Watkinson (1999, p. 63) makes the point that the professional development of all staff can assist in school improvement and that support staff 'directly in contact with the students can have a direct role in enhancing achievement'. The Chief Inspector's annual report for 1996/7 made the same point: 'Where Specialist Teacher Assistants (STAs) have been properly trained and deployed, they contribute significantly to standards in literacy and numeracy' (Ofsted, 1998, p. 19).

There is still much work to be done before the true potential of LSAs is harnessed. All too often LSAs are not used effectively in schools. Michael Barber's point that 'teaching assistants are least effective when they are used to supplement an inadequate teacher' (Barber, 1997, p. 232) is well made.

Jo Fletcher, a teacher at Lodge Park Technology College, makes a similar point:

> The skills of classroom assistants are often unknown or underused in schools. Although they were often felt to have similar personal qualities to teachers, they were sometimes expected to have similar skills without any training. Not only this, they were expected to show what was required of them within varying and diverse subject areas.
>
> (Fletcher, 1999, p. 128)

An evaluation of the specialist teaching assistants (STA) training scheme (Phillips, 2000) revealed high levels of satisfaction by the participants, increased skills and knowledge by virtually everyone involved. However, on the return to schools of the newly qualified STAs, satisfaction, effectiveness and contribution to school improvement depended significantly upon their deployment, which itself often depended upon the attitude of headteachers and classroom teachers. The key therefore may lie in the development of an appropriate culture.

## Developing a dynamic culture

In order to ensure that LSAs are fully utilised it is vitally important that an appropriate learning culture is developed and sustained in schools. All the time there is any sense of 'us and them' or mistrust or apprehension or misunderstanding about the most effective way for teachers and LSAs to work together for the students, the potential benefits to be gained from the effective development of all adults in schools in teaching and learning may be lost.

Teachers and managers need to be flexible, innovative and open to what might be described as revolutionary thinking about how best to utilise the range and variety of human resources open to them. Parker (1999, p. 9) recounts an incident involving Jan Mullen, an LSA who, as a 40-year-old mature student, joined her daughter's sixth form and after two years achieved a distinction in the advanced GNVQ business studies, which illustrates neatly how lateral thinking can produce better solutions.

> Jan was very familiar with the course, having both studied it and supported teachers delivering it. On one occasion a supply teacher arrived to take a Year 10 Group (15 year old students) and immediately confessed to Jan his complete ignorance of the subject matter. Jan's solution was simple. He stayed to support her and she delivered the lesson using support materials she herself had produced.

## CONCLUSION

Our research has indicated that many curriculum support staff currently employed in schools and colleges have a large number of the attributes mentioned above. Indeed, a number are frustrated at their lack of opportunity to use them. Issues such as pay and conditions and a qualifications pathway (ultimately enabling staff to become teachers if they so wish) will need to be addressed at a national level for their full potential to be achieved.

At national levels, studies of a number of developing countries reveal that one of the biggest issues faced by governments is the large numbers of *unqualified* teachers working in schools because the state training provision is unable to meet the needs of the schools. (See, for example, Middlewood (forthcoming) on South Africa, and Dalin *et al.* (1994) on Colombia, Ethiopia and Bangladesh.) If the argument is accepted that the purpose of provision in schools is to facilitate learning and apply resources as appropriate, it may be worth speculating as to whether developing models of a range of personnel support such as discussed in this chapter may not be a suitable and cost-effective way of proceeding.

Such range of provision in the UK may well be accompanied by a restructuring of the teaching profession as we have known it. Such restructuring seems appropriate and essential in a century where the emphasis is moving more heavily towards managing learning. The implications for leaders and managers in schools and colleges is that the starting point is *not* 'How can I make the *teaching* more effective here?' and providing assistance to the teacher, *but rather* 'How can *learning* be most effective here?' and providing a range of resources to enable this. These resources will surely include good teachers and effective curriculum support personnel of the kind suggested in this chapter. Even in the period of transition, recent research (Hartle, 2000) has identified three factors in classroom climate as significant to students' learning:

- lack of disruption
- encouragement to engage
- high expectations.

The appropriate use of curriculum support staff can only enhance the effectiveness of this climate for learning.

## REFERENCES

Barber, M. (1997) *The Learning Game*, London, Cassell.

Bush, T. and Middlewood, D. (1997) *Managing People in Education*, London, Paul Chapman.

Blunkett, D. (1999) Speech to North of England Conference, autumn.

Dalin, P. *et al.*, (1994) *How Schools Improve*, London, Cassell.

Department for Education and Employment (DfEE) (1998) *Teachers Meeting the Challenge of Change*, London, DfEE.

Duffy, M. (2000) So who's managing this lot?, *Times Educational Supplement*, 7 April, pp. 29–30.

Elkin, S. (2000) The supporting role, *Leadership Focus*, Vol. 1, no. 2, p. 35.

Farell, D., Balshaw, M. and Polat, F. (1999) The management, role and training of learning support assistants, *Research Report*, No. 161, London, DfEE.

Fidler, B. and Atton, T. (1999) *Poorly Performing Staff in Schools and How to Manage Them*, London, Routledge.

Fletcher, J. (1999) Managing teachers' time effectively through the improved use of classroom support staff, unpublished MBA dissertation, University of Leicester.

Hadow, G. (1931) *Primary Education, Board of Education*, London, HMSO.

Haigh, G. (1996) To boldly go beyond washing paint-pots, *Times Educational Supplement*, 9 February, p. 21.

Hargreaves, D. (1996) Teaching as a research-based profession: possibilities and prospects, *Teacher Training Agency Annual Lecture 1996*, London, TTA.

Hartle, F. (2000) How do effective teachers get better results?, *Headway*, no. 11. p. 5.

Kedney, B. and Brownlow, S. (1994) Funding flexibility, *Mendip Paper 62*, Blagdon, The Staff College.

Mercer, A. (2000) Class struggle, *Nursery World*, no. 2. March, p. 11.

Middlewood, D. (forthcoming) Teacher professionalism and development, in Lumby, J., Middlewood, D. and Kaabwe, S. (eds.) *Managing Human Resources in South African Schools*, South Africa, Amabhuku.

Mortimore, P. and Mortimore, J. (1994), *Managing Associate Staff*, London, Paul Chapman.

Moyles, J. with Suschitzky, W. (1997), Jill of all trades? Classroom assistants in Key Stage One, a report for Association of Teachers and Lecturers, London, ATL.

Naylor, D. (1999), The professional development needs of midday assistants, *Professional Development Today*, Vol. 3, no. 1, pp. 51–60.

Office for Standards in Education (Ofsted) (1998) *The Annual Report of Her Majesty's Chief Inspector of Schools: Standard and Quality in Education, 1996/97*, London, HMSO.

Parker, R. (1999) Learning support assistants: a way forward, *Headship Matters*, Vol. 1, no. 1, p. 9.

Passarello, E. (2000) Learning support, *Times Educational Supplement*, 2 June, p. 17.

Phillips, A. (2000) An evaluation of the specialist teaching assistant scheme, unpublished MBA dissertation, University of Leicester.

Times Educational Supplement (TES) (2000) Mum's Army comes of age, *Times Educational Supplement*, 2 June, p. 4.

Watkinson, A. (1999), The professional development of teaching assistants, *Professional Development Today*, Vol. 2. no. 3, pp. 63–9.

# 13

# THE MANAGEMENT OF RESOURCES FOR LEARNING

## Ann Briggs and Neil Burton

## INTRODUCTION

The effective management of resources for learning is an area upon which the student's learning experience heavily depends. The complex issue of the management of the human resource element – teaching and associate staff – is addressed in another volume in this series, *Managing People in Education* edited by Bush and Middlewood (1998). The resource of the learning environment – the classroom, workplace, seminar room – is discussed in Chapter 11. The focus of this chapter is that group of learning resources that are used to enhance the interaction between teacher or tutor and the learner. These learning resources – from expensive equipment down to individual textbooks – may be 'owned' at a whole-school or whole-college level, by individual departments or individual teachers, or – a common feature in many parts of the world – provided by the students themselves. The extent of the impact of learning resources on the learning process may vary from minimal – an individual worksheet used to support a classroom lesson – to central, as in the case of text-based distance learning. In this 'mix and match' environment, issues of resource accessibility, equity and effectiveness are paramount. The availability and distribution of funding influence the management of educational resources – this is typified by the balance between resource availability determining the nature of the curriculum and funding being sufficient to determine fully the acquisition of learning resources. In general terms, effective resource management can be enhanced by:

• management systems where resource decisions are included in whole-institution planning and decision-making

- good understanding by teachers as well as managers that particular patterns of resource can achieve success
- a focus on outcomes: the obtaining and deployment of the best possible resources for an effective learning experience.

## WHOLE-INSTITUTION PLANNING

When curriculum development is planned for a school or college – a change of syllabus, the introduction of a new subject area, a move to computer-based or resource-based learning – the costs of the change would normally be estimated and a budget allocated. However, concern has been expressed by researchers (Bullock and Thomas, 1997; Levačić, 1995; Thomas and Martin, 1996) about the effectiveness of links between school development plans and school budgets – a concern which has implications for the planned purchase of learning resources – and academic managers in higher education institutions have also been criticised for being 'unaware of the full costs of activities' (Joint Funding Councils, 1996, p. 6).

It is important that the strategic planning, together with the associated budget allocation, takes account of the whole implementation process. At its simplest level, for a new subject area or syllabus, new books and equipment may be needed, but a change in teaching approach or learner access to materials may entail changes to accommodation, and once the appropriate learning resources are in place, learners and teachers may both need to develop appropriate skills and understanding in order to make the best use of the new learning opportunities. So in terms of the cost calculations, it is not just the purchase prices of the new books and equipment that need to be identified, but also the costs of training staff to make effective use of the acquisitions, and the ongoing costs of storing, managing and maintaining them.

An example of this has been the drive for schools in England to ensure that they have a full range of ICT equipment, specifically computers. The government set targets for student access to ICT which encouraged schools to purchase computer hardware. In many cases, where the technical advice available in schools was limited, this led to inappropriate purchases and an overinvestment in equipment at the expense of training and maintenance – schools had the computers but were unable to either make effective use of them or ensure that they remained in working order. Clearly such a state of affairs is a very inefficient use of resources. Indeed, such inefficiencies were still prevalent in 1998 where primary schools in Brixton, London, were having rooms cabled to provide computer laboratories, due to the availability of ring-fenced funding, but were unable to purchase computers to put in them!

Management decisions can only effectively be made when adequate information is presented in an appropriate format. Resource-acquisition decisions based purely on purchase price may well prove to be a false economy.

Clearly the initial decisions to obtain new resources in order to support a curriculum development will be based and justified on educational grounds, but this will need to be within the funding that is available. Educational priorities will have to be determined at an institution-wide strategic level through appropriate decision-making processes within the school or college. These priorities will then need to be translated down to the departmental or cost-centre level – the level at which the learning resources are likely to be employed and managed.

Simkins (1998, p. 71) describes a range of competing pressures upon strategic resource management, including: 'the need to respond flexibly to changing environmental demands, while providing a reasonably stable resource environment to enable those responsible for undertaking the core activities of the institution, i.e. curricular and other provision for students, to work effectively'. In the UK, two factors have helped to focus attention upon strategic planning of learning resources, both of which impact upon the 'stable resource environment' and the 'core activities of the institution'. The first is the falling unit of resource, particularly evident in further and higher education, where 'the available resources per student have been steadily reduced, as a result of insistent demand to bring about efficiency gains and to reduce costs' (Cowan, 1994, p. 2). The second is the focus upon student- or pupil-centred learning, with its emphasis on individual enquiry: 'At the heart of any pupil-centred learning activity is a sequence of tasks requiring pupils to locate, select, interrogate, interpret and communicate knowledge and understanding' (Kinnell, 1992, p. 53). Both of these factors, combined with the growing importance of learning technologies, have created a shift away from the teacher as 'knowledge provider' to the teacher as enabler of learning and, consequently, as guide to the use of an increasingly wide range of learning resources.

To take a more detailed example: in response to the factors introduced above, a school or college may set up a learning resource centre, with books, paper-based and audio-visual materials, computers and on-line resources, to enable students to access a range of resources to support their study. For the venture to succeed, substantial consultation will be needed with teachers and managers, in order to 'build' use of those resources into courses in an effective and meaningful way. Whole-institution strategies such as the following would be appropriate (based on Briggs, 2000):

- Establish a school or college-wide understanding of the function of the resource centre, and allocate a budget.
- Give the resource centre manager membership of/access to the school or college's decision-making and developmental forums.
- Involve curriculum managers and classroom teachers in the development of the centre, and maintain their involvement in further planning and evaluation.
- Set up staff development opportunities for teaching staff and resource centre staff in relation to student-centred and resource-based learning.

- Welcome teachers into the resource centre, to provide specialist support for students and to advise on provision of resources.
- Liaise to create a variety of learning environments, flexible to learner need, and train resource centre staff, teachers and students in effective use of the centre and in accessing its resources.
- Devise and implement appropriate systems to plan, manage and monitor the learning of individual students.

Given this type of whole-institution involvement, effective development and use of a central resource can enhance the learning and teaching experience on a range of courses.

Whole-institution planning – based, for example on a commitment to enhance the use of learning technologies – can also involve decisions about substantial capital purchases such as computer suites, network cabling or upgraded reprographic and audio-visual equipment. Here difficult choices may be encountered, where competing or even complementary needs may have to be balanced against each other in an attempt to meet long- or medium-term benefits through a finite annual allocation. Once purchased, there can be an issue of 'ownership': who is responsible for the maintenance and booking procedures for a video camera which was purchased through cross-college funds, but which is housed in the art department? Do the sports teachers know of its existence and, if so, how can they borrow it? Who pays for repairs when the drama teacher drops it? It is upon such quandaries that the micro-politics of learning resource management are founded!

In the case studies described in Chapter 11, all three institutions had prioritised the management of resources in their strategic planning, and allocated their budgets accordingly. In the lower school, improved management of resources is part of the strategy to enhance the overall learning environment of the school. Central to this is the employment of a learning support assistant in the computer/library room, to manage the resources in preparation for the arrival of the class groups. A 'whole-school ethos' can be established in a room which is accessed in turn by all the pupils. 'Without her [the learning support assistant] the room would not be the success that we currently enjoy' (lower school headteacher).

In the secondary school, student access to learning resources in the newly created curriculum learning centres is a key element of the curriculum change. The five-hour 'contextualised learning event', which takes place each week, depends for its success upon teacher planning of the use of a range of different learning stimuli for the children. The learning centres provide access to some of these stimuli: they are 'well furnished, well equipped, with good artefacts or appropriate manipulatives, for whatever subject it is, within sight and easy to get at'. Once the school had prioritised the concept that children 'are different in their learning and in their needs for the things that we create for them', the teaching teams developed ways of 'creating learning experiences so that all of them can feel that "I can achieve" at their own different levels and in their own different ways, that they all have value' (secondary school vice-principal).

The further education college is committed to translating and transferring its learning resources into a format which can be accessed 'any time, any place, anywhere' by students who are within or remote from the college. For students studying away from the college, this meant allocating staff time and physical resources to creating computer-based teaching materials and offering on-line tutor support – in some cases face-to-face through the use of a digital camera – so that students have access to college staff to guide and encourage them in the use of the resources. For the students in college, lecturer time which had formerly been allocated to teaching course content is preserved for 'interpretation and application and evaluation . . . to develop seminar skills, presentation skills, discuss issues, really talk around subjects' which students have investigated themselves using a computer-based managed learning environment (FE college project co-ordinator).

In all three cases, accessibility to learning was a prime motivator influencing strategic planning which involved major changes to the management of learning resources.

## Resource prioritisation

Throughout the above examples there are references to prioritisation: that is prioritising educational initiatives and then ensuring that resources are made available to support those agreed priorities. Each provides an excellent example of priority-based budgeting, also referred to in the literature as 'programme planning budgeting' (Glover, 2000, p. 122). When educational establishments are inspected in England under the criteria laid down by Ofsted, they are expected to demonstrate that their educational priorities, as identified in their development or improvement plans, are fully supported and complemented by the priorities in their published budgets. The final measure of this 'effectiveness' is given in any inspection report by a comment on the 'value for money' being offered. Formal, public inspection of resource application and use provides a very strong pressure to conform to state or governmental educational priorities, such as the emphasis on technology described above.

There are two assumptions being made here that are by no means universal throughout all education systems. The first is that a school or college actually has sufficient resources to fulfil their basic educational remit – this is clearly not always the case, particularly in countries with very limited or poorly distributed finances. Second, the level of control that schools or colleges have over their resources to be able to make prioritising decisions. In some systems, South Africa for example, state schools have the decision-making powers to require parents to 'top-up' the fees that the school receives from the state.

Educational priorities can usually be addressed through the use of learning resources from either additional or reallocated funds. In both cases the actual cost of the priority is more than simply the cost of the resources and their support costs, but must also be considered in terms of the priorities that will no longer be resourced. For every use to which learning resources can be put, there is another use that will probably go unsatisfied – this is the 'opportunity cost' of resource decisions. In the prioritisation process, the opportunities that will be foregone will need to be considered in terms of their educational and resource impact. The act of prioritising the acquisition of one multimedia computer over the purchase of text-based reference materials for the same cost is one that needs to be judged in terms of the overall educational impact. The decision-maker will need to ask the question 'which will lead to the greatest overall improvement in educational opportunities in the long term?'

Once the educational priorities have been determined and clear goals set, funding will need to be allocated for learning resources to ensure that the goals can be reached. Not all goals will have a direct resource cost. It is quite possible that the existing learning resources are adequate for the purpose, but they may need to be reorganised or used more effectively by improving staff competence. Although actual costs are still quite likely, they may be much less than those likely to be incurred should completely new learning resources be required. For this reason, it is important that resource managers carefully audit the learning resources that are available so that they are fully aware of their potential. It may well be more cost (and educationally!) effective to adapt existing learning resources to a new or changed use, than obtain entirely new resources.

There may well come a point where, however educationally desirable a particular priority is, it may have to be rejected on the grounds of resource cost. To be able to make this decision both rationally and effectively, the resource manager will need to perform some form of 'cost-benefit analysis' (see Simkins, 2000). Here the manager will need to carefully ask two questions:

- Can we afford to do it?
- Can we afford *not* to do it?

In higher education, the cost of ensuring quality provision and assessment in most standard undergraduate courses may be considered to be high; but the cost of not ensuring appropriate standards will be even greater – the probable closure of the course. As with all resource decisions, the manager must prioritise in terms of:

- needs – essential resource requirements to meet basic standards of acceptability
- wants – desirable to enable identified higher goals to be met
- likes – non-essential, but would lead to the realisation of clearly defined educational strengths.

This prioritisation may take place at an institutional, departmental or individual class or teacher level. At an institutional level issues of equity and access will need to be addressed.

## TEACHER UNDERSTANDING OF PATTERNS OF RESOURCE

Learning resources rarely 'work' on their own: although there are notable examples of academic success achieved through independent study, most learners, depending on their preferred learning style, appreciate the guiding influence of a mentor or teacher, and the social encouragement of learning with others. The range of different learning stimuli referred to in the secondary school case study (in Chapter 11) includes people: teachers and learning assistants from inside the school, visitors and 'experts' from outside and other people's experiences shared on video. Creating a rich learning experience for a student group involves surveying the available resources, which are often scarcer than the teacher would wish, and creating an environment for learning and understanding.

This may involve managers and teachers in difficult choices: should the college cut the class hours for a certain subject and build in more independent study? The teachers may perceive that their subject is being 'eroded' or devalued, or they may see that students could access a wider range of resources outside the classroom than in it, and that a change of teaching style and approaches to learning would benefit the group. Should the primary school 'buy' a classroom assistant or a set of computers? The primary school in the Chapter 11 case study managed its budget to provide both, because they were complementary. Will the language learning equipment which a secondary school teacher wants to purchase this year be unused when that teacher leaves the school in a few years' time?

A further issue here is that of accessibility. Learning resources may be accessible or inaccessible to the learner: on open-access shelves or locked away in a filing cabinet. At a different level, however, the learning to be derived from those resources may be accessible or inaccessible. Agoulou and Agoulou (1997) define five types of inaccessibility when considering library resources in developing countries:

- Conceptual, where the materials are beyond the reader's comprehension.
- Linguistic, where resources are written in a language one does not understand.
- Critical, where the reader is not competent to analyse and evaluate the material, or to tell whether it is accurate.
- Bibliographic, where the user does not know how to use the available access tools.
- Physical, where the material is – deliberately or inadvertently – of restricted access.

This classification is equally useful when considering school or college learning resources, and it underlines the interdependence of the teacher, the student and the materials. Learning will be enhanced when materials are presented at a range of levels of comprehension and through a variety of media, suitable for the needs of the student group. Care needs be taken to avoid the 'language one does not understand', which may be literal, or it may be the coded language or jargon present in the resources, or in the terms in which it is presented to the learner. Less autonomous learners will need help in evaluating materials: for example, they may adopt uncritically a simplified version of a subject they are investigating or, very commonly, they accept unsubstantiated information from an internet site as being accurate and unbiased. Responsibility for bibliographical and physical inaccessibility lies with the teacher or resource manager: students will need training in the skills necessary to find resources and to locate the desired information, otherwise they may be deterred by their experience.

Accessibility is increased by teacher and manager awareness of these factors, and by action being taken to reduce any 'barriers' to learning inherent in the materials and the ways in which they are presented. It follows that where learning is teacher led or directed, student access is dependent upon the knowledge or competence of the tutor or teacher. Teaching staff will need to be aware of and possess the skills to make appropriate use of resources in order for learners to gain maximum benefit from them – unless students gain this awareness through other means.

## A FOCUS ON LEARNING OUTCOMES

Levačić (1995, p. 155) writing about the planning and evaluation of resource allocation, comments that decisions are based 'on professional judgments that the most beneficial learning outcomes would result from this particular pattern of resources'. Teachers, in many countries, are now encouraged – and at times required – to evaluate the quality of their teaching, and in some institutions the students also make formal evaluations of their learning experience. If these evaluations include a judgement of the effectiveness of the learning resources and the ways in which they are used, then future decisions about resource allocation could be more evidence based.

Dimmock (2000, p. 27) illustrates this situation by presenting a policy-making paradigm which is driven by student learning outcomes. These determine the learning processes and content, which in turn guide decisions on teaching methods and strategies. In Dimmock's paradigm, the final element is 'Leadership, management, resources, culture': instead of these being the shaping force of the school, they are themselves shaped by the school's primary focus upon student learning outcomes.

If the learning process is to be evaluated, the evaluation of outcomes should not simply be quantitative – how many students passed the examination, and at what level? – but also qualitative – what was it which best helped them to learn? Experienced teachers may feel that they have the answer; this understanding will be enhanced by consulting the students themselves. Through this process, the resource cycle of obtaining, allocating, using and evaluating can be applied to the learning resources as well as to the budget as a whole.

# BUDGETING FOR LEARNING RESOURCES

Obtaining funding or resources within an educational organisation will be subject to several different – sometimes conflicting, sometimes complementary – influences. These influences may be in the forms of systems and structures by which resource managers indicate the extent of their resource needs from an institutional budget – a rational system. Or the influences may be more arbitrary in nature – dependent upon the interpersonal and group relationships within the institution – a political system. Realistically the resource determination is likely to be some combination of the two. To acquire and organise learning resources, resource managers will need to adhere to departmental or institutional systems and fulfil the bureaucratic processes, but it is also likely that they will employ interpersonal skills to obtain support from the decision-makers for their requests.

Already assumptions have been made about the nature of funding resources. As Burton (2000, p. 261) suggests: 'the question being addressed is "how do we allocate the funds we have?" rather than "how much does it cost?".' Resource managers may ameliorate their funding requests on the basis of known funding availability rather than curricular need. The curriculum may be determined as much by what can be afforded as by what is educationally sound. For this reason the manager must determine the most resource efficient means of delivering the required curriculum. This may mean the reliance on 'outsourcing' as in the Israeli system curriculum resources (both human and material) as a more immediate and reliable means of addressing deficiencies in the curriculum provision. The lack of a teacher of Spanish may mean that a particular language course cannot be resourced by more traditional means, so students are required to use multimedia or web-based learning to meet some of the more subject specific elements of their course.

The structures by which resource funding allowances can be identified fall into one of three general approaches:

- Incremental budgeting – where resource funding is based upon previous requirements.
- Zero-based budgeting (ZBB) – where resource requirements are calculated afresh for each financial cycle.
- Priority-based budgeting – where funding priority is given to resources that help to meet predetermined institutional or departmental educational goals.

These systems are discussed in much greater detail by Davies (1994) and Levačić (1990), but in their pure forms it is unlikely that any will be used exclusively due to their inherent strengths and weaknesses. These are shown briefly in Figure 13.1.

The effective management of the school or departmental budget is a key element in the effectiveness of the resource manager. It is important that the manager determines the nature of the costs associated with particular learning resources – in particular the distinction between initial and recurrent costs (for example, maintenance). The expected serviceable lifespan of the resource must be calculated. Some learning resources, such as writing paper, are known to be consumables in the short term, but how frequently should the resource manager plan to renew computers or footballs?

Although the financial aspects of managing learning resources should not supersede the educational imperatives, funding does need to be recognised as a key enabling factor. Prudent financial management may help to ensure a more effective distribution and utilisation of resources for learning so that the educational benefit may be realised. It is unlikely that there will ever be sufficient funding of education for all resource requirements to be met, so decisions will always have to be made – the more competently the financial element can be managed, the more appropriate those decisions might be.

| Approach | Strength | Weakness |
|---|---|---|
| Incremental | Continues the status quo. It is quick and easy and transparent, but does assume that all costs are rising at the same rate. | Significant changes or priorities are difficult to manage. Any inefficiencies that are present are allowed to continue. |
| Zero-based | It does allow for new initiatives to be incorporated into budgets. It does require managers to justify their resource requirements. | Those managers that are better at completing the bureaucratic processes will come out best, regardless of actual needs – it becomes a rather political process. It is very time-consuming because everything has to be done anew each time. There is no consistency from one year to the next. As many costs are relatively fixed a true ZBB is not really feasible. |
| Priority-based | It certainly sets priorities, e.g. to work in a comfortable environment! It makes costs an issue at the point where the educational debate is taking place, e.g. the introduction of a new scheme, resourcing literacy developments | How are priorities ranked? What is the basis? Can 'lurch' as priorities change. Items which are not strictly a priority but have to be done, such as providing adequate lighting, must also be accounted for. |

**Figure 13.1** A comparison of different resource budgetary formats

# OBTAINING ADDITIONAL FUNDS FOR LEARNING RESOURCES

The alternative to distributing scarce resources as fairly and effectively as possible – working within a limited budget – is to expand the resource budget. If funding is insufficient for the learning resources that are necessary, then it may be possible for the resource manager to obtain more funding. Throughout history, schools and colleges have, to some extent, relied upon charitable or commercial donations to improve the quality of learning and teaching by the acquisition of further resources. Although Levačić (2000, p. 3) notes that the link between educational outcomes and resource expenditure 'are still subject to much controversy' there is an almost unshakeable belief that 'more resources equals better education'.

In educational systems where institutional funding is dependent upon enrolment, increasing student numbers can increase resource provision. In most cases it is unlikely that the additional cost of enrolling an extra student would exceed the additional funding received – though this is entirely dependent upon the individual learning needs of the student. Burton (1999, p. 137) questions the extent to which the variations in resource needs are accounted for in the public funding of education.

While educational funding via fees will focus on general resource requirements, educational establishments have occasional need for additional funding for specific, costly, learning resources that cannot be met from normal sources of income. A school needing to improve its provision for science through the building or refurbishment of a laboratory block can either attempt to 'save up' for the known future expense by retaining a portion of its income, or attempt to raise the funds independently of these more usual sources. Publicly funded schools may make a request for additional funding from the state, or, like privately funded schools, there may be an attempt to raise the necessary capital via means such as:

- enterprise – commercial activities
- support from companies
- sponsorship
- benefactors – parents, ex-students, local businesses
- bidding for funds (Anderson, 2000, pp. 48–54).

The last of these approaches, bidding for funds, is one that the DfEE are employing with increasing frequency. The DfEE make funding available for particular educational purposes, usually involving resource acquisition, and then require schools and colleges to bid for it. The rationale behind this is that it ensures that the funding is directed towards the educational priorities as determined by the government. A national priority say, to, direct resources towards ensuring that there is an adequate range of reading material in school, could be circumvented if schools were just provided with the funding in the hope that their priorities were the same. By requiring the school to place a bid for the funds, the school will have to explain how the funding will be used to improve the learning resources in that particular area and what the 'success criteria' will be. This also ensures that those schools that share these priorities are given preferential funding. Clearly this system does have problems which may prevent an equitable distribution of the available funds – the competence with which the bid is completed being the most significant.

The external determination of educational priorities and, in turn, the nature of the curriculum through accessibility of funding is one that needs to be explored at both the institutional and national policy level. At a time of greater self-determination for schools and colleges, the extent to which priorities are set at the national level needs to be taken into perspective.

## CONCLUSIONS

Learning resources do need to be considered in management terms. The links between the educational priorities and outcomes and the learning resources that are used to meet them must be confirmed and rationalised on both educational and financial terms. At the point of resource acquisition the manager must confirm the sustainability of both the curriculum development that they are there to support and the financial commitment for the short and long term. Learning resources need to be organised and made available to enhance the learning experience of students as effectively as possible. This will include taking responsibility for the costs of the training of staff and the maintenance and storage of the resources. Although these are specifically operational issues, the theoretical background to these issues is compelling and can lead to a clearer understanding of the nature of the management structures within the institution.

## REFERENCES

Agoulou, C. C. and Agoulou, I. E. (1997) A conceptual approach to the role of the library in developing countries, *Education Libraries Journal*, Vol. 40, no. 3, pp 13–21.

Anderson, L. (2000) The move towards entrepreneurialism, in Coleman, M. and Anderson, L. (eds.) *Managing Finance and Resources in Education*, London, Paul Chapman.

Briggs, A. R. J. (2000) Modelling: what's in it for me? The applicability of modelling to the management of accessibility, *Research in Post-Compulsory Education*, Vol. 5, no. 1, pp. 115–32.

Bullock, A. and Thomas, H. (1997) *Schools at the Centre: A Study of Decentralisation*, London, Routledge.

Burton, N. (1999) The efficient and effective deployment of staff and resources, in Brundrett, M. (ed.) *Principles of School Leadership*, Dereham, Peter Francis.

Burton, N. (2000) Costing initial teacher education, *Higher Education Quarterly*, Vol. 54, no. 3, pp. 259–73.

Bush, T. and Middlewood, D. (1988) *Managing People in Education*, London, Paul Chapman.

Cowan, J. (1994) The student and the learning process, in Adams, M. and McElvoy, R. (eds.) *Colleges, Libraries and Access to Learning*, London, Library Association.

Davies, B. (1994) Models of decision making and resource allocation, in Bush, T. and West-Burnham, J. (eds.) *The Principles of Educational Management*, London, Paul Chapman.

Dimmock, C. (2000) *Designing the Learning-Centred School*, London, Falmer Press.

Glover, D. (2000) Financial management and strategic planning, in Coleman, M. and Anderson, L. (eds.) *Managing Finance and Resources in Education*, London, Paul Chapman.

Joint Funding Councils (1996) Management information for decision-making: costing guidelines for higher education institutions, mimeo.

Kinnell, M. (ed.) (1992) *Learning Resources in Schools: Library Association Guidelines for School Libraries*, London, Library Association.

Levačić, R. (ed.) (1990) *Financial and Resource Management in Schools*, Buckingham, Open University Press.

Levacic, R. (1995) *Local Management of Schools: Analysis and Practice*, Buckingham, Open University Press.

Levacic, R. (2000) Linking resources to learning outcomes, in Coleman, M. and Anderson, L. (eds.) *Managing Finance and Resources in Education*, London, Paul Chapman.

Simkins, T. (1998) Autonomy, constraint and the strategic management of resources, in Middlewood, D. and Lumby, J. (eds.) *Strategic Management in Schools and Colleges*, London, Paul Chapman.

Simkins, T. (2000) Cost analysis in education, in Coleman, M. and Anderson, L. (eds.) *Managing Finance and Resources in Education*, London, Paul Chapman.

Thomas, H. and Martin, J. (1996) *Managing Resources for School Improvement: Creating a Cost-Effective School*, London, Routledge.

# GLOSSARY OF TERMS

| | |
|---|---|
| CACHE | Council for Awards in Children's Care and Education |
| CAT | cognitive ability test |
| CPD | continuing professional development |
| DfEE | Department for Education and Employment |
| EBD | emotional and behavioural difficulties |
| EMDU | Educational Management Development Unit |
| FE | further education |
| FEFC | Further Education Funding Council |
| GM | grant maintained |
| GNVQ | General National Vocational Qualification |
| HE | higher education |
| HEADLAMP | Headteacher Leadership and Management Programme |
| ICT | information and communication technology |
| IEP | individual education plan |
| IIP | Investors in People |
| KS | Key Stage |
| LEA | local education authority |
| LMS | local management of schools |
| LPSH | Leadership Programme for Serving Headteachers |
| LSA | learning support assistant |
| MBWA | management by walking about |
| MLD | moderate learning difficulties |
| NASEN | National Association for Special Educational Needs |
| NFER | National Foundation for Educational Research |
| NPQH | National Professional Qualification for Headship |
| NQT | newly qualified teacher |
| OBE | Outcomes-Based Education |

| OECD | Organisation for Economic Co-operation and Development |
| Ofsted | Office for Standards in Education |
| PMLD | profound and multiple learning difficulties |
| PSHE | Personal, Social and Health Education |
| QCA | Qualifications and Curriculum Authority |
| SAT | standard assessment task |
| SEN | special educational needs |
| SENCO | special educational needs co-ordinator |
| SLD | severe learning difficulties |
| SMSC | Spiritual, Moral, Social and Cultural |
| SMT | senior management team |
| STA | specialist teaching assistant |
| TOC | Target-Oriented Curriculum |
| TTA | Teacher Training Agency |
| TVEI | Technical and Vocational Educational Initiative |
| WWW | World Wide Web |
| ZBB | zero-based budgeting |

# INDEX

Adams, N. 123
Adelman, C. and Alexander, R. 98
Adey, K. R. 123, 130
Adey, P. and Shayer, M. 40, 47, 116
Agoulou, C. C. and Agoulou, I. E. 210
Ainscow, M. 150
Ainscow, M., Farrell, P., Tweddle, D.
  and Malki, G. 163
Alexander, R., Rose, J. and Woodhead,
  C. 140
Anderson, L. 59, 214
Armstrong, L., Evans, B. and Page, C.
  123, 124
Aspinwall, K., Simkins, T., Wilkinson,
  J.F. and McAuley, M.J. 74, 78, 79,
  85, 86, 87
Atkinson, R. L., Atkinson, R.C., Smith,
  E.E., Bem, D.J and Hilgard, E.R. 37

Baddely, G. 180
Baines, E. 64
Barber, M. 200
Beattie, N. 8, 15
Becher, T. 108, 129
Bell, L. 139, 150
Bell, D. and Ritchie, R. 123, 147
Bennett, N. 131
Bentley, T. 179, 181
Best, R. and Ribbins, P. 125
Blamires, M. 160
Blandford, S. 125
Blandford, S. and Gibson, S. 150
Blase, J. and Blase, J. 131

Blatchford, R. 29–30
Blunkett, D. 192
Boisot, M. 57
Booth, T., Ainscow, M., Black
  Hawkins, K., Vaughan, M. and
  Shaw, L. 157, 158, 160, 163
Boud, D. 14
Bowring-Carr, C. and West-Burnham, J.
  5, 6, 10, 118, 184
Brehony, K. J. 46
Briggs, A. R. J. 206
Brighouse, T. and Woods, D. 117
Brophy, J. and Good, T.L. 38
Brown, L. 45
Brown, M. and Rutherford, D. 177
Brundrett, M. and Burton, N. 22
Bull, T. 116
Bullock, A. 124
Bullock, A. and Thomas, H. 205
Burton, N. 212, 214
Bush, T. and Middlewood, D. 109, 190,
  204
Busher, H. 125
Busher, H. and Harris, A. 125, 142, 150
Busher, H. and Harris, A. with Wise, C.
  124, 127, 128
Busher, H. and Hodgkinson, K. 126
Busher, H. and Saran, R. 131
Butler, K. 115

Caldwell, B. and Spinks, J. 22, 38
Campbell, R. J. 39, 140, 141
Campbell, R. and Neill, S. 60, 66

219

Chan, Y and Watkins, D. 4, 7, 8
Charoenwongsak, K. 148
Cheng, Y. C. 147
Chomsky, N. 37
Clark, D. 4
Coleman, M. 84, 85, 86, 117
Coleman, M., Middlewood, D. and
    Bush, T. 142, 143
Cooper, P. and McIntyre, D. 129
Cordingley, P. 4
Covey, S. 112
Cowan, J. 206
Crawford, K. and Jones, M. 45
Creemers, B. 38
Crick, B. 45
cross-curriculum co-ordination 135–51
    in further education 144
    in primary schools 140–2
    in secondary schools 142–4
    role of co-ordinators in 135–6
    skills and competencies in 138–9
    versus the curriculum 137–8
Cumming, J. and Carbine, B. 181
Cunningham, I. 150
curriculum
    accountability for standards in
        110–13
    appropriate culture for 113–117
    and leadership of 20, 107–19
    and senior staff 107–9
        as role model 117–8
    definitions of x, xi, 4–5
    effective teacher for 114–17
    evaluation of 89–102
        agenda for 95–6
        community for 97–8
        external requirements in 92–3
        product 93–4
        process 94–5
        students' involvement in 98–9
        types of 90–2
        values in 97
    inclusion
        and individual school responses
            164–70
            and curriculum 165–9
            resourcing for 169–70
            roles and responsibilities in 165
        and practice 161–4
        arguments against 159–60
        in Newham, London Borough of
            160
        managing individual needs within
            155–170
        rationale for 157–9

management of 4, 5, 11
    and the subject leader 122–31
        role of 123–125
            and improving learning 130–1
            and progression 128–30
            in setting culture 125–6
            in shaping ideology 126–8
    monitoring of 70–87
        acceptability of 82
        areas for 78
        criteria in 81
        definition of 71–3
        effectiveness of 80–1
        focus of 78–9
        personnel involved in 76
        problems and difficulties in
            82–7
        purpose of 74
        reasons for 70–1
        reporting of 82
        review of 79–80
        target setting in 73
    state control of 4, 20, 25
    whole view of 109–10
curriculum organisation
    leadership and 20
    models of 17–33
        characteristics of 20–27
            open-ended v target-driven 25–7
            process v content 23–5
            student v subject focus 21–3
        in practice 27–34
    cubic curriculum 18, 19, 136
curriculum support staff 190–202
    and career opportunities 195–6
    as associate teachers 196–7
    effective management of 197–201
        and role clarification 197–8
    rationale for 191–3
    trends, practice and issues 193–5

Dalin, P., 201
Daniels, H., Visser, J., Cole, T. and de
    Reybelall, N. 163
Davies, B. 213
Davies, B. and Ellison, L. 56, 57
Davies, L. 43, 45, 46
Davis, A. 37, 41
Deal, T. 176
Dearing, R. 128
Department for Education and
    Employment (DfEE) 22, 37, 58, 65,
    67, 92, 96, 102, 125, 127, 129, 149,
    150, 155, 158–9, 160, 163, 191,
    214

Department of Education and Science (DES) 26, 92, 158
Department of Trade and Industry (DTI) 144
Deutsch, M. 46
Devoogd, G. 3, 8
Dimmock, C. 13, 22, 56, 67, 211
Dimmock, C. and Walker, A. 5, 8
Dimmock, C. and Wildy, H. 9, 10
Disability Discrimination Act 157
Duffy, M. 108, 109, 142, 191
Dunham, J. and Varma, V. 66

Earley, P. 58
educational managers
  core task of 4
Egan, K. 137, 138
Elkin, S. 195
Elliott, G. and Crossley, M. 117
Elmore, R. F. 147
Emery, H. 43
Everard, K. B. and Morris, G. 20

Farrell, P. 160
Farell, D., Balshaw, M. and Polat, F. 193, 195
Feiler, A. and Gibson, H. 159, 160
Ferguson, M. ix
Fidler, B. and Atton, T. 190
Field, K., Holden, P. and Lawlor, H. 146
Fielding, M. 122
Finn, B. 138
Fisher, R. 116
Fletcher, J. 200
Fletcher-Campbell, F., Tabberer, R. and Keys, W. 129
Fondas, N. and Stewart, R. 125
Foreman, K. 58
Foskett, N. and Hemsley-Brown, J. 63
Fraser, B. J., Rennie, L. J. and Tobin, K. 178
French Education Ministry 23
Friel, V. and Fagan, C. 45
Fullan, M. G. 47, 108
Fullan, M. and Hargreaves, A. 84, 141
Further Education Funding Council (FEFC) 156

Galton, M. 8, 21, 42
Gardner, H. x, 5, 94, 115, 185
Gibbs, G. R. 182
Gipps, C. 38, 41, 92
Gipps, C. and Macgilchrist, B. 41

Gipps, C., McCallum, G. and Brown, M. 41
Glover, D. 208
Glover, D., Gleeson, D., Gough, G. and Johnson, M. 122, 124
Goleman, M. x, 6, 116
Gray, J. 99, 176

Hacker, R. and Rowe, M. J. 140
Hadow, C. 191
Haigh, G. 192
Hall, V. 61
Hallam, S. and Ireson, J. 38
Hallinger, P., Chantarapanya, P., Sribooma, U. and Kantamara, P. 148
Halstead, J. M. and Taylor, M. J. 47
Handy, C. x, 6, 100, 112, 115, 124
Hanna, D. 40
Hannay, L. M. and Ross, J. A. 142, 159
Harber, C. 45
Hardie, B. L. 70, 73, 74, 76, 78, 82
Hargreaves, A. 111
Hargreaves, A. and Fullan, M. 177, 181
Hargreaves, D. 116, 178, 197
Harlen, W. and Elliott, J. 79
Harris, A. 130
Harris, A., Jamieson, I. and Russ, J. 78, 130
Harrison, B. T. 143
Harrison, G. 7
Hartle, F. 202
Harwood, D. 138, 141
Haw, K. 150
Hay McBer 176–7
Health and Safety Commission 125
Hohmann, M., Banet, B. and Weikert, D. 178
Holy Family College 70, 73, 74, 76
Honey, P. and Mumford, A. x, 115
Hopkins, D. 82
Hopkins, D., Ainscow, M. and West, M. 116, 123
Howard, T. 122, 124
Huberman, M. 125
Hustler, F., Milroy, E. and Cockett, M. 180

INCA 23
Individual Education Plans (IEPs) 22, 67
Investors in People (IIP) 190

James, M. 77
Jansen, J. and Middlewood, D. 108

Jeffery, B. and Woods, P. 96
Jensen, K. and Walker, S. 45
Johnson, D. 84
Johnson, D. W. and Johnson, R. T. 46
Joint Funding Councils 205
Jones, K. 46
Joy, P. 29, 30

Kantner, R. M. 177, 187
Kedney, B. and Brownlow, S. 192–3
Kelly, A. xi, 53
Kelly A.V. 37, 39, 45, 46–7
Kelly, V. 92, 93
Kemmis, S. and McTaggart, R. 82, 83
Keys, W. and Fernandez, C. 100
Kinnell, M. 206
Kogan, M. 98
Kouzes, J. and Posner, B. 113
Knight, B. 60

Law, S. and Glover, D. ix, x
Lawn, M. 140
Lawton, D. 23, 46, 108
learners
  concepts of 5
  views of 5, 7–8, 98–101
learning
  a holistic approach to 12–13
  and cultural change 11–12
  and emotional intelligence x
  and ICT x, 3, 15, 29, 32, 119, 192
  and multiple intelligences x
  and resources 13–14
  and school and classroom design
    178–9
  and systems 11
  and teaching ix, 8–9
  and twenty-first century 3–15
  beyond the classroom 179–81
  managing the planning of 55–68
    group planning in 65–6
    institutional focus on 58–63
    expectation issues in 62–3
    resources in 58–61
    management issues in 61–2
    the curriculum 63–5
      expectation issues in 65
      individual planning for 66–8
      management issues in 64–5
      resource issues in 64
  climate conducive to 175–7
  managing the environment for
    175–87
  managing the resources for 204–15
    additional funds for 214–5

and whole-institution planning
    205–10
  budgeting for 212
  prioritisation of 208
  teacher understanding of 210
new context for ix
paradigms of ix, 6–7, 9
virtual environment for 181–2
learning organisation 14
learning styles x, 22
Leask, M. and Terrell, I. 119, 131
Leask, M., Terrell, I. and Falconer, A.
  117
Lee, J. C. and Dimmock, C. 147
Lee, J. and Fitz, J. 36
Lee, B. and Henkhusens, Z. 164
Levačić, R. 40, 177, 205, 211, 213, 214
Lipsky, D. K. and Gartner, A. 163
Local Management of Schools (LMS)
  190, 195
London Borough of Newham 160
Lumby, J. 10, 12, 14, 144, 145

MacBeath, J. 20, 39, 100
MacBeath, J., Boyd, B., Rand, J. and
  Bell, S. 99, 100, 101
Macbeth, A. and Ravn, B. 116
Maden, M. 91
Manset, G. and Semmel, M. I. 160
Marsh, C. 57, 138
Martin, J. 77
Martinez, P. 111
Marton, F. 41
Mathematical Association 128
Mayer, E. 138
Megahy, T. 144
Mercer, A. 196
Middlewood, D. 116, 117, 201
Middlewood, D. and Lumby, J. 48
Midthassel, U. V., Bru, E. and Indsoe,
  T. 147
Midwood, D. and Hillier, D. 123
Mintzberg, H. 72
Morgan, G. 40
Morris, P. and Adamson, B. 20
Morris, T. and Dennison, W. F. 123–4
Morrison, K. 20
Morrison, K, and Ridley, K. 126–7
Mortimore, P. 113
Mortimore, P. and Mortimore, J. 118,
  191, 193
Mortimore, P., Sammons, P., Stoll, L.,
  Lewis, D. and Ecob, R. 43
Moyles, J. with Suschitzky, W. 198
Mullins, L. 111

Nash, C. 145
National Association for Special
    Educational
Needs (NASEN) 160
National Commission on Education
    (NCE) 101
National Curriculum vii–viii, x, 4, 19,
    22–3, 25, 36, 39, 55, 58, 108,
    128–9, 135–6, 140, 141
National Literacy Strategy 38, 141,
    144, 146
Naylor, D. 190
Newman, G. 77
Nias, J. 126
Nixon, J. 178
Norris, N. 94, 95

Office for Standards in Education
    (Ofsted) vii, 26, 36, 77, 78, 92, 96,
    98–9, 102, 141, 146, 150, 185, 200,
    208
O'Neill, J. 27, 141, 163
Ong, T. C. and Chia, E. 144
Organisation for Economic Co-
    operation and Development
    (OECD) 6, 161–3, 170
Osborn, M., and Black, E. 140
Osborne, J. 47
Owen, G. 143

Paechter, C. 112
Parker, R. 201
Parlett, M. and Hamilton, D.
    95
Parsons, C. 159
Passarello, E. 193–4
pedagogy
    definition of 4–5
Peck, B. T. and Ramsay, H. A.
    91
Pell, A. 5, 9
Pettigrew, A. and Whipp, R.
    20
Phillips, A. 200
Piaget, J. 41
Pitcher, T. 13
Pollard, A. 41

Qualifications and Curriculum
    Authority (QCA) 44, 135–6

Raffan, J. and Ruthven, K. 71
Ralph, M. 14
Randle, K. and Brady, N. 4
Regan, L. 5

Republic of Korea, Ministry of
    Education 23–4
Resnick, L. B., Bill, V. and Lesgold, S.
    47
Ribbins, P. 123, 124
Ribbins, P. and Marland, M. M. 143
Richards, C. 140
Richards, I. C. 163
Richmond, K. x
Riding, R. and Rayner, S. 22,
    129
Riley, K. xi
Robertson, D. 145
Rogers, C. ix, 41
Rogers, G. and Badham, L. 79, 80, 81,
    82–3, 85, 86, 87
Rosenholtz, S. 121
Rubin, J. 46
Rudduck, J., Chaplain, R. and Wallace,
    G. 99

Salim, J. and Chua, E. 144
Sammons, P., Hillman, J. and
    Mortimore, P. 38
Sammons, P., Thomas, S. and
    Mortimore, P. 78, 123
Satow, T. and Wang, Z. 4
Schein, E. 125
Sebba, J. and Sachder, D. 160
Senge, P. 14, 112
Silcock, P. J. 39, 45, 46
Silcock, P. J. and Stacey, H. 46
Silcock, P. J. and Wyness, M. 42
Simkins, T. 128, 206, 209
Siraj-Blatchford, I. 12–13
Siskin, L. 125, 126, 131
Skilbeck, M. 93
Smith, H. 163
Southworth, C. 14
Southworth, G. and Conner, C.
    135
Stake, R. E. 71, 74, 75, 94–5
Stoll, L. and Fink, D. 5, 6, 8, 10, 13,
    130, 131, 176
Sugimine, H. 6
Sugrue, C. 46
Sylva, K., Harry, J., Mirelman, H.,
    Brusell, A. and Riley, J. 38

Tan, E. 146
teacher
    role of 8–9
teaching and learning
    managers of 4, 9–10
    models of 35–48

learner-centred 39–44
  management implications of
    42–4
  practical reasons for 39–41
  theoretical reasons for 41
partnership approaches 44
  management implications of
    46–8
  practical reasons for 44–5
  theoretical reasons for 45–6
teacher-centred 35–9
  management implications of
    37–9
  practical reasons for 36–7
  theoretical reasons for 37
Teacher Training Agency (TTA) 38,
  123, 130, 140
Technical and Vocational Educational
Initiative (TVEI) 138–9
Thomas, H. and Martin, J. 205
Tillotson, V. 119
Times Educational Supplement (TES)
  94, 195
Tomlinson, H. 38
Tomlinson, J. 138–9
Tomlinson Report 156
Torrington, D. and Weightman, J.
  71
Trident Trust 181
Tyler, R. 57, 61, 93

United Nations Educational, Scientific,
  and Cultural Organisation
  (UNESCO) 158
Usher, R. and Edwards, R. 110

Vaughn, S. and Schumm, J. S. 159

Walker, D. 57
Wang, M. 179
Wang, J. and Mao, S. 7
Waring, S. 20
Warnock Report 158
Waters, M. 146
Watkins, C. and Mortimore, P. 4, 9
Watkinson, A. 200
Webb, P. C. and Lyons, G. 123
Weindling, D. 117, 119
West-Burnham, J. 20, 39, 71
West-Burnham, J. and O'Sullivan, F. 38
Weston, J. 144
Whalley, C. and Watkins, C. 112
Williams, C. 100
Wilson, J. 159
Wise, C. S. 131
Wolfendale, S. 116
Wragg, E. 18, 136, 179

Yamamoto, K. 21
Yui Chun Lo 147, 148
Young, M. 39, 41